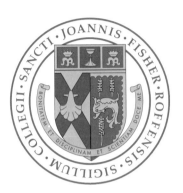

Growing and Knowing:
A Selection Guide for Children's Literature

Mary Trim

Growing and Knowing
A Selection Guide for Children's Literature

K · G · Saur München 2004

Bibliographic information published by Die Deutsche Bibliothek
Die Deutsche Bibliothek lists this publication in the Deutsche Nationalbibliografie;
detailed bibliographic data is available in the internet at http://dnb.ddb.de.

Printed on acid-free paper

Typesetting by Florence Production Ltd., Stoodleigh, Devon, Great Britain.

Printed and Bound by Strauss Offsetdruck, Mörlenbach, Germany.
ISBN 3-598-11581-4

Contents

List of Illustrations

Contributors

Mary Trim brings to children's literature a background of writing, teaching, training of teachers, a Master's degree in Educational Psychology (Sydney, 1982) and a PhD in Children's Literature (Loughborough, 1998). For the past thirty years she has lectured in children's literature at universities in Australia and England, while currently she works as a writer and consultant in language and literature. Mother of five, she has taught primary school in Australia, India and New Zealand, and her publications include academic articles, numerous short stories and poems for children, a children's literature video, *Longtime – Hesba Brinsmead's Mountains of Australia* and *The Rights of the Child: A Teacher's Resource,* 1989 (ISBN 0 949 346 04 7) written as a UNICEF Fellow.

Tricia Kings, writer of The Motivational Librarian, (i) Chapter Six, has been a primary school teacher and librarian; former Co-ordinator of Schools and Young People, Libraries and Heritage, Derbyshire. She is an expert story-teller and has also been involved with selection panels for the Carnegie and Greenaway Awards. Currently, she is Project Manager for an England-wide programme for librarians, 'Their Reading Futures', which is supported by The Arts Council of England and the DCMS/Wolfson Public Libraries Challenge Fund. Now living in Cornwall, but commuting all over England for consultancy assignments, she has a teenage son.

Sally Maynard, who writes Chapter 7, Electronic Books, is the Research Associate in the Library and Information Statistics Unit (LISU) based at Loughborough University. She also teaches a module entitled 'The Child and the Book' in the University's Department of Information Science. For her doctorate at Loughborough University her subject was a study of electronic books for children. She also holds a first degree in English from Southampton University and a Masters degree in Information Technology from Loughborough University. She is mother to two young sons.

Acknowledgements

I have benefited from the discussions and insights of former students, some now professional librarians, especially Rebecca Carrington, Joanna Dare, Angie Edmonds, Marion Howell, David Parker, Natalie Powell, Christine Thornhill and Suzie Schuetz. I am also indebted to school teachers who have cooperated brilliantly with me, especially Pat Eastwood, Christine Cox and Vivienne Barratt Peacock, and to a parent, Gudrun Middleditch.

I also thank Dr David Rudd, of the Department of Cultural and Creative Studies at the Bolton Institute, Rosina Perbedy, Development Manager with Libraries and Heritage, Derbyshire and Sheila Stainwright, Co-ordinator of the Boots Books for Babies Programme.

I also acknowledge the encouragement of Dr Eric Davies, Director of LISU at Loughborough University and Dr Margaret Kinnell Evans, whose professionalism, ongoing support and friendship I value. Thank you, too, to Len Eastwood for his willing assistance with photography. Finally, I should mention my husband, John Ballard Trim, who has had to tolerate my unavailability while the manuscript was in process, but who encouraged me all the way.

This book is dedicated to my mother, Harriet Matilda Buckingham, who shared her love of books with me.

Mary Trim

Illustration 1: Story-time with a board book and one of untearable cloth. Used by permission of Boots Books for Babies.

Illustration 2: Keren finds out about Harry Potter (black and white photo, by Len Eastwood).

Introduction

Stated simply, this is a book about childhood and children's literature. It aims to offer an interrelated framework of reference about both, in order that those who select books for child readers may do so with understanding, knowing *why* they select certain books and activities; recognising the links between content, method and developmental theory. Professionalism and good parenting moves beyond personal pleasure from reading – though this is a valid starting point – to a recognition of all that a literature experience can offer a child; to the ability to relate this broad awareness to a specific book. Such skill is based on, and enhanced by, a knowledge of child development and the sociological dimension that affect a child's place in the world.

The age group considered as children in this text is from 0–16 years, with those at the upper end sometimes referred to as young people. This is in harmony with the report, *Investing in Children: The Future of Library Services for Children and Young People* (1995) produced by the Library and Information Services Council (England).

As is now recognised, the hypothetical child reader often surprises an adult observer by asserting his/her own choices and responses to literature. So the one who has the responsibility of selecting books for children is perhaps to some extent like an angler who needs to respect the characteristics of marine life, to know baits and locations; or like a craftsman who values and polishes precious metals.

In a book that concerns literature it is appropriate to start with a story:

Once upon a time, there were some British university students enrolled in a course called *Childhood and Children's Literature.* Some had chosen the programme as an elective because they 'loved' books for children and 'couldn't wait' to get back to their childhood favourites to read them again as if re-entering childhood, though now with adult perception. They had marvellous memories of books they had treasured in their childhood and wanted to share their enthusiasm with children in society in the roles of librarians or teachers. Some of them, mature-age students, still owned books by such authors as Enid Blyton, Roald Dahl and L. M. Montgomery and, unswerving in allegiance, could quote chapter and verse like true disciples.

A few of the students came to the introductory lecture out of curiosity, or because of the good reputation of the module on the student grapevine, or to have respite from technology in an Information Science programme, while others recognised its value to intended teachers. Some had never read beyond children's basal readers in primary school, but there were reasons for this – often because their childhood homes had few books and lacked adult role models of interest in literature, or as individuals they had somehow been lost in a large class and had missed out on an invigorating reading experience. Now, however, they wanted to be initiated into Alice's Wonderland, or to go through the wardrobe that led into Narnia; or to find out what Harry Potter and Hogwarts' School of Witchcraft was really all about. They had heard the call of these and other worlds through film or television. So the three groups, plus the addition of others – some nondescript stragglers, an international group from France, a few from Hongkong, the African continent and other countries – waited on the first day of the semester with their pens or laptops ready. After a few sessions, as they began to read, they became less inclined to be mere scribes and started to ask pertinent questions and to offer their own insights. They had started the process of re-entering childhood reading, which Peter Hollindale suggests:

> *should be one of integration with the adult critical self, which leads to continuities and connections being accepted and better understood.*
>
> *Hollindale, Howells and Newby 1996, 65.*

A text book was available because many students like the security of having a recommended text to which they can refer. It was not followed slavishly during the semester, but was used from time to time for reference material and discussion questions. It also offered reading lists, many by American authors, unknown and unavailable in Britain.

These lists began a wish, expressed quietly at first with European politeness but with increasing crescendo as the months passed. "We would like a British or European text," they said. The next year a new class echoed the same remark; as did the next and the next . . .

And that is the end of the story. The students, both undergraduate and postgraduate, read with pleasure, developed in knowledge and critical skills, completed their courses and entered their professional work-places, where it is believed (through continuing feedback), that many are indeed living happily ever after because of the enrichment of their favourite literature programme. However, they never did get the text book they wanted. Of course they read much relevant and up-to-date material – primary texts, secondary references, journal articles and w.w.w. information. They began to recognise the significance of books in the overall development of a child; they understood the history of children's literature from mediaeval to contemporary times; they discussed children's 'classics' and award winners. So involved were they that they even continued their discussions with one another in lunch hour and coffee breaks. And they ritually insisted that what they really wanted was a book that gave an holistic approach to the subject of understanding and selecting literature for children; a text book they could own, that spoke to them in a clear, unified, up-to-date way. A Master's student spokesperson said pointedly, "Why don't YOU write it?"

This book is the answer to their repeated requests for a text book to which British students of children's literature can relate, yet one that others in such places as mainland Europe, America, Australia, the African continent, Canada and New Zealand and other parts of the world such as India, Japan and other parts of Asia will also find helpful.

1. Profile of Perceived Readers

This profile describes those who have an interest in two interrelated features. These aspects are:

- *firstly*, recognition of the power-potential of books in the life of child or adult, and the desire to effectively use books in a vocation;
- *secondly,* the desire to be communicators in the twenty-first century who can use technology in partnership with a firsthand knowledge of children's books.

It should be noted that those within this profile may sometimes be English Literature majors in adult literature, and practitioners of academic literary criticism. They will generally be students or professionals, in librarianship or education.

Yet the group may extend further to include all who work in some way with children, from early childhood through to those of primary and secondary school age. They may be pre-school teachers and play-group leaders, nurses in a paediatric ward, Sunday School teachers or social workers.

There is another group, a peripheral but important class of book enthusiasts and supporters, which extends beyond teachers and librarians. It particularly includes parents – not only those who are already convinced of the value of books but also those who have heard that reading makes a difference in children's education; who see a need for their sons and daughters to have a 'slice of the cake' that could lead to successful lives, wishing for their own boys and girls a positive share in the adventures of the 'wonderland' that is life experience. They may belong to a parents' discussion group initiated by a Parents and Teachers meeting, or, having been motivated by this text, decide to start one. Finally, come interested grandparents and others involved with children as buyers of book gifts.

These distinct groups share a common interest in childhood and books. They may, however, be involved in work places that do not share identical terminology, jargon and commitments. Teachers are wise to take the opportunity, if on offer to them (DfES 2002), to take part in a training module that seeks to cultivate better understanding of the library, but not all will become involved. This text endeavours to lead to homogenisation.

2. The History of Children's Literature

Texts other than this provide comprehensive histories of books for children, and some of these are listed, when appropriate, under books for 'Further Reading,' given at the end of each chapter. There are, however, certain points that should be recognised at the outset. *Firstly,* the history of children's literature is one of *diversity and change*, yet still rich in constants, as themes demonstrate. It dates back to hand-written parchment manuscripts of mediaeval times, to the first printing in English of the fifteenth century, growing and extending to the golden age of children's literature in the nineteenth century. At that time, with the expansion of educational opportunities, more children than ever before learnt to read, and publishing for children proliferated. After World War II came the communication explosion of the twentieth and twenty-first centuries, enhanced by technology. *Secondly*, literature for children over this long period reveals societal changes in attitudes and behaviour, both toward children by adults and by children themselves toward society. Initially, society was largely moulded by the Christian Church but, more recently, by the growing influences of postmodernism and multiculturalism.

There are excellent collections of children's literature from the past available in England which is often regarded by overseas scholars as a researchers' heaven. Most places require proof of identification, also a letter of introduction/recommendation and will charge a fee for a reader's card. Collections are both historical and modern in many locations.

For early books, some notable collections are:

- Oxford University's Opie Collection at the Bodleian Library;
- Renier Collection at the Victorian and Albert Museum, Kensington;
- Parker Collection at Birmingham Reference Library;
- Wandsworth Historical Collection at Putney, London;
- The British Library, London.

Excellent collections of twentieth and twenty-first century books for children include those with:

- The Reading and Information Centre of the University of Reading;
- The School Library Service;
- The Children's Book Foundation, London;
- The Department of Education Library, University of Cambridge;
- National Research into Children's Literature, 50,000 recent books, formerly held by the Young Book Trust, at Digby Stuart College, Roehampton.

3. Organisation of the text

The primary aim of this work is to function as a general, foundational guide *for the selection of children's literature* within the setting of understanding how children develop, matching suggested books to stages of growth. Serving more as an overview, it does not attempt to focus on specific concerns which are covered in other publications or university units. Basic to the premise is the recognition that the teacher and librarian need to know books, love books and share the best books that have shaped British and world thought. Every committed librarian and teacher who values the English language and literature will want to share this traditional passion and pass it on to the young.

This book offers a view of principles, possible choices, useful approaches and other relevant details. It is not intended in an arbitrary way, but rather as a smorgasbord of appropriate material – dishes to be tasted and tried, applying suggested ingredients and others of the practitioners' own choosing. It therefore considers issues that are important for the readership defined, not as a totally comprehensive approach nor as a seminal work, but to provide a useful overview or survey in textbook form, for use in the early twenty-first century.

3.1 Selection of Books

Examples of both classic and contemporary publications are cited, often in descriptive rather than analytical terms. As well as highly regarded literary works, popular books are also recognised as useful starting points, respecting the interests and reading competencies of all children. Recent publication dates of retellings and classics are provided, and the text refers to books that are available from publishers at the time of this publication (2003).

3.2 Structure of this book

The work is structured in two parts. Section One focuses on the 'Child, Growing and Knowing Through Books', beginning with a developmental basis in Chapter One and then moving through genres in Chapters Two to Four. In contrast, the second section focuses on the 'Professional, Knowing and Growing,' considering activities and inclusions, principles of selection and evaluation for library and classroom which will enhance professionalism and be meaningful to a child's experience in literature. The final chapter considers all communities in an increasingly multicultural world community.

Each chapter is organised to suggest guide lines for the evaluation and selection of types of books under discussion. Chapters end with (i) children's sayings, relevant to the topic of the chapter. First names only are given, with parental; permission (ii) Tutorial Topics (iii) Suggestions for further reading. (iv) Children's books cited. (v) Bibliography. The children's books cited focus largely on books published in Britain, mainly by British authors, though some highly regarded books by international authors are also included. Books published in both the past and present receive consideration. Bibliography is placed at the end of each chapter for easy retrieval.

It should be pointed out that, because of the breadth of subjects covered in this text, it offers an overview, rather than an in-depth analysis of the topics. The references for further reading, along with classes in particular subjects, will augment and answer further questions. However, for the student in library studies whose subjects are mainly technology related, or for the student teacher who majors in a particular discipline, or for the professional librarian or teacher who wants a reference point, this text offers guidance.

4. Prerequisite Knowledge

4.1 Key Stages of Literacy

It will be helpful to readers of this text if they approach it with some knowledge of what are known as 'The Key Stages of Literacy', advocated by the British *National Literacy Strategy Framework for Teaching* (DfEE 1998a), emphasised in classroom curriculum as a prescribed programme: a dedicated hour a day, at least, for literacy. These are seen as keys to opening avenues of learning, each key expanding and building on the preceding one. Speaking, listening and writing are included at each step, but in this context we focus on the Reading Keys, all related to both fiction and nonfiction at each step. It must be recognised from the outset however, that while the categories are descriptive of the norm, there will be individual differences for various reasons so that some students will be ahead while others may lag.

Preceding the Key Stages are the *Foundation* Years of 3–5 year-olds who enjoy picture books, building on a foundation of picture stories, rhymes and songs begun with 'First Books for Babies'.

Key Stage 1 concerns 5–7 year-olds who develop interest and pleasure in reading as they learn to read with confidence and independently. Teachers will employ different teaching strategies, including re-emphasis on phonological and phonemic awareness, but these will largely focus on words and sentences. Children will be encouraged to work out the meaning of straightforward texts and talk about the content.

Key Stage 2, like Key Stage 1, covers the primary school years, but concerns the growing child from 7–11 years. It leads the child progressively on to enjoy reading and using books of many genres, themes and writing styles; of texts that increase in length from which the child can reflect meaning, analyse and discuss. Teachers are trained how to break the stages into steps, so that, by Year 6, children have achieved tackling books in chapters and can sit for periods of individual sustained reading. Librarians can depend for selection more on categories, such as are described by the BookTrust. It must never be forgotten, however, that not all children fit in with what is prescribed and their own judgement of what they like to read is worth respect.

Key Stages 3 and 4 generally apply to secondary school students. At Stage 3 in the lower secondary school years, the student reads a wide range of texts independently, enjoys reading, has developed particular genre and/or author interests and knows how to use texts for study purposes. Moreover, students have become responsive and critically discriminating, able to perceive layers of meaning.

Recommendations and suggestions in this text relate to the key stages system so the following categories and terms are used, wherein ages are only approximate:

- Books for Babies/Infants, 0–3 years;
- Foundation Years, 3–5;
- Key Stage 1, 5–7 years;
- Key Stage 2, ages 7–11;
- Key Stage 3, adolescence; lower secondary
- Key Stage 4, to about age 16 – GCSE level, and young adults in late high school years.

While the ages sound prescriptive, a wise adult will recognise children's individual differences and also heed what the children themselves select.

4.2 Literary Criticism

Professionals benefit from some understanding of ways into literary criticism, which influence the style in which they write book reviews, as teachers and librarians frequently must. Reviews are sometimes written from a purely gut response, declaring what the reviewer likes or dislikes and general comments about the book without any basis of critical judgement. This type of review may have its usefulness, but the skill of the true professional will be honed by knowledge of the history and practice of academic criticism. Some institutions offer specific, in-depth courses in Literary Criticism. The following is an overview of various viewpoints.

Methods concern: (i) The traditional, *extrinsic approach,* a historical-bibliographic method, common until about the 1940s. It emphasises concern with the author, with questions of origin, authority and the relationship of ideas of Western metaphysics (Ideas about cause, time, space and theism). It dwells on archetypes and expects a single inter-pretation of the text.

(ii) In contrast is the *intrinsic method,* known as Formalist, Structuralist, Post-structural Poetics, Linguistics or Narratology, depending on the emphasis, and it began in the 1940s and 1950s. It sees the text as self-sufficient and autonomous, standing on its own feet in its own right, moving away from the author's intentions.

(iii) A third method of literary criticism, called *Reader Response* is neither extrinsic nor intrinsic to the text in scrutiny, but focuses on the reader and his/her interpretation, bringing personal insights influenced by a background of experience in the world. (It resembles the gut response of the uninformed writer, yet the enlightened reviewer will identify and control the method of Reader Response, so that it is more than passionate description). Such things as reader's age, culture, socio-economic environment, and awareness of various 'isms' all contribute to the perceptions expressed in a reader's response, be they child or adult reviewer. For example, diversity of background makes the view of child from a Western materialistic, urban, perhaps Humanistic community quite different from that of the child in a non-industri-alised, rural, religious society. Reader Response began in the 1970's and is commonly applied in the twenty-first century.

(iv) Another method, *Deconstruction,* is part of Post-Structuralism ideology. It questions common interpretations of a text and the authority of the author. To construct is to build, but Deconstruction uses the technique of dismantling the recognised building and empha-sising a new form. In this way, for example, the seventeenth-century favourite with children, *Pilgrim's Progress,* is admirably retold and adapted in the twentieth century, but with new emphases – a type of deconstruction. For example, the picture book, *The Evergreen Wood,* is about animal characters, Christopher (a mouse) and and his companion, Deathly (a black rat) who are bound for the Evergreen Wood to escape the effects of pollution in the Dark Wood and the evil behaviour of hawks, weasels, rats, wildcats and foxes. The retelling parallels the shape structure of Bunyan's work, but the cross where Christian loses his bundle and is greeted by three white shining ones is replaced by a white lamb – minus ministering lamb-angels, and the delightful animal symbols, trying to fulfil Bunyan's agenda really lose the Christian message that a seventeenth-century child would have recognised. In the same way, *Joe Burkinshaw's Progress*, another Bunyanesque redaction, makes the city of Sheffield Joe's 'celestial city', a deceased brother, his 'Evangelist', and it is through reading, not via crossing the river (of death), that he achieves salvation – a different, deconstructed story. Enid Blyton's attempt to retell the story for children, *The Land of Far-Beyond,* moves even further in highly imaginative but extraneous detail before the final chapter attempts to resolve everything by 'the Prince of Peace, the Prince of Love.'

As librarians and teachers establish regular habits of reading children's literature they will soon identify a product of deconstruction if they have also read the template. It can then become information that becomes part of their framework of understanding, or it may be applied in direct instruction when it is needed.

(v) *A New Historicist Approach,* sometimes called 'Cultural Materialism' or 'Cultural Poetics' is a more current, holistic approach that seeks to integrate text and socio-historic contexts. This method, as well as earlier models, may be taught at undergraduate or postgraduate level, depending on the university and its course structure.

Readers may well ask if literary theory has any useful purpose. R. McGillis answers that question in a challenging and inspirational way:

> *So what good is literary theory? Will it keep our children singing? Well perhaps not. But understanding something of literary theory will give us some understanding of how the literature we give our children works. It might also keep us engaged with the texts that surround us, keep us singing even if it is a more mature song than we sang as youthful readers of texts. As long as we keep singing, we have a chance of passing along our singing spirit to those we teach.*
>
> *McGillis 1996: 206.*

5. Conclusion

A procession of librarians and teachers, and those training for these professions, have shared in the making of this book; parents and also children have been involved. In the twenty-first century it is usual for children to share their view of books and to help in the selection of awards, but this is a late twentieth century development in the field of children's literature. For instance, in 1985 in New South Wales, Australia, child involvement was still uncommon. 'Should the Children Choose?' is the title of an article published following Book Week of that year in Australia (Trim, 1985). It urges the Library Association to involve children more, for children had already to begun to write book reviews which attracted interest and comment. This custom is now encouraged in classrooms and in a number of publications, such as *Books for Keeps,* and by the book awards chosen by children themselves.

Libraries today seek to work 'proactively to create the best possible reading experiences for young people', as the programme for librarians, *Their Reading Futures, (TRF)* underlines in all its inservice training sessions throughout England. It was designed to take public libraries' work with children to a new level. The project has a three year programme, 2001–2003. It is co-ordinated by LaunchPad, the library development agency, in partnership with:

- ASCEL, the Association of Senior Children's and Education;
- SCL, the Society of Chief Librarians;
- CILIP;
- YLG, the Youth Libraries Group of CILIP;
- Books for Students;
- The Arts Council of England, Literature Department.

Educators also recognise the importance of books in children's lives from a young age and seek to deliver fulfilment of government policies regarding literacy.

To select books for children with enlightened discrimination and insight is, for all concerned – whether they are trainee librarians and teachers, or professionals, parents, or interested policy makers and bystanders – more than ever a pressing and important objective. The desire of any community is that their children may indeed grow into mature and wise adulthood, building stable lives for themselves and the world of the future.

Some Children's Sayings

"I hope it's library today." Sally, 6 years

"I'm gonna read a lo' o' books. It's gonna be *cooool*!" Abram, 10 years

Tutorial Topics

1. **Identify** where and why you fit into the profile of readers of this text. Listen to peer discussion and not similarities or dissimilarities.
2. **Describe** a special book you recall from childhood. Examine your reasons for remembering that book in particular. If you cannot recall a book from your childhood experience, consider an adult book you have read recently, or, find a children's book you have never read and get absorbed in it. What 'doors' did it open for you?
3. **Read** a picture book or a short story to any child. Be sure to have a parent's or teacher's permission to do this. Observe the child's responses, record them and report back to your tutorial group. What conclusions about children's responses to story do you reach as a group?
4. **Discuss** the implications of one of the following quotations, applying them to any books you know:
   - A book is a friend whose face is constantly changing. (Andrew Lang, *The Library*)
   - The true university of these days is a collection of books. (Thomas Carlyle, *The Hero as Man of Letters*).
   - The only important thing in a book is the meaning it has for you. (Somerset Maughan, *The Summing Up*).
5. **Analyse** what your personal, environmental background contributes to your reading insights.
6. **Respond** to the quotation from McGillis, 1996, 206, regarding literary theory. Which theory or theories interest you most, and why?

A USEFUL TIP: Start an annotated bibliography, using either a card system or data base. You will find it very helpful for reference purposes. No-one can remember *everything!*

Further Reading

Hollindale, Peter, with Rhanon Howells and Jacqui Newby. 'Re-reading the Self: Children's Books and the Undergraduate Readers.' In *Signal,* January 1996, 62–65.

Hunt, Peter, ed. *An Illustrated History of Children's Literature,* London and New York: Oxford University Press, 1995.

Hourihan, M. *Deconstructing the Hero: Literary Theory and Children's Literature.* London: Routledge, 1997.

JOURNALS. *Books for Keeps,* or *Carousel,* or *The Lion and the Unicorn,* or *Orana* or any journal about Children's Literature. See Reetz, M. *Professional Periodicals in Children's Literature: A Guide.* Munich: Internationale Jugendbibliothek, 1994.

Russell, David L. *Literature for Children: a Short Introduction.* New York, Longman, 2000.

Bibliography

Blyton, Enid. *The Land of Far Beyond.* Dragon/Grafton Books, 1986,126.

Buckton, Chris. NLS Trainer's Cassette 4, Side 1 (DfEE 1998).

Darton, F. J. Harvey. *Children's Books in England: Five Centuries of Social Life.* 3rd edition, revised by Brian Alderson. Reprinted with corrections. London: British Library, 1999.

Graham, Judith and Alison Kelly. *Reading Under Control: Teaching Reading in the Primary School.* Reprint. David Fulton Publishers, 2000.

Goodwin, Prue. 'Knowing about Children's Literature'. In *Books for Keeps.* No. 123, July 2000, 1.

Hendrickson, L. *Children's Literature: A Guide to the Criticism.* Boston, MA: G. K. Hall, 1987.

Hollindale, P. *Signs of Childness in Children's Books.* South Woodchester: Thimble Press 1997.

Hourihan, M. *Deconstructing the Hero: Literary Theory and Children's Literature.* London: Routledge, 1997.

Hunt, Peter, ed. *Literature for Children:* Contemporary Criticism. London: Routledge, 1992.

—— *Children's Literature: an Illustrated History.* Oxford: Oxford University Press, 1995.

Hurlimann, Bettina. *Three Centuries of Children's Books in Europe.* Translated and edited by Brian Alderson. London: Oxford University Press, 1967.

Key Stage 3 National Strategy: managing the seond year. DfES, 2002.

Key Stages. See <http://www.nc.uk.net>

Korky, Paul. 'Windows into Illustration: Korky Paul'. In *Books for Keeps,* September 2002, 7.

McGillis, R. *The Nimble Reader*. New York: Twayne, 1996.

Parry, Alan and Linda. *The Evergreen Wood*. Hunt and Thorpe, 1994.

Piaget, J. *The Moral Judgement of the Child.* New York: Harcourt Brace Jovanovich. 1932.

Townsend, John Rowe. *Written for Children.* Sixth edition. London: The Bodley Head, 1995, reprinted 1997.

Trim, Mary. *Incite,* 25 October, 1985, 12–13.

Veeser, H. A., ed. *The New Historicism*. London: Routledge, 1989.

Watson, Victor, ed. *The Cambridge Guide to Children's Literature in English.* CUP, 2000.

SECTION ONE

THE CHILD:
GROWING AND KNOWING
THROUGH BOOKS

CHAPTER ONE

The Developing Child

The child-development point of view begins with the recognition of the uniqueness of childhood. Children are not miniature adults but individuals with their own rights, needs, interests, and capacities. This concept suggests a need for literature that captures the wonders, humour and disappointments of childhood.

Huck 1976, 21.

NOTE: This chapter is not intended to give full instruction on all the specifics that concern child development, psychoanalytic theory, or how the child learns to read. Further details will be part of other academic programmes. For librarians, teachers and parents, an overview of child development provides a framework from which to base selection of children's literature and to help in the recognition of what aspects of development particular books may offer the child reader. Use this chapter as a smorgasbord of ideas, studying what is applicable to the adult's need.

1. The Uniqueness of Childhood

Every childhood is unique, the writing of a first chapter in a new biography. Nevertheless, childhood can be mapped out in a general way that is relevant to all children, based on anecdotes, observation, empirical study and scientific theories of child development. Certainly childhood is a time of amazing change and growth as each tiny bud of human potential unfolds. In accordance with usual practice, childhood is seen as extending to 16 years of age.

Many excellent text books, videos, Chartered Institute of Library and Information Professionals (CILIP) and Department of Education publications as well as journals, newspapers and web sites give detailed information concerning child development. These studies particularly focus on the areas of language, cognition, personality and social development, all of which interact to have some bearing on children's literature. From this knowledge arise certain principles which can affect book selection by librarians and teachers and all those adults who buy books for children's reading. They may also be kept in mind in observation of children's choices, always recognising that children can surprise, having different perceptions from adults. One example concerns the first Harry Potter book which won awards decided by children, but not those finally adjudicated by adults.

1.1 Physical Development

is one aspect to consider in the selection of books for Children.
(i) *Manipulative skill and fine motor control.*
Books that infants will want to grab and hold for themselves need to suit the limited manipulative dexterity of tiny fingers and hands and compulsions to suck or chew or throw. Therefore lightweight yet sturdy books of untearable cloth, or thick cardboard (known as board books) such as Dorling-Kindersley's *Touch and Feel Kitten* and MacDonald's *Let's Try* or Rebecca Elgar's *Jack – it's a rainy Day* are suitable. Board books have the advantage of having endurable thick pages and can be wiped clean after use.

As the infant becomes toddler and pre-schooler and grows increasingly into the wonder of books, he/she is ready and more able to lift the flap, as in Cimarusti and Petersen's *Peek-a-Moo*, to pull the tab, as in Elgar's *Jack – It's a Rainy Day* and to manage the holes or other moving parts of novelty books, of which there are many available.

(ii) *Attention span* and the ability to sit still long enough for a picture book (without need for a drink or to go to the toilet or just wriggle around) is another aspect of physical development through the years of infancy and the Foundation Stage, although it is also related to developing thinking skills and concentration. Attention varies from child to child but increases with age, practice and increasing interest in topics that relate to a range of life experiences, both ordinary and extraordinary. Such are portrayed, for example, in playing peekaboo, in Ross's *Peekaboo Baby; or* going on a picnic as in Hutchins' *We're*

Going on a Picnic; or starting school, as in *I spy Schooldays* by Wick and Marzollo. Fussy eating is the focus of Child's *I will not ever NEVER eat a tomato*. The very ill child, fearful of death, is the theme of Hoban's *Jim's Lion*, an unsentimental yet sensitively illustrated picture book, while *There's a House inside my Mummy* by Andrea Giles is a way of explaining the birth of a sibling.

Attention is also affected by how interest-holding are the illustrations, the perspective, language and way a story is told. Winners of the annual Greenaway and Carnegie awards are indicators of the highest standards.

(iii) *Visual attention* is important for the school-age child, but the pre-school child can be *prepared* by home and/or nursery experience with books. For whole-class or group learning-to-read activities in the Literacy Hour, teachers frequently select books that have been enlarged, sometimes as big as 60 × 45 cm, often 30 × 36 cm and 50 × 36 cm. These are the Big Books, available from numerous publishers, which make visual attention easy and inviting. Use of rhythm, rhyme, repetition, patterned language and predictability also help young ears to tune in and develop listening skills and ongoing attention. Presented in fiction and also non-fiction, traditional tales, or very popular stories such as McKee's *Not Now Bernard,* Big Books can also be used with dramatic effect in a library display. Small versions of the Big Books are suited to being held by individual children so should be on library shelves.

(iv) *Growth and change*. Children are like green runner beans that grow longer and fuller, and children's literature frequently reflects this and can enrich the Personal, Social and Health Education programme (PSHE) which starts in year 1 of primary school education. For Key Stage 2 children, E. B. White's *Charlotte's Web* is a classic example of story that depicts growth and change, the story of an eight-year-old who rescues a runt pig from slaughter, through whom she meets Charlotte, the spider and other barn animals. But at another level it is also a fable of a child growing up with changing interests and friendships, who becomes part of the cycle of life with its theme of death and rebirth. *Where Babies Come From*, by Stones, a non-fiction picture book, answers questions of origin in an informative, yet sensitive way, using accurate presentation and correct terminology. Fine's *Flour Babies,* which depicts young Simon taking on the awesome responsibility of a baby, draws attention to the need for care that contributes to growth and change over time.

Books which reflect the *physical change* of pubescence (shape and weight, pimples, puberty, feelings about themselves and friendships between sexes) are sought after by the late Key Stage 2 and Key Stage 3 readers. Sex education and talks with peers and mother contribute some knowledge, but a book about it all is highly regarded. Judy Blume's recognition of this is indicated in several of her long-popular, fiction titles, for example: *Are you there God? It's Me, Margaret,* (focus on girls); *Then Again,Maybe I Won't,* (focus on boys). Thompson's *Have You Started Yet?* is an example of non-fiction that explains menstruation in a open way and, as the author suggests, it is also a book for boys to read.

Examples of informative books that use photographic illustrations depicting young people are: What *Do You Know About Relationships? Let's Discuss, Love, Hate and Other Feelings* and *Let's Discuss Sex and Sexuality*, by Sanders and Myers. These texts may be included in the PSHE programme but should be available to young readers who want to see and read for themselves. Other information books which are about the growth, curiosity and embarrassment of teenage years are met in such as *Cool and Celibate? Sex or No Sex,* by Dr David Bull, Fisher's *Living with a Willy,* and Asquith's, The *Teenage Worrier's Pocket Guide to Mind and Body.*

For older, secondary-school age teenagers at Key Stage 4, there is a range of fiction available that matches with their sexual awareness and experimentation, emphasised through education and the influence of peers, media and society generally. Doherty's *Dear Nobody* considers the theme of teen pregnancy as does *Don't Look back* by Chick, and, particularly for boys, *Shadows,* by Bowler and Ure's *Just Sixteen.*

2. Language Development

> *Children pick up words as pigeons pick up peas.*
> *Anonymous English source, 17th century*

2.1 The Theorists

Chosen for emphasis in this text are **Vygotsky** and **Cambourne and Turbill.** An overview of the considerable body of research concerning language development, coming especially from the varied perspectives of linguists, psycholinguists and educators, is useful to a professional who is involved with children's books and learning.

Russian-born, *Lev Vygotsky* ((1896–1934) researched in the 1920s and is respected for his theory of *Social Constructionism* which influences current ideas for language development in Early Years education and the primary classroom. He emphasises:

- the student's *Zone of Proximal Development* by which he means that some tasks are too difficult for the child to master alone, but allow her/him to work independently until help – frequently of social influence – enables the child to attain a higher level of ZPD.
- Use 'Scaffolding', meaning a changing level of support provided by peers or adults, in much the same way that scaffolding supports a building under construction.
- Respect an interactive, interpersonal language environment. This includes the use of private speech and allows for talking to oneself as many children do, associating thought and action.

2.2 *The implications of Vygotsky's theory*

For librarians and teachers is, firstly, to intervene when needed and to allow library and classroom not to be 'no talking' areas, but those where students share verbally; where the private speech of a child is acceptable. It can be heard as a child searches for a book: "Um, um, Dinosaurs, where are you?' Or, "No, that's not right. I'll try the next shelf . . .'

Secondly, there is the assuring role of literature itself, that, in the genres of Fairytale, Fable, and Realistic Fiction or Fantasy, constantly depicts the lives of fascinating characters, animals, adults or children, whose actions are often inadequate for their task, but by which, with some peer or adult assistance, they learn. Thereby the young child can meet Archie of Ezra Jack Keats' *Pet Show*, who is determined to take part in the local pet show even when his own cat runs away; who is encouraged in societal activity that demands some divergent thinking by adults. They can also relate to Peter who longs to be able to whistle to Willie, his dog, so he practises and practises until, *heigh-ho*, suddenly, out comes a real whistle, the story of *Whistle for Willie*. Ezra Jack Keats' portrayal of the under- sevens is absolutely true to life – and in these books, true to a black American community. These kids demonstrate their zone of proximal development as they model inexpertness that becomes expertise with effort; which is modelled, initially for Willie, by another boy whose dog runs straight to him when he whistles.

The same pattern can be seen in the *Josie Smith* series of eight or more books about a five and a quarter year old girl who, as experience accumulates, growing into independence and autonomy, explores her place in the world, assisted by adults and peers. Books by Jacqueline Wilson, such as *Double Act* and *The Suitcase Kid,* move the reader on to the typical zonal experience of ten year olds, all written with the eye of an accurate observer who is also sympathetic to the inexperience of the pre-teen. *For children of ten and older, Skellig,* Carnegie Award winner of 1999, portrays the contribution to deeper understanding that comes to the hero, Michael, through an extraordinary creature that he discovers in his garage, a bluebottle eating half-angel and an unusual girl, Mina, who is home-schooled and loves Blake's poetry. Even the famed Harry Potter and his school friends depict their own zones of proximal development as they depend on each other to find answers to wizardry and human relationship problems.

The adolescent struggle is grippingly developed in *Junk,* the Carnegie Award winner of 1997, which concerns house squatting, thieving, drug addiction, prostitution and pregnancy. Immature the 14 year-old teenagers, Tar and Gemma are, but they naively imitate an adult world, and in the pain and downward spiral of their runaway existence, move on toward self-knowledge, empathy and wisdom. For the reader who knows little of the dark world of addiction, the use of different voices in first person narration, is a device which allows

> *the twisted voice of heroin itself to come through. Heroin begins as mother, lover, best friend . . . and ends up like a soldier holding a gun to your head. There's no need to moralise about it. Why go on about the obvious? The readers aren't so stupid.*
>
> Burgess 1997, 1

Burgess' use of this narrative device subtly portrays the negative and positive effects of society, revealing that both types of experience, demonstrated in peer influences, have an effect on cognitive development as well as affecting emotions and personality.

2.3 Cambourne and Turbill

are two Australian educators who identify seven optimal conditions for language and literacy growth. Though they have their basis in Whole Language Philosophy, they are also in harmony with teaching and library practice in affirming, welcoming environments.

*Cambourne and Turbill's Conditions for Language and
Literacy Growth (1987).*

(i) The primary condition is that of IMMERSION. From birth, a child is immersed in a flood of meaningful spoken language. The developing infant becomes bathed in the sounds, meanings, cadences and rhythms of the language they will acquire.

The same principle applies to library and classroom where the child should be surrounded with bright, clear signs and bulletin boards, story-reading-telling opportunities and projects such as treasure hunts through books.

(ii) The second condition is that of DEMONSTRATION, a term which originated with the psycholinguist, Frank Smith. This means that from other speakers come examples of the spoken form of the language. It is frequently related to action, such as in: "Pass the rice, please"; consequently the rice or salad or potatoes or whatever has been requested is passed to the speaker. It may be related to sound: "Oh, there's someone at the door" or, "The telephone's ringing." Modelled speech that is easily taken in is usually informal and brief.

In the classroom, teachers and students are active demonstrators of oral language examples of commands, questions and instructions. They can also provide speech models through the language of story. In the library, a quieter place, there is a particularly library-based vocabulary: "Are you looking for *fiction or non-fiction?*" or "Oh, this book is *overdue*. There is a small *fine* to pay." Or, "Did your teacher specify any particular *genre?*" or, "Today we are going to follow a *story trail!*" or "Do you know about our *DELTA* programme?" (Libraries frequently develop their own county-specific terms, such as used in Derbyshire to promote their own Derbyshire Learning and Technology Access: DELTA).

(iii) Thirdly, Language in the home, library or classroom is employed for REAL-LIFE purposes. With this in mind, children at school are encouraged to write genuine plans, to record about past or coming events of consequence, of visits to special places such as theme parks or zoos or grandparents' home; of celebrations, of birthdays and festivals. Attention is drawn to diaries, calendars, weather reports, and to books and publications of all kinds. Similarly, stories that resemble real life, or are true accounts, demonstrate language for real purposes.

(iv) RESPONSIBILITY is Cambourne and Turbill's fourth condition, for when children initially *learn to talk* there are no controlled lessons in prescribed structures. The children use language conventions – questions, demands, commands, statements – that suit their needs and readiness, experimenting with vocabulary and syntax. Different speakers take different routes through their innate language skills, responding to, and receiving from their environment, so that, as Hitchcock states:

> *children are active participants in their own language and literacy development; they build theories and test hypotheses as they construct meaning about their world.*
>
> 2001, 151.

It should be recognised that an admission of the importance of Responsibility which reflects psycholinguist theory and the 'top-down', Whole Language approach to literacy, which has been used in Britain, Australia and New Zealand and other countries since the 1980s, does not discount the twenty-first century's 'bottom-up' emphasis. This is a move back to skills and stresses a significant recent development in the area of phonics; that 'phonological and phonemic awareness can make towards success in reading.' Graham and Kelly 2000, 11.

When the principle of Responsibility is applied to literature in the classroom and library scene, children are encouraged to self-select the books they want to read. Ongoing skills-instruction, dictionary use and one-to-one support should always available.

(v) The fifth condition is that of EXPECTATION for every parent expects his/ her child to speak and to become part of an interactive environment. As Brian Cambourne says,

> *We 'give off' expectations that our children will learn to walk and talk, and they do, even though it's quite often painful (walking) and very complicated' (talking).*
>
> Butler and Turbill 1984, 7.

In the classroom, success is assumed and teachers set clear goals for what the children will achieve. Similarly, the librarian believes that every child-seeker will find a book that pleases them, ('the right book for the right child') which will contribute to some aspect of development.

(vi) Condition six seems to come easily to parents. Note the importance of APPROXIMATION whereby young learners are not expected to display perfect competence immediately. Parents are delighted when their offspring try to make meaning, and they reward them with praise and positive responses. Even abbreviated, unstructured statements can be rich in meaning, such as "Doing?" or "Mummy sock." In the home, approximation is welcomed and receives encouraging response! In classroom and library, positive reinforcement of a child's approximations in oral expression and reading skill are the norm, for they are not wrong but a step toward the acquisition of more sophisticated word recognition and perception, especially as modelling and immersion apply.

FEEDBACK is the seventh condition worthy of notice wherever language is developing. When the young child says "Doing?" the parent or caregiver will usually extend the brief utterance by modelling an appropriate response, such as "I'm doing the ironing," or I'm changing a tyre." If the child pronounces, "Mummy sock," the feedback would probably be, "Yes, that's Mummy's sock," but gesture and circumstances add their own meanings. Furthermore, despite many examples of feedback of language, no parents or caregivers in early childhood expect instant change. They know that immature structures will persist for a long time until one day *goed* becomes *went* and *buyed* becomes *bought*, especially as the positive models of books, library and classroom instruction continue to apply. Nagging makes very little difference until readiness prevails. Feedback also applies in the exchange of opinions about books.

2.4 *Books and Language Development*

Young they may be, but babies soon become interested in books, whether introduced in the stage of babbling at 3 – 6 months (Bloom), or at nine months (as with the Books for Babies scheme), the time when infants are at the verge of uttering their first word (usually from 10–13 months). Illustrations make their eyes light up, prompting goos and gurgles and reaching out to touch. The baby is alert, ready to absorb and respond, according to his/her innate 'wiring' for language, as described by Chomsky. This experience supplements the immersion of everyday language in the home and adds further demonstration, modelling and feedback. Not only does the rhythm, rhyme, repetition and humour of the language of story stimulate and excite, but a contrasting mood that uses gentle, musical and poetic language can also soothe and comfort. As Vygotsky pointed out, children's development is proximal, so of course the infant does not understand everything at once, but wooed by story, with the guidance and assistance of adults and more skilled children, his/her language will thrive.

As the child continues to grow physically, so will language, into the two word stage and beyond, with each child demonstrating his/her innate capacity (as described by Chomsky) to apply morphological rules. The classic experiment by Jean Berko-Gleason (1958) demonstrated how pre-school and first grade children were able to generate plural and other forms of syntax, even with fictional language. All children can do this, but it is a fact that the child who has been stimulated by the additional experience of book experience from an early age does it in an outstanding way. This is evidenced by the longitudinal study of Professor Barrie Wade and Dr Maggie Moore concerning book experience by pre-schoolers in Birmingham, England. It clearly shows at school commencement the superiority in literacy and mathematics of a child who has been immersed in the language of literature. Such superiority, according to Walter Loban's longitudinal study, makes for excellence in reading and writing in sixth grade. Other studies show that reading and writing development are rooted in oral language (Gavelek and Raphael, 1996; Nagy and Scott, 2000). Santrock emphasises that

> *For children who have participated extensively in print-related interactions in their homes and communities, literacy often comes quickly in school. However, many children who have not participated extensively in lap reading and similar literary experiences in pre-school will take longer to develop literacy skills (Hiebwert and Raphael, 1996).*
>
> Santrock 2001, 75.

At Bingham, Nottinghamshire, I observed the eagerness and participation of 28 babies and toddlers, accompanied by 32 parents and grandparents, at a Boots Books for Babies session in the town library. I watched their little faces light up as they fixed their eyes on a Big Book, listened to several stories, including Walking *through the Jungle* and *Peek a Moo*. Then they joined in action rhymes, infants jigging on a parent's knees, or two and three year olds moving with animation to the finger rhymes, 'Two little dickie birds' and 'This little piggy went to market.' Singing followed, the children using instruments for small hands, then colouring a given picture, looking at books, playing with soft toys and jigsaws if they chose and, to end the session, a biscuit and orange juice. It was a happy, interactive scene. One young father who attended with his three-year-old wanted to tell me, meanwhile beaming at his son, "It's amazing what he knows; what he can say!" His pregnant wife added, patting her abdomen, "We want the next one to have the same start with books." Other young parents nodded and smiled in agreement.

Many delightful board books, and other formats, are available for infants as 'tasters' and 'starters', such as those written by Helen Oxenbury. Her books, *Dressing*; and *Working* clearly picture recognisable aspects of a baby's life and environment, each with a baby hero. As Dorothy Butler says in her fine work, *Babies Need Books*, babies love to be held, so in the warm, safe relationship of one-to-one story experience, the caregiver shows the picture and tells the name of the item as it is called in that family, putting it into a simple sentence which might be: "Look at the baby/ baby's shoes/socks." Or, " There's the baby's potty. See, he/she's sitting on the potty/ now it's time to have a bath/ to go to bed." There is no written text, just pictures of the familiar and the assurance of love and care, given by the close proximity of the reader and recipient in their loving relationship. It is well recognised that, as Butler claims, 'language learning has a great deal to do with emotion and the development of relationships' (20). Bookstart type programmes in Britain, Australia, New Zealand and other places all recognise the value of books for little people as a tremendous launch to life.

2.5 Milestones of Language Development and their Implications for Selection of Children's literature[1]

Infancy: **0–24 months.**	Language learning starts at birth when babies are aware of sounds about them, apparent by their body language. By three months they turn to a speaker and respond to a soothing voice. 3–6 months: cooing; discrimination of vowels. Babbling expands to include sounds of spoken language. Turn-taking is evident. First words are spoken at about 10–13 months. Understands about 50+ words by 12–18 months. *Vocabulary expands* to about 200 words. Combines two words, as in subject and action ("Mummy gone." "Want teddy") by 24 months.

[1] This is a composite model based on Bloom, Chukovsky, Lindfors, Norton, Santrock and personal but unpublished research.

Implications	Provide simply illustrated concept books that include familiar food, places, animals and body parts; also Mother Goose rhymes. Read books with recognisable action pictures. Enjoy colour and humour together.
2 years	Vocabulary increases rapidly to about nine hundred words; correct use of plurals and past tense; some prepositions. Can identify and name actions and body parts. Enjoy starting to count and 'write'.
3–4 years	Utterances increase to 3 – 4 morphemes in a sentence. (Morphemes are the building blocks of the English language, e.g. *play* is one morpheme; can be changed to *playing* (two morphemes). Vocabularies increase to about fifteen hundred words. Uses past tense, *wh* questions, negatives and imperatives, adjectives, adverbs, pronouns and prepositions. Some children start to read simple words, and to write, using invented spelling.
Implications	Read stories about families, child heroes, pets, outings; also rhymes, riddles and poetry (See Chapter 2).
5–6 years	Vocabulary reaches about 10,000 words; can co- ordinate simple sentences. Enjoy dramatic play. Starting to read.
6–8 years	Conversational skills improve; many new words; use complex sentences. Reading skills and interest increasing.
Implications	Offer literature that is relevant to the interests of school-age children, both stories and information books. Move past dependence on picture books. Continue offering poetry, especially humorous verse and story poems.
9–11 years	Children start to relate concepts to broader ideas; start to use synonyms when defining; conversational strategies improve.
11–14 years	Abstract words are added, used and understood, along with complex grammatical forms. Can understand metaphor and satire.
15–20 years	Now young adults.
Implications	Approaching, or advanced in, puberty so relevant literature should be displayed where children and young people can find it easily Provide books about

contemporary and historical life. Broaden the range of genres. Males start to prefer information books; females continue an interest in family stories and the novel. Interest in poetry wanes.

2.6 Reading Skills: There's More to Reading than Meets the Eye!

Methods of teaching reading skills have changed over time, yet children have always learnt to read, suggesting that any one method alone is not superior. In the seventeenth century some very young children were able to read, and this is still so today for a minority. The Alphabetic method, the Look and Say approach, 'Language Experience' and 'Whole Language' – each have come and gone in classroom fashion. Methods and attitudes vary to some extent from country to country and from culture to culture. This text considers theory and practice in the Western World.

It is clear that children need to develop skills of *cueing*: the ability to use clues or signals which the brain receives and acts upon when one reads. A somewhat similar process happens in speech when he speaker sends and receives auditory cues. As Vygotsky pointed out in 1962, there is a real association between inner speech and thought, and these come together in the cueing system.

2.7 The Cueing System

(i) The Semantic Cueing System. By this, readers draw on meaning from a text through what they understand from life experience. If the child has had varied experiences, words in print will convey meaning because personal involvement with 'mother', 'cat', 'pizza' brings their images to mind. If the child has had personal experience enriched through story, s/he has vicarious experience to draw on also.

(ii) The Syntactic Cueing System. This concerns the rules of the language of the environment in which an infant grows and develops speech. As the child is immersed in everyday language of the home and beyond, these rules are constantly being demonstrated. They concern such things as word order. Is the order *subject-verb-object*, as in I like pizza, the English format? They also concern the placement of describing words – the adjectives- and how plurals are made, and how

tense is denoted in a sentence. It is when the child knows these rules by osmosis and having applied already to speech, that h/she predicts easily what a sentence is telling in print. Sound and letter recognition will play a part, but so does prediction stimulated by knowing what to expect.

(iii) *The Grapho-Phonic Cueing System* concerns how a word is written and how it sounds. Two year old David began to identify any word in print that he saw starting with K as 'K Mart', name of the store where his parents took him shopping, where he knew the big red sign. He was applying innate visual recognition of the graphic form to experience. When started exclaiming 'K Mart, K Mart' and pointing to the K on Kellogg's Cornflakes, he was applying phonic knowledge.

Again, as with the other cueing systems, pre-reading experience flows on to make competent readers. Pre-reading experience will include the sounds of language related to words on a page when a story is read, and the bold titles of favourite story books that small people begin to recognise and 'read,' It will also include other forms of language experience that emphasise the grapho-phonic dimension, such as 'writing' letters and 'stories' about drawings from an early age.

Reading and Writing flow from oral language skills, developed in environments such as Vygotsky, Cambourne and Turbill describe. As Chomsky has shown, young children are 'wired' for language and have the innate potential to cope with an abstract symbol system.

One recent development is the reawakening to the contribution of phonological and phonemic awareness. This means that phonics, the relationship between letter symbol and sound, needs to be known by a reader and taught by a teacher. Thus teachers of the British National Curriculum are required to teach phonic skills as part of a learner's repertoire of strategies.

3. Cognition

> *My life through its first years . . .*
> *The way I travelled when I first began*
> > Wordsworth

Students who have already studied Piaget and other child developmentalists will find the following a review, but related to children's literature. To some other readers it may be new.

The Theorists: Piaget, Gibson

Current understandings about children's minds and how their thinking and learning skills develop (i.e. cognitive or intellectual abilities) are largely based on the theories of two psychologists: the Swiss *Jean Piaget*, (1896–1980) and the neo Piagetians who adopt but modify his theories. James Gibson, a more recent theorist, holds views which are influencing attitudes to cognition in early childhood.

3.1 Piaget

Piaget was a *Constructivist* in view point, believing that while infants' cognitive potential was innate, they were born with few abilities and must establish their minds by constructing meaning through interaction with the environment. He theorised that children organise their thinking into what he called *schemas*, meaning a 'concept or framework that exists in an individual's mind to organise and interpret information.' How children adapt and apply their schemas focuses on two main processes which he identified as *assimilation* and *accommodation.* By assimilation he meant what takes place when a child receives new information and *adds* it to what is already known. By accommodation he meant how the child *adjusts* to the new information which contributes to broadened understanding and, thereby, application.

Piaget also believed that cognition develops in a sequence of age-related stages, beginning at birth to about two years, a period when the infant is forming an understanding of the world through his senses. He calls this the *Sensorimotor Stage.* Even in the first month cognition is taking place, evidenced in the baby showing recognition of familiar voices and how s/he turns or quietens when hearing these voices. The infant also fixes a gaze on patterns and faces. There is little opportunity for books at this time for the infant mainly sleeps, eats and cries, and the mother is adjusting to a new and demanding schedule. By three months and over, however, the building blocks of language, cognition and symbolic development are emerging, in cooing, gurgling and chuckling; in use of tone and volume without the use of consonants; crying noisily for needs to be met; smiling and laughing as a response; becoming interested in playthings. And why not books? Mothers, like Gudrun from Leicestershire, England who introduced simple picture books to her twins at three months, and Carol from New South Wales, Australia, report that their little ones responded very positively at this early age. Leila Berg pointed out in 1977 that reading and loving go together, which describes the relationship of a baby in a mother's arms, cradled by language, smiles and caress.

By six months and over, as assimilation and accommodation continue, so does cognition, associated with language and symbolic development. Now the baby shows an increasing ability to concentrate on interesting objects, including bold pictures in books. This is why Books for Babies programmes that promote introducing books to infants, frequently advocate books for the nine months old infant. Right in harmony with the infant's innate ability to grow in cognition via sensory stimulation are concept books like *Touch and Feel Kitten*, a Dorling Kindersley board book, which introduces actual textures for the infant to feel, along with photographs of several adorable kittens:

> *Come and meet your favourite kittens!*
> *Stroke my **soft** silky fur.*
> *Touch my **rough**, pink tongue.*
> *Look at our two **smooth** tags.*
> *Feel my **hard**, yellow food bowl.*
> *Touch the **scratchy** straw basket.*

Another example, *Tickle Tickle Tom* by Alex Ayliffe links the language of a concept text (body parts) with the game of touching (sensory activity), so reader and child can play along with Tom:

> *Tom can tap his **nose***
> *touch his **toes** . . .*
> *shake his **head***
> *or **nod**, instead . . .*

When the baby approaches one year to about fifteen months, s/he understands use of familiar everyday objects; understands everyday words and simple commands; is starting to speak occasional words and can play 'pretend' games; will pat books and look curiously at pictures on the page. Gudrun, mother of the twins referred to earlier, writes:

> *The girls are really book mad now and are only 14 months old. They have a little table and chairs in their bedroom which we bought for when they are about two or three, but they love it already and sit at it studiously examining all their favourite books. On our magazine table in the lounge our National Geographic*

magazines have been replaced by Peter Rabbit, One Duck Stuck, Peekaboo Baby! *and many other baby books.*

This progression of expanding schemas continues into the 18 months-and-over period when s/he now has between 20 and 50 recognisable words – though vocabulary acquisition varies from child to child – and is starting to thread words together in 'telegraphese' communication: "Pussy come" or "Want drink." Now s/he enjoys picture books, will point to favourite pages or characters and may name some objects on the page; will also laugh at the humorous or unexpected and find it very funny if a dog is called a horse! The simple one sentence text of Hutchins' *Rosie's Walk* in which Rosie outwits a fox, and the humour of *How do I eat it?* and *How do I put it on?*, both by Shigeo Watanabe are perennial favourites with this age group. More recent publications that suit them are *Shrinking Mouse* by the author of *Rosie's Walk*, and Lawrence's *Baby Loves* with its humorous illustrations and lively text.

The *Preoperational Stage* lasts from about two to seven years. Operational has the prefix, pre, to indicate that, according to Piaget's theory, young children cannot understand/ perform mental operations that are reversible for it involves back-to front, reasoning and thinking. An example sometimes given is that if asked to walk home from a friend's house, the preoperational thinker probably would reply that he didn't know the way because he had never walked home before.

Such seemingly illogical behaviour (from an adult perspective) is demonstrated vividly and lovingly by Ezra Jack Keats in the behaviour of his picture book characters. These are children who behave and think just as their picture book audience does, all at the preoperational level. For example, Peter, in *The Snowy Day* by Ezra Jack Keats, runs outside to explore the strange snowy world that arrived outdoors in his neighbourhood while he slept. Page after page depicts his experimentation:

Crunch, crunch, crunch, his feet sank into the snow. He walked with his toes pointing out, like this. He walked with his toes pointing in, like that. Then he dragged his feet s-l-o-w-l-y to make tracks . . . He picked up a handful of snow . . . He packed it round and firm and put the snowball in his pocket for tomorrow. Then he went into his warm house.

The inevitable happens, unforeseen by a preoperational child, as the snowball melts away to nothingness, the reverse to his immediate, straightforward experience:

Before he got into bed he looked into his pocket.
His pocket was empty. The snowball wasn't there.
He felt very sad.

Egocentricism, also demonstrated in Keats' characters, is typical of this second stage of cognitive development when children's perception is always self-centred; when they relate to characters who behave as they do, or might enjoy trying, themselves; when they play *beside* another child, rather than *with* them. They also recognise the egocentric and imaginative behaviour of animal heroes, whether they are a bear (as in the *Mr Bear* series by Debi Gliori), a badger (as in *Bedtime for Frances* by Russell Hoban) a rabbit (as in *Goodnight Little Rabbit* by Marie Wabbes) or a wombat as in *Wombat goes Walkabout* by Michael Morepurgo, or any other animal hero – and they abound!

At this stage the child begins to think intuitively, and symbolically to represent mentally an object that is not present; follows simple stories and enjoys repetition. By age seven the child's interest in talking, listening, reading and writing are becoming established and s/he will be learning to listen attentively to stories and poems, and also using picture, context and phonic cues in reading. Old favourites like Burningham's *Mr Gumpy's Outing,* and Hutchins' *Good-night, Owl!* never fail to please pre-schoolers and beginning readers, as does the humour and amazing appetite of The Very *Hungry Caterpillar.* Devotees of the hungry caterpillar may also enjoy Carle's collage-based work, *The Very Clumsy Click Beetle,* and others in the 'very hungry' series.

There is an abundance of literature for the blossoming Preoperational child as s/he develops during this five year stage from being a listener only, to being an active beginner reader who can now use picture, context and phonic cues for prediction, in group reading situation, with a reading partner, or in moments of quiet solitude. Watch out for annual award winners and lists in journals and on web-sites that will extend their young horizons and bring a taste of honey.

The Concrete Operational Stage is the third Piagetian phase of cognitive development, lasting from about seven to eleven years. Now the child is 'operational' and uses concrete objects that s/he can see and handle, as a way into further understanding. Now they can also do and apply mentally what they could previously do only physically, and they can reverse operations. This means that they begin to develop a time sense so that they can accept the time shifts of stories like the ever-popular *Tom's Midnight Garden,* by Philippa Pearce, or for a mature reader, the historical setting of World War II and the location shifts of *Goodnight Mr Tom* by Michelle Magorian. They are also moving away from egocentricism, so can identify with different points of view and life styles that reflect other cultures, as in John Steptoe's *Mufaro's Beautiful Daughters: An African Tale.*

The Formal Operations Stage, identified by Piaget, may begin at ages 12, or higher. Children now move on cognitively, being more able to understand principles, abstract language and concepts, see another's point of view and become concerned with personal identity and society. Many books address these issues, suited to the adolescent and young adult.

3.2 *James Gibson*

holds views which are receiving attention, especially in the area of early childhood. He disagrees with Piaget's *constructivist* view that infants have each to *construct* their understanding of the world. In contrast, James Gibson a *nativist* in theory, argues – with experimental evidence to support his claims – that the infant has many innate abilities. Stephanie Thornton sums up in the closing paragraph of her work:

> *Present theories of intellectual development draw on data which were simply not available to Piaget. One wonders what he would have made of it, had he the methodological tools in use today. As it is, one can only stand in awe of his achievement. For, despite all the radical change in how we now see the detail of the process of intellectual development,* **the broad outlines of our understanding, and the philosophical questions shaping our agenda for research are still recognisably Piagetian.**[2]
>
> *Thornton, 2002*

How then, does Gibson's view contribute to the selection of children's literature? One suggestion is that infants can cope with picture books from even earlier than most imagine or propose, as some mothers who use colourful books with their babies from six weeks on have already discovered. Baby Billy lives in Canada; at seven weeks of age he watched intently and listened with obvious pleasure as the sounds of language washed over him and illustrations held his gaze.

---

[2] Bold is mine – M. Trim.

4. Personality

> *Personality refers to distinctive thoughts, emotions and behaviours that characterise the way an individual adapts to the world.*
> Santrock 2001, 151.

4.1 Theorists: Erikson, Lacan, Maslow

Personality development is like a climbing plant that intertwines with other aspects of human development, yet psychologists are interested in identifying its particular characteristics (Rychman, 2000).

Erik Erikson (1902–1994) was an early theorist who, like Piaget, recognised stages of human development, his focus being on a developmental unfolding of the personality through *eight psychosocial stages*, for which he identifies the positive and negative possibilities of each. The first of these is *Trust versus Mistrust* which occurs in the child's first year, a marvellous time for an adult to introduce an infant to the joyous world of picture books in a loving, bond-establishing, safe relationship.

Erikson's second stage concerns the toddler years and concerns those 'terrible twos' who discover that they can assert their independence, sometimes stamping their feet, or running in the direction they choose, thereby exerting some power in their environment. Theirs is the stage of *Autonomy versus Shame and Doubt*. Many books depict this new independence of action and imagination, sometimes depicted through young animal characters, as in Mahy's *A Lion in the Meadow*. Erikson suggests that at this stage a sense of shame and doubt develops where there is too much restraint and punishment. So little people need not only the reassurance of loving caregivers but also the added modelling of affirmative attitudes of picture book settings, heroes and heroines.

Three other psychosocial stages cover: (i) the three to five year old (*Initiative versus guilt*) for whom the world is widening and growing more challenging, with adults expecting children to take care of themselves and their belongings. Picture books for this age group express their expanding skills, imagination and ambitions for interaction. One aspect is portrayed in *Murphy's All for One*, about Marlon, an only monster child, eager to make new friends and extend his horizon, yet still needing assurance of continuing mother-love. He wants someone to play with and meets up with three other little monsters: Alligatina,

Boomps-a-daisy and Basher, who play as their names suggest. They do not really want him in their game which changes too fast for Marlon to keep pace with. But he is discovering that for monsters, as with children, making friends can be a roller coaster ride. Many writers and illustrators like the Ahlbergs, John Burningham and Anthony Browne are well tuned in to the needs of children whose initiative needs to be encouraged.

(ii) *Industry versus inferiority*, Erikson's fourth psychosocial stage, is about the middle and prepubescent childhood years, which extend to about eleven years of age. The child is usually now established as reader, each with an individual reading age. This is an enthusiastic, responsive group whom many teachers love to teach. They are active, mastering knowledge and intellectual skills, keen to achieve, like their fictional book heroes of whom there are many. The older child of this group enjoys horror as in the *Point Crime* series (Scholastic) and humour as in the non-fiction *Horrible Histories* or *Horrible Science* series, also published by Scholastic.

(iii) The adolescent, teen years stress the *Identity versus identity* crisis of the pubescent young person. Like many of Judy Blume's characters, or those for older readers by Jacqueline Wilson, as in *Girls Out Late* and *Girls in Love* young people are often in confusion, experimentation and foolishness, trying to find out who they are and where they are headed in life. A teacher, librarian or parent who understands the dilemma, noise and precariousness of this age, one who can display or gently suggest books that are relevant to contemporary life and increasing maturation, can be of real service to this group as they move beyond childhood. One novelist, Linda Newberry, writes especially for the latter subset as she writes about young people who are teetering on the cusp between childhood and adulthood.

4.2 Basic Behaviours

Psychoanalytic theorists such as Freud and Jung have contributed their particular insights into how the unconscious operates and influences the self. Their assertions affect the adult critic, but they do not appear to bother children. When young readers look at little Mickey with his penis, displayed in Maurice Sendak's *In the Night Kitchen*, they accept that Mickey is a tubby little boy, not unlike themselves. Based on observation and anecdotal evidence, it is clear that most children accept the story literally as just the adventures of a little boy in a mixed-up, exciting sort of dream. It is one which bypasses parents, focuses on bakers' night activity, the child's involvement with rising dough and milk, then finishes up with an omnipotent Mickey safe in his own bed. Some older girls giggle at the bare body; other children put the book aside as 'boring' or 'not interesting.' There may be some whose experience has prepared them to sense a deeper, symbolic layering, as Bettelheim's theories suggest. It is not uncommon for adults, however, reading at more than one level, to raise eyebrows, or to frown and question as they immediately relate to sexual innuendo, identifying transfer of the author's own infantile sexuality (Freudian theory).

4.3 Lacan and Maslow

Along with Karen Horney, Melanie Klein and Donald Winnicott, *Jacques Lacan* revised some of Freud's views, but he elaborates on three stages of development, distinguishing between an infant's development of the imaginary, the symbolic and the real. He proposes that the imaginary, or mirror stage, starts at about six months when the infant receives the *imago* of its own body, thus the appropriateness of introducing infants of this age to books that emphasise body parts, such as Watanabe's *How do I put it on?*

Maslow reacted against Freud's pessimism and limited sampling, pointing out positive aspects of the developing ego with its propensity for self-realisation and symbolic play. From Maslow, a Humanist and Existentialist, comes a hierarchical model which emphasises the uniqueness of an individual, the rational and self-determining nature in response to environmental surroundings.

This is a useful model that shows the progression of basic needs, which, as they are met, con tribute to a balanced personality. The Maslow pyramid (1954, 1971) frequently shown within a triangle, begins from the base with the needs for physical care in the newborn, then proceeds through to the highest level which concerns every individual's need for knowledge and aesthetic fulfilment.

SELF-ACTUALIZATION NEEDS

Aesthetic and Cognitive Needs
Need to Know and Understand
Need symmetry and beauty
Esteem Needs

Approval and Recognition
Belongingness Needs
Love Affection Acceptance
Safety Needs
Physical and psychological safety
Physiological Needs
Food Drink Warmth Sleep
Shelter

Children's literature is full of examples that portray and help to fulfil this pyramid of human needs. Different readers will no doubt discern different emphases, yet the following are possible readings from (a) picture stories (b) other. Throughout life these needs must be met and each level contributes to a higher level of well-being.

NEED	CHILDREN'S LITERATURE
1. Physiological	(a) *Newborn* by Kathy Henderson Illustrated by Caroline Birch (Frances Lincoln) (b) *Have you started yet?* by Ruth Thomson, illustrated by Jane Eccles (Macmillan)
2. Safety	(a) *The Angel with a Mouth-Organ* by Christobel Mattingley (Hodder and Stoughton) (b) *How to Cross the Road and not turn into a Pizza* by Anne Fine (Walker Books)
3. Love, Affection, Belonging	(a) *I love Hugs* by Laura Jones (Scholastic) (b) *The Railway Children* by Frances Hodgson Burnett
4. Esteem	(a) *I'm Happy* by Karen Bryant-Mole & Mike Gordon (Wayland) (b) *King of Shadows* by Susan Cooper (The Bodley Head)
5. Self-actualization	(a) *The Shopping Basket* (Red Fox) (b) *Tumbler* by Liz Filleul, illustrated by Susan Field (Lion Books)
6. Knowing, Understanding	(a) *Alfie's Numbers* by Shirley Hughes (Bodley Head)

	(b) *I Have Lived a Thousand Years* by Livia Bitton-Jackson (Simon & Schuster)
7. Love of Beauty	(a) *Play with Me* by Marie Hall Ets (Puffin Books)
	(b) *The Secret Garden* by Frances Hodgson Burnett, illustrated by Shirley Hughes (Victor Gollancz)

4.4 Current researchers

consider there is an important 'big five' in personality development: emotional stability, extraversion, openness to experience, agreeableness, and conscientiousness (Costa, 2000; Costa and Marcie, 1995; McNulty, 2000). Critics of the 'big five' say that there are further aspects that contribute to personality, factors that should not be overlooked, such as the place of happiness and sadness, joy versus anger and the contribution of self- assertiveness. Others point out that temperament is closely related to personality; that children may classify as:

- An **easy child,** generally positive who quickly adapts to new experiences and regular routines;
- A **difficult child** who tends to react negatively, showing aggression, lacking self-control; slow to accept new experiences;
- A **slow-to-warm-up child** who has a low activity level, tends to be negative and does not adapt well.

    Chess and Thomas 1977: 218–216; Thomas and Chess 1991.

As children encounter literature, they constantly meet both positive and negative demonstrations of all the given factors and personality types, which reflect the diversity of real life behaviours and personalities. Many characters, but not all, are emotionally stable, some are confident extraverts, others are shy introverts, while others may be very agreeable or disagreeable, conscientious or couldn't-care-less. In real-life, too, as well as a diversity of personality types, behaviour is never completely static or one dimensional, and this movement between the socially/ ethically/ morally desirable and that which contributes to a less balanced personality, makes a story valid and acceptable. As librarians, teachers and parents should recognise, true-to-life but fictional demonstrations of behaviours may stimulate readers' role-modelling, thought, questioning and discussion. Victorian writers, especially of an Evangelical persuasion, tended to show only the positive, while the perspective of the twenty-first century offers struggle, 'warts and all'. The resolution, however, in children's literature is the ultimate option of what is good.

5. Social Development

Theorist: Bronfenbrenner

An important name in the field of social development is that of Urie Bronfenbrenner (B. 1917) who devised the *Ecological Theory* which emphasis the social context in which children grow up and persons who influence them. He describes five types of systems of which the primary system, called a *microsystem*, is the one that most affects children and especially relates to literature. This is the environment where the child spends most of his/her developmental years: with family, peers, in school and the neighbourhood. This, of course, is the setting of many stories for children.

Others agree agree that the concept of personality, or self, is *socially constructed*. Social development depends on Socialization, which, putting it simply, is all about getting along with other people in one's community:

> *Parents cradle children's lives, but children's development is also shaped by successive choirs of peers, friends and teachers. Children's small worlds widen as they become students and develop relationships with many new people.*
>
> Santrock 2001, 81.

Children's literature contributes to social development through its vivid portrayal of the beliefs, values and behaviours of society, demonstrated with effect by characters with whom the reader bonds. It may be through some of the true-to-life characters of author Jacqueline Wilson, such as Daisy, in *Sleep-overs*, and her acceptance of, and love for, disabled sister Lily. Another influence could be through the story of fourteen-year-old Terry Blanchard who turns to the popular musician Bruce Springsteen and his music for help in his teenage confusion; who recognises people in his community who can benefit from a 'lip-synch' concert which he initiates. For pre-schoolers, the Seventies child's manners were reinforced via the social importance of saying 'please' in

The Elephant and the Bad Baby by Elfrida Vipont. For the Seventies/ Eighties child, *Dogger*, portrayed the need for security and its achievement. For the Millennium pre-schooler, *Frog and a Very Special Day* underlines the importance of friendship, shown through a community of animals.

Beyond the immediate, familiar society are the unknown beliefs, values and behaviours of other cultures, which, again, are revealed to children through story. Understanding cross-cultural variation is important in the world of the twenty-first century and the International Board of Books for Young People (IBBY) contributes through its emphasis on bringing books and children together. Through their awards, honour lists, biannual congresses held in different countries, seminars and workshops, books that represent a world literature for children are promoted, opening doors into new perception and pleasure. Permanent collections of their Honour Books are housed at: the International Youth Library, Munich; the Swiss Children's Book Institute in Zurich; the Bibiana Research Collection in Bratislavia. Books translated from other languages also help to build bridges between cultures, and this activity is expected to expand in the twenty-first century.

Children do indeed choose to read about children from other cultures. Primary School children enjoy the humour and lively characterisation of *Jamela's Dress*, by Niki Daly, noting details of everyday South African life. Books read by older children, written by Bernard Ashley, depict a South London scene that is foreign to most white Anglo children, as in *Little Soldier* and *Tiger without Teeth*.

In Wales, Alison described her response to *Chinese Cinderella*, the moving story of Adeline Yen Mah's childhood in China:

> *The many emotional tales in* Chinese Cinderella *is going to bring a tear to every reader's eye, as it did to mine. The way in which the book was written made me want to keep reading and never put it down.*
>
> Alison 2000, 16.

6. Moral Development

Theorist: Kohlberg

How children think about moral issues interested Jean Piaget (1932 but Lawrence Kohlberg is the theorist who is most recognised for developing the theory and for the dilemmas he proposed. His emphasis is that moral development unfolds in stages. He does not prescribe ages.

In Kohlberg's Theory (1976, 1986) Level One, *Preconventional*, is characterised by children's obedience because adults tell them to obey, and in a second phase they obey when it is in their best interest to do so. This is demonstrated in picture books for the preschooler in a character like Max who makes his decision to leave *Where the Wild Things Are*, to return to an acceptance of home and the cooperation it requires.

By Level Two, *Conventional*, the child has moved on, usually to adopt his/her parents' moral standards; wanting to be regarded as a 'good boy' or a 'good girl.' This characterises the school child, especially those at Key Stage One and in *Lucy and Tom go to School* by Shirley Hughes it is implied that Lucy cooperates with her teacher and school friends. In a second phase of Level Two, the child is making moral judgements based on understanding, duty, law and justice. This resembles the 7–11 years, Key Stage 2 reader who seeks to be treated fairly and who has to learn to comply. In *Instant Sisters* by Rose Impey, two girls are forced to live together when their parents' marriages fail. Before they learn to adapt, much bitchiness takes place.

By Level Three, *Post Conventional*, the adolescent and young adult is moving more and more toward abstract reasoning in decision making, such as Melvin Burgess portrays in his hard-hitting novels for young adults. However, whatever stage of moral development a child has reached, the literature they read for pleasure or for study will reveal possible models or anti-models.

Faith development, important in communities, is also recognised as developing by stages. This dimension is elaborated in Chapter 8.

7. Case histories

Many reports show the positive outcomes of matching a child's developmental need with an appropriate text, such as those concerning Jacob, Caroline and Becky.

Three and a half-year-old Jacob lives in Australia. His Daddy, his favourite 'mate', walked away from the family home, never to return, leaving him alone with his mother. Immediately he started having nightmares about monsters and was consumed by fear that Mummy would leave next. His personality dramatically altered as giant monsters appeared in his room and started to devour him, changing him from a happy three-year-old into an angry child, riddled with fear. Then his mother began to read *Where the Wild Things* are by Maurice Sendak.

Jacob wanted it read to him over and over; he kept the book under his pillow; he drew pictures about it; he knew it word for word. Over a few weeks, like a miracle it seemed as if the former Jacob returned, from across the sea of fear, as did his hero, the 'wild thing', Max. He assured himself that he could be another 'King of the Monsters', sure of the certain love of his mother and the changed, but now accepted, home environment.

Six-year-old Caroline lives in England. She is an only child of nervous disposition with a keen imagination, much loved, but living in a somewhat unsettled and lonely home life due to frequently changing child-sitters and the absence of both her young parents who work long hours. For more than a year her favourite character in book and video was Dorothy of *The Wizard of Oz*. Caroline insisted on dressing like her heroine, danced down her own 'red brick road' and knew the tin man and other characters as her special friends.

Her complete absorption in Baum's story demonstrated her entry into symbiotic thought, typical of Piaget's Preoperational Child, and also linked with the power of fairy tales to heal disfunction. Baum himself said that:

> *The winged fairies of Grimm and Andersen have brought more happiness to children's hearts than all other human creations ... "The Wonderful Wizard of Oz" ... aspires to be a modernised fairy tale, in which the wonderment and joy are retained and the heartache and nightmares are left out.*
>
> Baum 1900, Intro.

Becky is an English girl in secondary school, a fan of 'Posh' Beckham'. After she read Victoria Beckham's autobiography, a book that gripped her interest throughout, she identified with the bullying of Victoria's story and her deeply based determination to fly' – to succeed in life. It spoke to her of own self-esteem and ambition, helped to clarify her goals and made her smile through tears.

Conclusion

8. Principles Underlying Book Selection for the Developing Child

- Some key words: Uniqueness; stages not ages; interest and readiness; scaffolding.
- 'The right book for the right child at the right time.'

Children's Sayings

"Not *that* one! *This* is the book I want!" Laura, 16 years.

"Grandma gave my cousin a *Horrible Science* book for Christmas, then my cousin gave it to me because she *hated* it but I like it!" Warren, 12 years.

"Hey, hey . . . I just read about *The Worlds of Chrestomanci*.[3] Kinda weird – this fella Christopher, like me, kinda c-oo-l." Abram, 10 years.

Tutorial Topics

1. Randomly select two picture books. What aspects of child development do you recognise in each book? Identify these and give a theoretical and/or experiential basis for your answer.
2. Do you recall any book from your childhood that you now believe was important to your personality, social or cognitive development? Explain your conclusions.
3. Select one of the following: *Charlie and the Chocolate Factory* by Roald Dahl, or *Peter Pan* by James Barrie or *Kit's Wilderness* by David Almond, or two texts by Maurice Sendak from: *In the Night Kitchen*, or Where *the Wild Things are*, or *Outside Over There*. Discuss your chosen reading in relationship to an aspect of child development. Can you identify any relationship of the text to psychoanalytical theory?
4. Compare and contrast the work of any two theorists. Suggest how their work contributes to understanding children and their literature.

Further Reading

Berg, Leila. *Reading and Loving*. London: Routledge, 1997.
Bettelheim, B. *The Uses of Enchantment*. New York: A. A. Knopf, 1976.
Bosmajian, H. 'Charlie and the Chocolate Factory and other excremental visions,' in *The Lion and the Unicorn* 9:36–49, 1985.

---

[3] Jones, Diana Wynne. *The Worlds of Chrestomanci: The Lives of Christopher Chant*. London: Collins, 2000.

—— 'Reading the Unconscious: Psychoanalytical Criticism. In *Understanding Children's Literature*, Peter Hunt, ed. London: Routledge, 1999.

Bruner, J. S. *Child's Talk. Learning to Use Language*. Oxford University Press, 1983.

Byrnes, A. *The Child: An Archetypal Symbol in Literature for Children and Adults*. New York: Peter Lang, 1995.

Elkin, J. and R. Lonsdale. *Focus on the Child: Libraries, Literacy and Learning*. London: LAPL, 1996.

Lee, V., Das Gupta, P. *Children's Cognitive and Language Development*. Blackwell, 1995.

Thornton, Stephanie. *Growing Minds. An Introduction to Cognitive Development*. Basingstoke: Palgrave/Macmillan, 2002.

Tucker, Nicholas. *The Child and the Book: a psychological and literary exploration*. Cambridge: Cambridge University Press, 1990.

—— *The Rough Guide to Children's Books 5–11 Years*. Penguin, 2002.

Whitehead, Marian. *Supporting Language and Language Development in the Early Years*. Reprint. Buckingham: Open University Press, 2001.

Children's Books Cited

Manipulative **Skill and Fine Motor Control**
Touch and Feel Kitten, a Dorling Kindersley Book.
MacDonald, Amy. *Let's Try*. Walker.
Elgar, Rebecca. *Jack – it's a Rainy Day*. Kingfisher.

Attention Span
Andreae, Giles. *There's a House inside my Mummy*. Illustrated by Vanessa Cabban. London: Orchard Books, 2002.
Child, Lauren. *I will not ever NEVER eat a Tomato*. Illustrated by Lauren Child. London: Orchard, 2001.
Hoban, Russell. *Jim's Lion*. Illustrated by Ian Andrew. London: Walker Books, 2002.
Hutchins, Pat. *We're Going on a Picnic*. London: Red Fox, 2003.
McKee, D. *Not Now Bernard*. London: Andersen Press, 1996.
Ross, Mandy. *Peekaboo Baby*. Illustrated by Kate Merritt. London: Ladybird, 2001.
Wick, Walter and Jean Marzollo. *I Spy Schooldays*. London: Scholastic, 1999.

Growth and Change
Asquith, Ros. *The Teenage Worrier's Pocket Guide to Mind and Body*. London: Corgi, 1998.
Blume, Judy. *Are you there God? It's Me, Margaret*. London: Macmillan, 1998.
—— *Then Again, Maybe I Won't*. London: Macmillan Children's Books, 1998.
Bowler, Tim *Shadows*. Oxford: Oxford University Press, 2001.

Bull, David. *Cool and Celibate? Sex or No Sex.* London: HarperCollins, 1998.
Chick, Sandra. *Don't Look Back.* Women's Press. Livewire, 1999.
Doherty, Berlie. *Dear Nobody.* London: Puffin, 2001.
Fine, Anne. *Flour Babies.* London: Puffin, 1994.
Fisher, Nick. *Living with a Willy.* London: Macmillan, 1994.
Sanders, Pete and Steve Myers. *What Do You Know About Relationships? Let's Discuss, Love, Hate and Other Feelings.* London: Franklin Watts, 1994.
Thomson, Ruth. *Have you Started yet?* Illustrated by Jane Eccles. London: Macmillan Children's Books, 1995.
Ure, Jean. *Just Sixteen.* London: Orchard Books, 1999.
White, E. B. *Charlotte's Web.* Illustrated by Garth Williams. Reprint. London: Penguin, 1977.

Books and Language
Cinarusti, Marie Torres. *Peek-a-Moo.* Illustrated by Stephanie Petersen. Andover: Ragged Bears, 1999.
Lacombe, Julie. *Walking Through the Jungle.* London: Walker, 1995.
Oxenbury, Helen. *Dressing.* London: Walker, 1999.
—— *Working.* London: Walker, 1999.

Proximal Development
Almond, David. *Skellig.* London: Hodder Children's Books, 1998.
Burgess, Melvin. *Junk.* London: Puffin. 1997.
Keats, Ezra Jack. *Pet Show.* Puffin Books.
—— *Whistle for Willie.* Puffin Books.
Wilson, Jacqueline. *The Suitcase Kid.* London: Doubleday, 2001.
—— *Double Act.* London: Corgi, 1996.
Nabb, Magadalen. *Josie Smith.* London: HarperCollins, 1994.

Cognition
Ayliffe, Alex. *Tickle Tickle Tom.* London: Orchard, 2000.
Burningham, John. *Mr Gumpy's Outing.* London: Red Fox, 2001.
Carle, Eric. *The Very Hungry Caterpillar.* London: Hamish Hamilton, 1995.
—— *The Very Clumsy Click Beetle.* London: Hamish Hamilton, 1999.
Gliori, Debi. *Mr Bear's Picnic.* London: Orchard, 2001.
Hoban, Russell. *Bedtime for Frances.* Illustrated by Lillian Hoban. Red Fox, 2002.
Hutchins, Pat. *Goodnight Owl.* London: Jonathan Cape, 1993.
—— *Rosie's Walk.* London: Bodley head, 1989.
—— *Shrinking Mouse.* London: Red Fox, 2001.
Keats, Ezra Jack. *The Snowy Day.* London: Picture Puffin, 1969.
Lawrence, Michael. *Baby Loves.* London: Dorling Kindersley, 2000.
Magorian, Michelle. *Goodnight Mr Tom.* Oxford: Oxford University Press, 1998.

Morepurgo, Michael. *Wombat Goes Walkabout*. Illustrated by Christian Birmingham. Picture Lions, 2000.
Pearce, Philippa. *Tom's Midnight Garden*. Illustrated by Susan Einzig. Oxford: Oxford University Press, 1998.
Steptoe, John. *Mufaro's Beautiful Daughters; An African Tale*. Hodder Children's Books, 1991.
Wabbes, Marie. *Goodnight Little Rabbit*. London: Walker, 1987.
Watanabe, Shigeo. *How do I Eat it?* Reprint. London: Puffin. 1983.
—— *How do I Put it On?* Reprint. Puffin, 1984.

Personality
Mahy, Margaret. *A Lion in the Meadow*. Illustrated by Jenny Williams. Picture Puffin.
Murphy, Jill. *All for One*. London: Walker, 2002.
Wilson, Jacqueline. *Girls Out Late*. London: Corgi, 2000.
—— *Girls in Love*. London: Corgi Juvenile, 1998.

Basic Behaviours
Sendak, Maurice. *In the Night Kitchen*. London: Red Fox, 2001.
Watanabe, Shigeo. *How do I put it on?* Illustrated by Yasuo Ohtomo. London: Red Fox, 1993.

Social Development
Ashley, Bernard. *The Little Soldier*. London: Collins Educational, 2001.
—— *Tiger Without Teeth*. London: Orchard, 1998.
Daly, Niki. *Jamela's Dress*. London: Frances Lincoln. ISBN: 0 7112 1449.
Hughes, Shirley. *Dogger*. London: Red Fox, 1993.
Velthuijs, Max. *Frog and a Very Special Day*. London: Andersen, 2001.
Vipont, Elfrida. *The Elephant and the Bad Baby*. Illustrated by Raymond Briggs. London: Puffin, 1973.
Wilson, Jacqueline. *Sleep-overs*. London: Doubleday, 2001.
Yen Mah, Adeline. *Chinese Cinderella*. Puffin.

Case Histories
Sendak, Maurice. *Where the Wild Things Are*. Puffin Books in association with Bodley Head.
Baum, L. Frank. *The Wizard of Oz*. Ware: Wordsworth Editions Ltd, 1993, Intro.
Beckham, Victoria. *Learning to Fly*. Penguin.

Bibliography

Alison. 'Good Reads.' *Books for Keeps*, May 2000, 16.
Baum, Frank L. *The Wonderful Wizard of Oz*, 1900. (rpt). New York: Dover, 1960, iii.

Berko-Gleason, J. 'Language.' In M. H. Bornstein and M. E. Lamb, eds, *Developmental Psychology*, 4th edition. Mahwah, NJ: Erlbaum.

Bloom, L. 'Language Acquisition in its Developmental Context'. In W. Damon, ed., *Handbook of Child Psychology*. 4th edition, Vol 2. New York: Wiley, 1998.

Bowen, Caroline. <http://members.tripod.com/Caroline_Bowen/Browns Stages.ht,>

Bronfenbrenner, U. 'Ecology of the Family as a context for human development: Research perspectives.' In *Developmental Psychology*, 22, 723–742.

Brown, H. and Brian Cambourne. *Read and Retell*. Portsmouth, NH: Heinemann, 1987.

Burgess, Melvin. In *Background Information. Library Association Carnegie Awards*. Library Association, 1997.

Butler, Dorothy. *Babies Need Books*. Pelican, 1982, 20.

Butler Andrea and Jan Turbill. *Towards a Reading-Writing Classroom*. Sydney: PETA, 1984.

Cambourne, Brian. 'Language Learning and Literacy.' In Andrea Butler and Jan Turbill, *Towards a Reading-Writing Classroom*. Sydney: PETA, 1984, 7.

Cambourne, B. and Jan Turbill. *Coping with Chaos*. Portsmouth, N.H.: Heinemann, 1987.

Chess, S. and A. Thomas. 'Temperamental individuality from childhood to adolescence.' In *Journal of Child Psychiatry*, 16, 1977, 218–226.

CILIP. Chartered Insititute of Library and Information Professionals. CILIP is used in this text.

Chomsky, N. *Syntactic Structures*. The Hague: Mouton, 1957.

—— *Language and Mind*. New York: Harcourt, 1968.

Costa, P. NEO 'Personality Inventory' in Kazdin. A., ed. *Encyclopaedia of Psychology*. Washington, D.C: American Psychological Assn and Oxford University Press, 2000; Costa, P. T. and Marcie, R. R. 'Solid Ground on the Wetlands of Personality: a reply to Black. *Psychological Bulletin,* 117, 1995, 216–220; McNulty, J. 'Five Factor model of personality.' In Kazden, A., op. cit.

Erickson, E. H. *Identity: Youth and Crisis*. New York: W. W. Norton, 1968.

Gavelek, J. R. and T. E. Raphael. 'Changing Talk about Text: New Roles for Teachers and Students.' *Language Arts* 73, 3, 182–192.

Graham, Judith and Alison Kelly, eds. *Reading Under Control: teaching Reading in the Primary School*, 2nd edition. London: David Fulton Publishers, 2000.

Gudrun. In a personal report to M. Trim.

Hitchcock, Anita Marie. 'Individual Variations.' In Santrock, John W., op. cit, 151.

Huck, Charlotte S. *Children's Literature in the Elementary School*. 3rd edition. New York: Holt, Rinehart and Winston, 1976.

Jung, C. G. *Man and his Symbols*. New York: Doubleday, 1964.

Kohlberg, Lawrence. *Essays on Moral Development: The Philosophy of Moral Development*. New York: Harper and Row, 1981.

Lacan, J. *Ecrits*, translated by Alan Sheridan. New York: W. W. Norton, 1977.

Lindfors, Judith Wells. *Children's Language and Learning*. Englewood Cliffs: Prentice-Hall Inc., 1980.

Loban, Walter. *Language Development: Kindergarten Through Grade Twelve*. Urbana: National Council of Teachers of English, 1976.

Maslow, Abraham H. *Motivation and Personality*, revised edition. New York: Harper and Row, 1970.

Nagy, W. E. and Scott, J. A. 'Vocabulary Processes.' In M. L. Kamil *et al*, eds: *Handbook of Reading Research*: Vol III. Mahwah, N.J.: Lawrence Erlbaum.

Norton, Donna. *Through the Eyes of a Child*. 3rd edition. New York: Macmillan, 1991.

Piaget, Jean and B. Inhelder. *The Psychology of the Child*. New York: Basic Books, 1969.

Ragoff, B. 'Cognition as a Collaborative Process.' In W. Damon, D. Kuhn and R. S. Siegler (Eds). *Handbook of Child Psychology*. 5th edition, Vol. 2. New York: Wiley, 1998.

Ruddell, R. B. *Teaching Children to Read and Write: Becoming an influential teacher* (3rd edition). Boston, MA: Allyn and Bacon, 2002.

Rychman, R. M. *Theories of Personality* (7th edition). Belmont: Wadsworth, 2000.

Santrock, John W. *Educational Psychology*, New York: McGraw Higher Education, 2001, 63.

Stone, Rosemary. 'Authorgraph' No. 120: Magdalen Nabb. In *Books for Keeps*, January 2000, 12–13.

Thornton, Stephanie. *Growing Minds*. An Introduction to Cognitive Development. Basingstoke: Palgrave/Macmillan, 2002.

Vasta et al. *Child Psychology: the Modern Science.* New York: John Wiley and Vygotsky, L. S. 'Thinking and Speech'. In R. W. Riba and A. S. Carton, eds, *The Collected Works of L. S. Vygotsky*. New York: Polonium, 1987.

Wade, B., and M. Moore. 'An Early Start with Books: literacy and mathematical evidence from a longitudinal study.' *Educational Review*. Literacy and Schooling, 50/2, 1998.

—— *A Gift for Life: Bookstart the First Five Years*. London: Booktrust, 1998.

Wordsworth, William. *The Prelude*, Kb 2. L 3–4. Oxford University Press, 1970, 20.

CHAPTER TWO

The Knowing Child

Much have I travelled in the realms of gold,
And many goodly states and kingdoms seen.
                                                    Keats

There are various routes that a child reader – or an adult professional – may follow when setting out on a journey into literature. It does not really matter which route is chosen, for there can be many beginnings and many endings, byways and highways all contributing pleasure and insight. The traveller may not appreciate all the possible sights along the way, but as James Stephens said:

> *The head will not hear until the heart has listened. And what the heart knows today the mind will understand tomorrow.*
                                                    The Crock of Gold

Moving away from metaphor, It is the *genres* that provide the various routes and landmarks of literature. This Section, Chapters Two to Four, considers the different categories into which genre may be organised. This chapter focuses on the earliest forms of literature, then expands to consider the first form most children encounter.

1. Traditional Literature

Traditional Literature is the first category (i.e. genre) which everyone who is involved with selecting and presenting literature should know.

Graham and Kelly emphasise its knowledge as essential for the teacher who wishes to reach the high standards of initial teacher training – and thereby in later practice – prescribed in governmental statutory requirements (circular 4/98 (DfEE 1998b). Documents from CILIP, as in the 2002 report on library services, stress high quality bookstock, of which traditional literature is a part. It has been a tremendous influence on scholars of the past and contributed to European and Western culture. It is the prototype for all literature and encompasses a number of disciplines.

> *It has been recognised that the study of folklore and its literature synthesises the disciplines of anthropology, sociology, psychology linguistics and literature.*
>
> Saxby 1979, 2.

1.1 Traditional literature Attempts Answers

Every society and culture has its own responses to the 'big questions' that concern humankind's origin, purpose and ultimate destiny, groping to find words and symbols that explain the mysterious, and the majesty of mysticism which they sense but dimly. In the stories of great deeds, tales of the high and low born person and fables of the wise and foolish lie socio-cultural attempts to explain, instruct or amuse. These answers contribute – even in a modern world – to the language, customs, religions, art, dress, values, outlook and uniqueness of its people. Cultures differ in specifics, but one thing worthy of respect is certain, regardless of size, a group's culture influences the behaviour of its members, as studies by Berry and Matsuomoto show.

1.2 Traditional Literature Contains Three Categories

Explanations from the past can be divided into three types: *myths* which are those concerning creators (gods) and creations; *legends,* which focus on larger-than-life heroes and their exploits; *folklore*, a term coined in 1846 by W. J. Thoms (according to Mae Durham Roger), which includes *folk and fairy tales, and fables.* Each type originates from people who displayed humankind's need to impart and receive stories that helped make sense of the world and their role within it.

1.3 Traditional Literature is Regenerative

A society's answers and values modify and develop, due to the passing of time and the interaction of new influences, but the underlying answers of traditional literature perpetuate and are retold in contemporary idiom and art for subsequent generations. Although traditional literature started as an oral form for a mixed audience, since the nineteenth century at least when the Grimm brothers published their *Marchen* which were traditional tales from Germany, more and more traditional literature of local and international origin has been largely taken over by children, the reason no doubt being that children continue to enjoy such stories. "The impulse to story' is how the English author Edward Blishen described his urge to write (29) and the impulse to *receive story* characterises children of the past and present, whether at Tudor fairground, in baronial hall or castle inglenook, beside a cottage hearth or in a terrace house bedroom of the twenty-first century; or devouring the rich flavour of story in media, classroom or library.

1.4 Components of Traditional Literature

(i) Mythology

> *It has always been the prime function of mythology and rite to supply the symbols that carry the human spirit forward.*
> *Joseph Campbell 1973, 11.*

Myths attempt to answer humankind's primitive questions of *who, how, where when and why*. For example, the story of Pandora's Box from the ancient Greeks tells how Prometheus and his brother Epimetheus made living creatures, while from the Hebraic past comes the story of the Garden of Eden. These and other cultural traditions account for the origin of the world and its people; they concern natural phenomena and describe emotions, portrayed through deities, humans or animals in an earlier world or elsewhere. At the deepest level, they satisfy the psychic need to know – the self, others, the example of heroes, the world – even to worship or emulate. As such they embody dogma and are frequently sacred.

   Of the traditional forms, myths are at the most elevated level, concerning the stories of gods, of super heroes and amazing supernatural feats and journeys in far distant, undated time. When referring to traditional literature, think of 'myth' as a traditional story used to explain origins, rather than an outright invention or fiction which is another definition. Elemental truths about the human psyche underpin mythology. According to Jung, they are fundamental expressions of human nature. He sees them also as a

> *direct expression of the collective unconscious . . . found in similar forms among all peoples and in all ages, and when man loses the capacity for myth-making, he loses touch with the creative forces of his being. Religion, poetry, folklore, and fairy-tales, depend also on this capacity.*
>
> Fordham 1985, 27.

Leon Garfield and Edward Blishen's work that won the Carnegie Medal for Children's Literature in 1970, *The God beneath the Sea*, is an excellent introduction to the older child or young adult reader who wants to explore Greek mythology. In imaginative and vivid prose it presents the omnipotence of Greek gods, their autocratic, sometimes vindictive natures: Part 1: *The Making of the Gods*; Part 11: *The Making of Men*; Part 111: *Gods and Men*.

Published in the 1990s and more recently, other books bring the era and ethos of Greece and Rome to life. For the young in Foundation years and Key Stage 1, these include, Kimber's *A First Book of Myths*, Amery's *Greek Myths for Young Children* and *One-Hundred-And-One Read Aloud Myths and Legends* by Verniero et al, suited for 4–8 year olds. For the upper primary school reader, *Greek Gods and Goddesses* is written with a light touch by the award winner, Geraldine McCaughrean and illustrated in a bright and interesting way by Emma Chichester Clark. The same author writes *Greek Myths and Roman Myths*, retelling them in McCaughrean's inimical style, while *Gods and Goddesses* by John Malam is also for older children, didactic but useful for school projects. In the Wayland's 'Ancient Greece' series is *Daily Life* by Stewart Rodd which contains a fine collection of photographs. Ross also writes *The Original Olympics* which gives an informational background to the modern Games and describes how the first athletes competed. One other work by McCaughrean is worth noting: *The Greeks on Stage*, which children and teachers can use as dramatisations of a possible twenty-five myths. Lively and fun for modern children, yet retaining some of the grandeur of the old stories, characters like Apollo, telling his tale as a ventriloquist, and *Across*, who mimics the sounds of aeroplanes, feature among the gods and mortals to be acted.

Older publications that are well received are collections of Greek and Roman myths with large colourful illustrations, by D'aulaire; also stories by the historical writer, Rosemary Sutcliffe, such as *Black Ships before Troy*: *The Story of the Iliad*, and *The Wanderings of Odysseus*: *The Story of the Odyssey*.

Another award winning author of children's books, Peter Dickinson, retells stories from the Old testament of the Bible in his work, *City of Gold*, writing imaginatively from witnesses' points of view and depicting the Hebraic view of the nature of deity. The tone varies as each witness speaks. It begins with grand oratory, tinged with longing and nostalgia by a Babylonian nobleman who tells the story of 'The Fall of Man', concluding with a hope for, and a sense of, a deity who has a caring nature:

> *Even now, sometimes looking at my Lord's garden here in Babylon, I dream that … time must already have begun – or perhaps God has given leave for the wind to blow here some seeds out of Eden, to show my Lord that he has God's blessing to us poor Hebrews in our exile.*
>
> *Dickinson 1980, 16.*

The first chapter of the book is the story of 'The Fall of Man.' It ends with 'The Fall of the City', told to a class of boys in Babylon. The reader can hear the speaker's ring of confidence in his voice as he passes on from experience in his own youth the assurance of faith and nationhood:

> *One night as I lay in the desert … I looked up at the stars and wondered … But as I was lying there, unable to tell star from star because of my tears, I heard a quiet voice speaking in my heart. "I am here," it said. … "My city will rise again!" … Next day I laughed and sang while we marched until my friends decided I had gone mad with sunstroke. But I shouted to them the words that God had spoken until they too laughed and sang. Think now of those men laughing on the long and burning road. They were your very fathers!*
>
> *Dickinson 1980, 180.*

Palestinian culture, like any other, has its own oral tradition, rich in stories from people of an ancient past. An enthusiastic Palestinian teacher, Jehan Helou, is Director of the Tamer Institute for Community Education which promotes literacy and reading and publishes Palestinian books by and for children. From one of Jehan's students comes a modern-day version of oppression and a young person's dream. It can be compared/contrasted with Dickinson's Old Testament, Jewish portrayal:

> *A beautiful house, nice clothes, and a city with wonderful views ... many things I used to dream about, but the occupation has destroyed all our dreams. The Intifada started, and we heard only the sound of bullets in the streets, the thunder of fighter planes in the sky and waves of dead and injured ... Now wherever I go, I carry a bullet with me, a gift from the occupation.*
> *Kifah Al Aaraj, age 14.*

Biblical stories from the Hebrew tradition feed into the Christian tradition of the West, but Islam, too, has its stories from the past on which to nourish its children, discussed further in Section Two, Chapter Eight: Communities.

From Nordic mythology, as told by Olivia E. Coolidge in *Legends of the North* comes a picture of northern deities: Odin, the mightiest, who believes that the lesser gods should know their realm and often walk among men; and Thor, god of war, red-haired and fierce-eyed, who rides in a chariot drawn by red-eyed goats. Despite his warlike nature, he shows attributes of loyalty and courage, and there is humour in his actions and responses. For example, when searching for his lost hammer and Freyja, the goddess of beauty gently asks him where he put it, he shouts at her, rather like a frustrated father or child that if knew where it was he would not need to hunt for it! And again, when he decides to dress as a beautiful bride in order to to soften the heart of Thyrm – the giant who has stolen his beloved hammer – he wears a veil to cover his distinctive eyes, hair and beard. Not exactly a cuddly god, but one who depicts some human characteristics, who could be an ancestor of Hagrid of *Harry Potter and the Philosopher's Stone*. Like Thor, Hagrid is enormous in stature, has a shaggy mane of hair and beard and eyes that glinted under the hair, 'like black beetles.' (Rowling, 1997, 39).

Hagrid's resemblance to Thor, although a lesser figure, is unsurprising. This is not to suggest that Hagrid is directly derivative, but well-read authors cannot help but be influenced by their perceptions of mythical stereotypes, coupled with their own imaginations. Norse mythology is known to have influenced Shakespeare as he wrote

Hamlet; characters and countryside descriptions in Tolkein's *Hobbit* and *Lord of the Rings* resonate with echoes from his familiarity with Anglo-Saxon literature, linked with his knowledge of English landscape, while C. S. Lewis delighted in mythology from his schoolboy days when he chose *Teutonic Myth and Legend* as a prize, as Walter Hooper discloses. Lewis's range of characters and settings in his Narnia series for children are seen by many readers as a synthesis of his wide reading, his classical scholarship and appreciation of Norse, Teutonic and Hebraic literature.

This chapter has discussed briefly the mythology of only a few of the cultures that Europe represents. Going back to the metaphor of routes of travel, the Nordic tradition might represent the frozen north, the European route the cool to mild zones, while the Islamic and Jewish traditions are from paths where hot sun beats down on sand and palms. Yet whatever route is chosen, there are the points of commonality which Campbell identifies, which make myth and legend an important component of reading for today's children who live in an increasingly complex world.

The topic of mythology raises serious questions. Do myths have any real significance to readers in the twenty-first century, or are they fascinating but out of date, as some might regard a vintage car? Is a knowledge of ancestral and other cultures important? Do old ideas about existence retain relevance? Do they challenge and expand the imagination? Joseph Campbell's argument is worth consideration: that myths have four important functions which continue to make them important. These functions, restated, are:

(1) a mystical one that allows people to experience the awe of the universe
(2) a cosmological one that shows the shape and mystery of the universe.
(3) a sociological one that supports and validates a certain social order.
(4) a pedagogical one that teaches people how to live.

Norton 1991, 259–260.

1.5 Legends

Legends are usually linked to, and published together, with mythology, for they concern journeys and exploits by heroic, almost godlike though human characters who resist evil in the world in a far distant time. Some are religious figures such as martyrs and saints, as with Joan of Arc of France. Many of their deeds have come down through epic poetry, such as via the Greek epics *The Iliad* and *The Odyssey*.

The former is an account of the Trojan War from which we know the cunning ruse of the wooden horse. The latter tells the journey of Odysseus, King of Ithaca, known to the Romans, later, as Ulysses. Last of the victorious generals to leave Troy with his team of warriors in a fleet of twelve ships, ten years of struggle pass before he reaches his home and beautiful wife. What a man; what a legend! During the journey, he is delayed by hostile gods, imprisoned and caught in storms sent by the evil god of the sea, Poseidon. Yet he is also assisted by the good, as with a goddess who appeared to him as a gull in his moment of greatest danger. "Put on this belt and swim ashore," she says. He defeats the one eyed Cyclops, resists enchantresses – the Sirens and Circe – and sails on as warrior- conqueror.

This story has all the features of legends: The resolute hero, his difficulties and temptations as he is assailed by evil forces, his cunning strategies to fulfil his task, his courage. Add to these the other side of the coin: miraculous interventions and his ultimate arrival at the journey's end where he resumes rulership. Rosemary Sutcliffe's versions, mentioned under Myths, are lit by her imagination and literary competence.

From the Nordic tradition comes the story of the warrior, *Beowulf*, who struggles against evil in the forms of a monster and dragon. In the British Isles, where the Celtic people maintained the oral tradition before the Roman invasion, the Romans left behind an inheritance of their myths and legends – largely taken over from the Greeks – which they emphasised in their worship, statues, artefacts, vocabulary (e.g. "By Jove!) and way of life, influences which persist into the twenty-first century. Havelock the Dane is a legendary figure of medieval romance from the era of Saxon and Viking wars.

Cuchulain was the great Irish hero of stories in old manuscripts, and other Irish legends and legendary characters are today depicted in *Lady Gregory's Irish Legends for Children*. In England, *Bevies of Hampton*, *Guy of Warwick*, *King Arthur* and *St George* (another dragon slayer) and *Robyn Hood*, hero of the common people, were popular through ballads and story. Sir Bevies of Southampton did exploits of tremendous valour, 'rescuing the distressed, destroying Monsters and Tyrants, gaining kingdoms and converting Infidels to the Christian Faith . . . (14).

1.6 Folk tales

Stories about ordinary people ('Folk') abound in every culture but operate at a lower level than myth or legend, giving insights into life and human nature through tales about the adventures of animal or human characters. Common characters are people with exaggerated human foibles, coming from countryside, city or castle: farmers, weavers, shoemakers, kings, princes and princesses. Reflecting their oral genesis, these tales give little detail regarding character and setting, just the information that is essential to the plot, one which is characterised by challenge, conflict and action. The result is a satisfying, easy-to-listen- to, simply-told story wherein good is rewarded, evil is punished and the foolish exposed; whereby contrasts are demonstrated between good and evil, wisdom and folly, cowardice and bravery, and laziness and resourcefulness. The effect draws in a circle of listeners, and when it is applied in print carries a charmed young reader on to the always marvellous and predictable conclusion.

We can understand children's fascination for stories that end happily ever after, with their rightful consequences achieved, when we balance this view alongside Piaget 's stages of Morality Development. He saw the early stage of Heteronomous Morality as operant between the ages of four to seven years, when young children believe that justice and rules are unchangeable properties, over which people, especially children, have no control. This attitude changes slowly as the growing child experiences education and more of the world, so that by about ten years of age, children reach the stage of Autonomous Morality. Now they realise that rules and laws are created by people themselves and that consequences result if obeyed or broken. From this age on, folk tales will be taken less seriously, rather like Santa Claus, though the references will never be completely forgotten, perhaps continuing in the mind as part of the universal collective unconscious on which Jung laid considerable stress:

> It has contents that are more or less the same everywhere and in all individuals. It is, in other words, identical in all men and thus constitutes a common psychic substrata of a suprapersonal nature which is present in every one of us.
>
> *Jung 1968, 4.*

O'Connor explains further:

> The mind, through its physical counterpart the brain, has inherited characteristics or innate predispositions with which to respond to

> *life's experiences . . . Through the collective unconscious, each indi-*
> *vidual is linked not only with his own past, but the past of the*
> *species . . . It can also be seen as a reservoir of latent images.*
>   O'Connor 1985, 21.

There are elements that repeat over and over again in the Folk Tale genre. These are called motifs. Some of these, with examples from well-known stories, are

(i) Beings who hinder: ogres, witches or giants as in Jack the Giant Killer.

(ii) Beings who help: seven dwarfs, elf shoemakers.

(iii) Extraordinary animals such as the cat in the French Puss in Boots and the wolf who eats up Red Riding Hood's grandmother and then impersonates her.

(iv) Magical spells and transformations, as in Grimms' story of The Frog Prince, or The Sleeping Beauty.

(v) Quests to fulfil and rewards, as with The Little Hen and the Grain of Wheat (from the English collection of Joseph Jacobs) and The Twelve Dancing Princesses (from the German Grimm Brothers).

(vi) Repetition of key sentences, as with the wolf who will huff and puff and blow down little pig's house; with the Story of the Three Bears.

(vii) Use of the numbers three (pigs, bears, billy-Goats, sisters etc.) and seven (dwarfs, days, years).

(viii) Kindness brings rewards. From the brothers Grimm is the story of the Golden Goose and the despised third son whose simple-mindedness, which is really virtue, is rewarded when he marries the King's daughter and at the King's death, becomes King of the realm.

1.7 Cumulative Tales

For simplification, the principal divisions of Folk Tales are : firstly Cumulative Tales that keep adding characters or speeches in a sequential way. For example,The Gingerbread Boy who runs away from the little old woman and the little old man, shouting

> *Run! Run! as fast as you can*
> *You can't catch me, I'm the Gingerbread Man!*

He uses this rhyme to taunt other pursuers: cow, horse, threshers, mowers, while their names get added, one by one, to the record of each sequence of his running away. To the last group, the mowers, the boy again addresses his teasing lines, saying:

> *I have run away from a little old woman, a little old man,*
> *a cow, a horse, a barn full of threshers,*
> *And I can run away from you, I can!*
>
> *Bryant 1974, 7.*

Only the fox outwits him and discloses the comeuppance and naivety of a Gingerbread Boy who can never run again.

The cumulative technique is used by authors today, such as John Burningham, for example in *The Shopping Basket*, a story in which young Steven meets a bear, a monkey, a kangaroo and other animals that accost him in a similar, repetitive manner. *Mr Gumpy's Outing* is his earlier example, about Mr Gumpy and his boat. "May we come with you?" ask some children, with the same request repeated by a rabbit, cat and other animals, all of whom are told how to behave, which of course they do not do. So into the water they fall and must walk across the fields to have their tea – told in the twentieth century in an age-long tradition.

1.8 Wonder Tales

form a second category. These are frequently called 'fairy tales' and tell of extraordinary, often magical happenings. *Cinderella* is such a tale, one that, like creation myths, appears in many parts of the world and is frequently retold for today's children. Back in 1893 Marian Cox found 345 variants of the Cinderella motif dating back to China in the 9th Century. Here is the theme of rags-to-riches transformation by a fairy godmother, but it may also be, at a deeper level, an exploration of sibling and sexual rivalry, as Bruno Bettelheim points out in his book, *The Uses of Enchantment*.

To many children the Cinderella story will be one of simple pleasure as a pumpkin becomes a golden coach – according to the Charles Perrault version from France in the late seventeenth century – and six mice become horses, and a rat and lizards turn into footmen . . . Other children may receive subliminal messages, sensed only dimly, but important to their development as individuals.

> *Applying the psychoanalytic model of the human personality, fairy*
> *tales carry important messages to the conscious, the preconscious*

and the unconscious mind, on whatever level each is functioning at the time. By dealing with universal human problems ... these stories speak to his budding ego ...

Bettelheim 1976, 6.

Cinderella is popular as a classic fairy tale, and, as John Gough points out, is the progenitor of many modern stories which he sees as falling under the theme of 'Rivalry, Rejection and Recovery.' As examples he refers to Frances Hodgson Burnett's *The Secret Garden*, *A Little Princess* and *Little Lord Fauntleroy*. He also cites examples by Kipling, Nesbitt, Hoban, Mahy and others, pointing out that at the root of these stories is a character's concern regarding parental acceptance, a distress that Bettelheim drew to attention in his work, *The Uses of Enchantment*.

Other fairy stories feature giants and dwarfs, elves and goblins, witches and demons, monsters and dragons, all scary characters, briefly. At a safe distance to consider and accept, they represent powerful human emotions that even young children have experienced, sensed or observed: insecurity, sibling and other rivalry, jealousy, how it feels to be a loser or winner, and how love makes living joyful. Yet the important feature of fairy tales is their resolution, so that fear can be endured and even enjoyed, for 'they lived happily ever after,' which children soon learn to chorus. Acquaintance with the fairy tale genre and its far-removal from reality, carries along with it prediction of outcome. There is also the reassuring certainty that goodness and the ever important hero can overcome evil.

1.9 Beast Tales

These appear in every culture, usually with animals that can speak. Their identity is determined often by the country of origin of the tale, for hippopotomi, elephants or wolves are not inhabitants everywhere! English Fairy Tales collected by Joseph Jacobs, include English animals as in *The Three Little Pigs*, *Henny Penny*, *Dick Whittington and his Cat*, *The Fish and the Ring* and *The Magpie's Nest*. *Little Red Riding Hood* is an example where a beast interacts with a child and her grandmother, killing and consuming the latter. As Peter Hunt comments:

It is a sociological and historical oddity that children's literature has come to include and absorb these (initially) crude, violent and sexu-

ally-charged texts, but by understanding their structures, and then relating them to broader cultural movements, they may be seen as other than they are generally supposed to be.

Hunt, 1999, 10.

Hunt also refers to Zipes' reading of *Little Red Riding Hood*, one that links with psychoanalytical theory, described in Chapter 1. Zipes claims it is a reflection of men's fear of male and female sexuality; that one positive feature of the story is that it warns about possible sexual molestation, which in a time of an increase in pedophiles is very relevant.

1.10 Humorous and Noodlehead stories

are another subset of fairy tales which depict foolishness and are early versions of cautionary tales. An example from Garner's collection from England and Wales is the tale of *Loppy Lankin* where the witch's daughter measures the inside of the oven where Loppy is to roast, but ends up with a push from Loppy, inside the oven herself, while he escapes. Told with cumulative use of rhyme, the tale also rings with the recognisable device of pantomime, as shown in the dialogue:

> *"Where shall you do for your roasting?" Loppy said . . .*
> *"I'll use the oven," says the daughter.*
> *"I'm too long to fit in the oven," says Loppy.*
> *"No, you're not," says the daughter.*
> *"Yes, I am," he says.*
>
> Garner, 1992, 139.

Hans in Luck, told by the Brothers Grimm, is another such folktale. Hans earns a piece of silver after working at a job for seven years. He exchanges it for a horse, the horse for a cow, the cow for a wheelbarrow, and so on, each time thinking how lucky he is. Ultimately he has nothing but a common rough stone that he throws into a pond. Now he is free of worry and exults in his good luck. The tale raises the question whether it was really good luck or the outcome of foolishness? Likewise, *Lazy Jack*, from Jacobs' English collection, in which Jack may seem to behave very foolishly, yet his act of carrying a donkey on his shoulders rather than riding it causes a rich man's mute daughter to laugh and recover her speech. Hence the happy ending in which Jack becomes son-in-law to the rich man and marries his daughter. That story is full of humour, and the ironic twist at the end may seem, in modern terms, as good as winning a lottery. It leaves the question, does laziness and noodleheadedness pay? It can certainly prompt laughter.

Hans Christian Andersen is one notable writer who built on the fairy tale foundation, writing many stories that have become absorbed into its tradition, for example, *The Tinder Box*, *The Emperor's new Clothes*, and *The Ugly Duckling*, some that are favourites. From Margaret Mahy's *The Other Side of Silence* comes a more contemporary, less obvious example. Here the hero is a girl called Hero who becomes a regular visitor to eerie Credence House which contrasts with another house, called home. The sparseness of detail, but the subtlety and wit, along with the depth of insight into family relationships, have many resonances of the root of fairy tale, now seen flowering into a novel.

1.11 Fables

The most well-known collection is associated with the name of Aesop, perhaps a Greek slave, six centuries B.C. There are numerous editions and retellings available, with or without illustrations, some as a complete set, others as single stories. They are about animal characters which talk and act as if they were humans, as in Aesop's fable of the *Fox and the Grapes'* about a hungry fox who tries to reach some grapes, finds them too high to reach, then consoles himself, by suggesting that the fruit was probably very sour. A satire of human behaviour, the conclusion is that 'Some people pretend to despise the things they cannot have.' Some of Aesop's fables focus on people to make a moral point, as with the story of the shepherd boy who called "Wolf", deceiving his hearers several times, so that when a wolf really came:

> *The boy screamed and called for help. But all in vain! The neighbours, supposing him to be up to his old tricks, paid no attention to his cries, and the wolf devoured the sheep*

> *MORAL:*
> *Liars are not believed even when they tell the truth.*
> *Bloomsbury 1994, 97.*

The fables of Aesop may have even been caricatures of contemporary, well-known people in public life, sent-up with some affection, or lampooned with a sting, in the way cartoonists do today with politicians and others. They are centuries old in origin, yet even today children read such stories as the 'Town Mouse and the Country Mouse' and recognise that people have preferences, some choosing a safe, dull life rather than a rich and dangerous one.

While the first fables were written in Greek, then translated into Latin, they were translated into English and printed by William Caxton in 1484, so children have been reading *Aesop's fables* in the English language for over five hundred years. In France, the seventeenth-century French poet, La Fontaine, wrote fables in verse form, drawing largely from Aesop.

Other examples are the well-known but longer fables which come from India, as in the Jatakas, animal stories that relate to the Buddha, and the Panchatantra, a work designed for young princes. In Australia, Djugurba: *Tales from the Sprit Time* and *The Rainbow Serpent* by Dick Roughsey and Percy Trezise, embrace both myth and fable.

Richard Scarry, Paul Galdone, Brian Wildsmith and Tomi Ungerer are some of those illustrators who have recreated old fables for modern children, being part of the regenerative chain of traditional literature that still endures. Authors use the form to create their own fables, such as Geraldine McCaughrean does in *The Stones are Hatching*. More than fable, however, it uses the style of Folk Lore with its use of characters such as the Horse, the Fool, the Maiden and the Green Man of rural legendry. Linda Newberry says:

> It's a horror story, an elemental struggle, a road movie, an environmental fable, a search for identity.
>
> 2000, 16.

1.12 Traditional Literary and the National Literacy Strategy

> So why, when we no longer believe there are gods living at the top of Mount Olympus, are we still telling their stories? Because they are full of the things that fascinate anyone, in any country, at any time.
>
> McCaughrean,1992, 7.

The British National Literacy Strategy of prescribes that children should study myths, legends, folk tales, fairy tales and fables, starting in Reception Class in Years 1, 2, 3 for 5 – 8 year olds, and in Year 5 for 9 – 10 year olds. Thus modern children may become afire with imagination similar to that kindled in, and by, former literate generations who, in maturity, appreciated adult literature of the West with its subtle references to traditional sources. Today's children become enthused about the Olympic Games and respond to film heroes like Russell Crowe who featured as the enslaved general with right on his side in the epic film *Gladiator*. They can also be fascinated by the heroic Argonauts who set sail in the Argo to find the Golden Fleece, and the supermen, Prometheus, and Odysseus, or Noah of the Hebraic flood story with its rainbow and dove, and Joseph with his multi-coloured coat who features in so many school productions of the musical by that name.

Moreover, knowing traditional literature gives the dedicated child reader a level of appreciation that will carry over to the writing of modern acclaimed children's authors such as C. S. Lewis, Alan Garner, Susan Cooper, Margaret Mahy and Philip Pullman who draw on traditional sources in a layered effect that adds richness to text and makes it Literature. More than that, however, they will know the underpinnings of European culture which is built on the Bible and the myths and legends of Greece and Rome. Nevertheless, as multiculturalism increases through-out the world and is promoted in several disciplines in schools, traditional literature from the East and Middle East may homogenise with that of the Western world, modifying the shape of international thought and behaviour in the twenty-first century.

In order for librarians and teachers to know which books to select, they are advised to sample them for themselves as far as possible. How else can they efficiently teach or encourage child readers? There are also reference books and web sites that will assist. *Giants, Monsters and Dragons – an encyclopaedia of Folklore, Legend and Myth*, may be helpful.

Some questions for the book selector of Traditional Literature to ask are:

- Does this version suit the needs and interests of the children?
- Is the quality of writing and presentation in harmony with criteria that staff have established?
- Do we have a balanced selection and resources such as tapes, CDs, reference books and electronic portrayals (see Chapters 4 and 7), should I wish to use them?
- Can I present this material in a way that will attract today's children?

2. The Picture Book

> *Picture Books can be deceptive. There may be more to them than
> first meets the eye. Good picture books deal with important human
> issues and can convey quite complex ideas despite their economic
> use of words.*
>
> Baddeley and Eddershaw 1994, 1.

Picture Books are not just books with illustrations. There may be a
minimal amount of text, or no text at all. Pictures tell the story.

For infants, picture books are the usual introductory genre, associated initially with a close, warm relationship, often on a parent's or
caregiver's knee, often at bedtime when love is affirmed before darkness descends. The line and shape of illustrations attract a young child's
eyes, and are usually bright, as in Vagnozzi's *Sleepy Baby* and *Morning
Baby*; are often very beautiful, as with Jan Barger's *Snuggle Nuzzles*;
or depict great fun, as with Jez Alborough's *Fix-it Duck*. Often used
are nursery rhymes, favourites for generations, with which a baby may
have already have familiarity through song or by use of rhymes and
finger-plays. Early picture books are designed to be childproof, made
of untearable fabric, or are sturdy board books which can withstand
repeated readings, throwings, suckings and fingering.

2.1 Concepts

Early picture books teach **concepts**, naming such things as food, toys,
body parts, names of animals and pets, and identify items in and
outside the home; they introduce counting and the alphabet; they
describe interesting people and places, modelling vocabulary and attitudes. The pictures are usually large and relate to a baby's world, as in
Baby's World – Baby's First Word and *Picture Book*.

2.2 Story

As well as the concept books there are those that contain a **story**, sometimes without words as in Jan Ormerod's *Sunshine* and *Moonlight*,
which graphically show details of a preschooler's daily rituals and inter-
actions at morning and evening. Or there are many with a minimal
amount of words, in which pictures really tell the tale.

2.3 Novelty books

for young children sometimes lack the artistic sensitivity and subtlety of good picture books, but they are designed to be novel, to intrigue young minds and to inveigle young fingers into lifting flaps and finding secrets hidden away among illustration and simple story. These began in nineteenth-century England, but re-emerged in the 1960s and have proliferated since. The main forms are:

(i) Shaped books, like *Tug Boat*; and *Kippers Box of Books* which includes four cube sized books that teach concepts, colours and counting.

(ii) Folded leaf books, where by simple or intricate folding a second picture hides under another, as in *Spotted Yellow frogs*.

(iii) Hole books which allow children to spy at other aspects of the story. Eric Carle's *Very Hungry Caterpillar* and the *Ahlberg's Peepo!* have been two of the better ones of this type.

(iv) Lift the Flap; Pull the Tag. For example, Matthew Price's *My Daddy* invites little fingers to lift back a series of pictures of an achieving child: on a motorbike, on a swing,, skiing and flying. Answering the question, "Who comes . . . with me? The picture under the flap assures the answer with one word :'Daddy.' Others, such as by Lucy Cousins, use both flaps and tags, as with the ingenious Maisie books.

(v) Pop-Ups do exactly as the name implies. Numbers of these have come from Asian and other markets. Their function is largely to astound and entertain, though a few attempt to instruct. *Go with Christian*, a retelling of the *Pilgrim's Progress* for the young, illustrates how amazing pop-up features can minimalize serious topics and purpose. They are fun, yes, but gimmicky. A regular diet of Novelty Books would be like eating pink fairy floss for daily nourishment.

Gradually, the infant moves on to the picture story. This is also a picture book, but one with increased text, in which art work and narrative support each other. They are not easy to write, despite their simplicity, as many author-illustrators recognise. The good ones apply the literary devices of rhythm, rhyme and repetition, repeated in patterns similar to those in folklore. They also use apt expression with onomatopoeia, simile and memorable language. The old favourite, *Drummer Hoff*, uses some of these devices in the cumulative style of folklore as,

> General Border gave the order,
> Major Scott brought the shot,
> Captain Bammer brought the rammer,

Sergeant Chowder brought the powder,
Corporal Farrell brought the barrel,
Private Parriage brought the carriage,
but Drummer Hoff fired it off.
            Emberley, 1984, n.p.g.

At school, when reading skills are formally introduced and become established, Picture Storybooks, which have strong story lines that are complemented by illustrations, often becomes early reading books. They continue to elaborate on the world of the child, depicting such aspects as family life, nature, realistic and fanciful animal and monster stories, tales of other times and places, the humorous or fanciful, and include the evergreen stories found in myth, legend and folklore. They use dialogue with natural sounding language and do not talk down to older children. Some examples are *We're Going on a Bear Hunt* and *My Cat likes to Hide in Boxes*.

Illustration 3: WE'RE GOING ON A BEAR HUNT c. 1989, Helen Oxenbury. Reproduced by permission of Walker Books Ltd. (black and white photo, by Len Eastwood).

2.4 Criteria for Selection of Picture Books, Nursery to Key Stage 2

Graham and Kelly suggest that:

- Stories need to be emotionally true and reflect the child's world, as in Cooper's *Pumpkin Soup and Floury* and Pinkeye's *The Patchwork Quilt*;
- stories should allow for a child's ability to predict, something they delight in even when the story is a familiar one, such as Jasper's *Beanstalk* and *All in One Piece*;
- recognise that the child enjoys finding secrets concealed under flaps, holes, folded pages and movable parts, especially when the novel elements are an integral part of the narrative, as in *Maisiy Goes Swimming* by Lucy Cousins;
- recognise that books which assume children's prior knowledge of nursery rhymes and traditional tales, which they can apply to the text, flatter young readers and they respond with satisfaction. The Ahlbergs do this well, having had a teaching background. See *Each Pear Plum* and *The Jolly Pocket Postman*;
- illustrations are important in the picture book genre. They indicate a feeling of time, place and mood that may augment the text, making a different emphasis from the language. For example, see Brown's *A Dark, Dark Tale* and Wildsmith's *The Christmas Story*;
- Illustrations often contain secrets that children are pleased to discover. Hutchins' *You'll Soon Grow Into Them Tiitch* and Prater's *Once Upon a Time* are good examples.

2.5 Big Books

are a major resource in the early years of education, being used in the shared reading slot of the Literacy Hour. They are picture stories, traditional, rhythmic, predictable and use literary devices such as patterned language and repetition that encourage children to join in with pleasure. Even children at the back of a group can see the large print, and the voice of a shy child is supported by the chorus from the class as they all join in recitation of the text.

Some Big Books are from conventional sized children's literature that has been converted to large size. From these, children can proceed to the small size versions, reading them for themselves, whereas previous to the Big Book experience they may have been stories to which they listened only. This method of teaching reading has been shown to be very effective in New Zealand and Australia, dating back to Don Holdaway's enthusiastic involvement and promotion in the 1970s before publishers became involved. This contributed to New Zealand's highly acclaimed success in teaching reading, which attracted overseas' observation and research. In present-day Britain, Big Books contribute to the literacy of young children as they respond positively to the picture book genre.

2.6 *Picture Books for Older Children*

Picture books are not limited to the very young. Christobel Mattingly's *The Angel With a Mouth-Organ* is one example of a picturestory for an able reader in the upper grades of primary school at Key Stage 2. It is also well received in a teacher's oral reading at story time for younger children. A story from a setting of war and recovery, it uses the device of starting with present time in a setting that is familiar to a child, that of decorating a Christmas tree, then moving back into the story of a Christmas past. Bombs, destruction, separation, disaster, death . . . all are portrayed with sensitive, yet honest artistry of language and illustration. It is a beautiful family story that an older primary school child can read and be stirred by. At the level of subtext there is opportunity for much personal awareness.

Another remarkable picture story for older primary school children is *The Sea People* by Jorg Muller and Jorg Steiner. This is an example, not of family solidarity in times of pressure as with The Angel . . . , but focuses on relationships in society. It offers tremendous scope, through simple yet elegant narrative and detailed, large illustrations, for insightful reading by older students, for class discussions about society, for dramatic interpretations and children's own versions. It begins, in the fairy-tale mode with 'Once upon a time', referring to two islands in the sea, one bigger than the other. This beginning, that carries a sense of remoteness, introduces the people of the Greater and Lesser Islands, their life styles, ambitions, fears, conflicts, doom and destiny, in which an old man, blind in physical sight, but profoundly wise in insight and prophecy, is a key figure. Resolved, yet unresolved, the story ends open-ended, allowing for imaginative ownership of the text through discussion, application and prediction:

> *However, that is still not the whole tale.*
> *Often enough the blind man did not tell the end of his stories, and so it is with this one.*
> *It is about the world, and as long as this world exists, the story goes on and on, and who knows how it will end?*
>
> > *Muller and Steiner, n.p.g.*

A picture story published in the twenty-first century, but with a topic from the past, is *Pirate Diary: The Journal of Jake Carpenter*. It is especially good for older primary school age boys, for it moves away from settings in the family or general society, as are the examples given above, and emphasises manly valour. Set in the eighteenth century, it is a rollicking adventure of life at sea, recounted in day-by-day segments which may encourage the participation of readers who are reluctant to read lengthy passages. The pictures are large and colourful, with the crew's facial and other characteristics indicating their dispositions: eager, mean, grim, fearful, cruel, suffering . . . Intense conflict as pirates take over the vessel is portrayed in a highly dramatic and colourful double-page spread, as is a detailed and open-sided view of the vessel, the Greyhound, with a key to the parts of a typical sailing ship, while another double-page spread graphically depicts a great storm where men and boys struggle to resist the challenge of the elements. Exciting, yet with informative details, plus notes and maps that give an illustrated history of piracy and the lives of the most famous rogues, it is a quite marvellous, true-to-life, historical picturestory. Through it a modern boy, in the shelter of his own computerised classroom or bed room, can vicariously sleep in a hammock, eat hard-as-nails ship's biscuits (with worms), climb a main mast, and feel a menacing pirate captain's face so close that his red whiskers tickle the chin.

Good picture stories for older children, like those mentioned, carry the hallmark of insightful, imaginative writing coupled with skills in illustration, true to the principles of the criteria already cited in relationship to picture books for younger readers and the evaluation questions which follow.

Pam Baddeley and Chris Eddershaw are teachers in Gloucestershire, England, who have used picture books effectively with 4 – 12 year olds. Their work, *Not-So-Simple Picture Books*, helpful to teachers and librarians, exemplifies texts and techniques of presentation for children of Reception Class through to older years. Its appendices record the discussions of 10–11 year olds regarding David McKee's *Not Now Bernard* and a list of some of the best picture books they know and recommend.

2.7 Book Illustration

Ideas about picture book illustration vary, and entire books are written on the subject, but there are at least three areas for the artist to consider, of which the professional teacher or librarian needs some general awareness in order to evaluate quality. These concern: (i) the visual elements, related to line and linear emphasis, colour, shape, space, perspective, patterning and texture. (ii) Design/composition which is a combination of the visual elements and placement of texts – formally or informally. (iii) Artistic style in which individual differences feature.

Each book illustrator has his/her own individual style, just as writers do with words. Styles vary in composition, technique, emphasis, use of materials and effect. This means that illustration can be approached by the artist, and studied by the critic, from any of these views. Diversity of style is demonstrated by past illustrators of renown, such as Greenaway, Beatrix Potter, Edward Ardizzone and others. Especially for the modern child, it may be that the reader learns to adjust to a different medium and mood with almost every new picture book experience.

Modern artists suit the mood of their work to the contemporary child. The first Children's Laureate, *Quentin Blake*, whose child or adult faces often look as if a child drew them, features impish, child-like humour with action and complex detail that make one warm to the characters. His recent work, *Loveykins* expresses his idea of people being bird-like; has them outlined in black watercolour pencil, then brushed over later with watercolours. John Burningham, whom Blake describes as 'The poet of the picture book form' (3), also uses water-colours, but with more rounded characters in what feels like a welcoming, slightly tilted world of texture and detail. Then there are those of bold and unconventional surrealism, as by Anthony Browne, which contrasts with Helen Cooper's reassuring, apt-for-bedtime, fantasy-reality mix that depicts children solving their own problems. Others display close attention to realistic detail, yet tempered with an imaginative artist's eye, as does long-time favourite Shirley Hughes, while Helen Oxenbury is noted for her witty and animated watercolours. Another style that depicts a carefree mood comes in the form of wildly anarchic scribbles, as used by Korky Paul, or, from the German illustrator, Klaus Baumgart, the 'gently vibrant and magical', according to David Blanch (12), a reassuring style that is winning him popularity all over the world. One artist whose work has a tremendous amount of fine detail, and can convey a marvellous sense of humour and the absurd, is Fritz Wegner whose artistry has supported writing by esteemed authors such as Leon Garfield and Allan Ahlberg.

Others use photographic reference in illustration as does P. J. Lynch, winner of the Mother Goose Award in 1987 and the Kate Greenaway Medal 1995 and 1997, but he does not suggest that using photographic reference become a replacement for good drawing practice. John Burningham, too, uses a combination of drawing and photography in Cloudland and Whadayamean. On the other hand, Shoo Rayner, creator of the spoofy animal detective series, *The Rex Files*, is an example of the contemporary children's book illustrator who draws straight into a computerised painting programme; he considers the question, 'Is Computer Art Creative' and describes the process he has worked through (8–9). Others, like Mel Gibson of the Write Away project, use a comic form.

2.8 Comic books

Prize winning writer Philip Pullman admits to being a fan of comics when a boy, finding Eagle and other British comics of the 1950s intoxicating, glamorous and funny. Writing in *Carousel*, he says:

> *I think it was the sheer speed of the storytelling as much as anything else. I liked the instantaneous way the pictures could show what was happening, without the need to assemble a picture in my own head by reading line after line of prose.*

He adds that 'it's no longer eccentric to suggest that comics can be the subject of serious discussion', drawing attention to titles by Roger Sabin and Scott McCloud.

Certainly comics and also graphic novels, with their highly or darkly colourful, in-your-face, all-over-the-page illustrations which use technology, virtural reality, fantasy and horror, have a following of young people; and it appears that more and more libraries are diversifying to stock them. David Wenzell's depiction of Tolkein's *The Hobbit*, is an example that gives the classic for children a fresh perspective. Whether one objects on the grounds of violence, sexism, or that they are just 'not literature', nevertheless they are a twenty-first format that has arrived and is popular. Perhaps they reflect a changing world society where nothing is 'precious' or confined to an elitist audience any more.

2.9 Evaluation Questions

- Does the art work 'vivify, quicken and vitalise'? – as Maurice Sendak suggests (3).
- Do the illustrations enhance visual awareness? – a class room goal that is important to Jane Doonan.
- Does the artistic style chosen by the illustrator harmonise with the author's literary style, stimulate aesthetic appreciation, delineate and develop characters, fit with historical, cultural and geographical detail? – criteria given by Donna E. Norton, (147).

Children's Sayings

"I hope you find the *Shoemaker and the Elves* in your library. I thought it was marvellous." Simon, 8 years.

"I chose *I like Books* because it's got a picture of a monkey and Mummy says I'm a monkey." Maisie, age 6.

"I like *Animalia* because it's funny and they've put tons of effort in it." Callum, 7 years.

"*The Ultimate Alphabet* is full of different paintings, like a puzzle book and you've got to find all these things in that picture." – Stephanie, aged 10.

After reading *The Little Red Hen*, retold by Vera Southgate; illustrated by Stephen Holmes:

"I think the pictures should have more colour, because nearly every picture in the book is either red, yellow, brown or green." Berin, 9 years.

"Hi, it's me again, Adam. I'm reading *The Amazing Maurice and his Educated Rodents* now. I think it's a sort of fairy-tale. Cool! (I've got a cat, too)." 10 years.

Tutorial Topics

1. Browse in the Myths and Legends section of your library. Select a book that appeals to you. You may wish to discover about the following mythical heroes: Theseus who fights the Minotaur, or Jason and the Golden Fleece, or the amazingly strong Heracles, or Orpheus who descends into the Underworld, all characters from Greek mythology? Or your choice may concern heroes from other traditions. Write or discuss what these stories might offer child readers. Consider if you would, or would not, select the book you selected for a child to read, and give reasons for your answer.

2. If you prefer a narrative for older readers, try Rosemary Sutcliff's *The Sword and the Circle* (1981) which vividly brings to life the story of King Arthur and his knights of the Round Table, presenting a feel of the mystery and mystique of Camelot. Do you know of sites in Britain where it is claimed these events happened? Talk about them; visit; sketch, take photos, write down your impressions . . . Get enthused about Myth and Legend!

3. Are the heroes of Traditional Literature whom Campbell suggests are portrayed as symbols – warrior, lover, tyrant, redeemer, saint . . . of any relevance to modern secular and technological society?

4. Read two stories from the Folklore tradition. What typical characteristics do they depict? Discuss reasons why the 'crude, violent and sexually -charged texts' (Hunt, 1999, 10) should be retained or excluded.

5. Read a modern picture book that tells a traditional tale. Identify its essential characteristics.

6. Discuss Jung's view that every person needs a myth to live by.

7. Evaluate the style of a contemporary illustrator of picture books. Note the techniques used and the mood evoked.

Further Reading

Genres

Norton, Donna E. *Through the Eyes of a Child*. An Introduction to Children's Literature. 3rd edition. New York: Merrill, 1991. Chapters 5–12 concern genres.

Traditional Literature
Berg, Leila. *God Stories: A Celebration of Legends*. London: Frances Lincoln, 1999.
Bettelheim, Bruno. *The Uses of Enchantment*. New York: Knopf, 1976.
Gough, John. *Rivalry, Rejection, and Recovery: Variations of the Cinderella Story*. In Children's Literature in Education, June 1990, 99–107.
Meigs, Cornelia et al. *A Critical History of Children's Literature*. Revised edition. London: Macmillan, 1969, Chapters 1–2.
Spawforth, Tony. *Imaginative Time Travel: The Greeks and Romans*. In Books for Keeps, No. 124, September 2000, 4–6.
Zipes, J. Ed. *The Trials and Tribulations of Little Red Riding Hood,* 2nd edition. New York: Routledge, 1993.
—— *Happily Ever After*. Fairy Tales, Children and the Culture Industry. New York: Routledge, 1997.

Picture Books
Cianciolo, Patricia. *Picture Books for Children*. ALA, 1997.
Baddeley, Pam and Eddershaw, Chris. *Not So Simple Picture Books*. Stoke on Trent: Trentham Books, 1994.
Doonan, Jane. *Looking at Pictures in Picture Books*. Stroud: Thimble press, 1993.
East, Kathy. *Inviting Children's Authors and Illustrators: A How-to-Do-It Manual for School and Public Librarians*. London: Neal Schuman, 1995.
Gifford, D. *Discovering Comics*. Revised edition, 1991. Prices Risborough: Shire, 1971.
Lewis, D. *The Constructedness of Texts: Picture Books and the Metafictive. Signal*, Number 62, 131–146.
Magic Pencil: children's book illustration today. Selected by Quentin Blake. The British Library: 2002.
Sendak, Maurice. *Caldecott & Co: Notes on Books & Pictures*. New York: Farrar, Straus and Giroux, 1988.
Watson, V. and Morag Styles, eds. *Talking Pictures*. Pictorial Texts and Young Readers. London: Hodder and Stoughton, 1996.

Children's Books Cited. A Selection Guide

Myths and Legends
Amery, Heather, ill. Linda Edwards. *Greek Myths for Young Children*. London: Usborne, 1999.
Barber, Antonia. *The Mousehole Cat*. London: Walker Books, 1990.
Coolidge, Olivia E. *Legends of the North*. Boston: Houghton Mifflin, 1951.
Dickinson, Peter. *City of Gold and Other Stories from the Old Testament*. Illustrated by Michael Foreman. Pantheon Books: New York, 1980, 16.

Garfield, Leon and Edward Blishen. *The God beneath the Sea*. illustrated by Charles Keeping. Carousel Books, 1977.

Jaffrey, Madhur. *Seasons of Splendour*. London: Puffin, 1985.

Kimber, Kevin et al. *A First Book of Myths for the Very Young from Around the World*. London: Dorling Kindersley Publishing, 1999.

Lady Gregory. *Irish Legends for Children*. Cork: Mercier Press, 1995.

Malam, John. *Gods and Goddesses*. London: Wayland, 1999.

McCaughrean, Geraldine. *Greek Myths*. Illustrated by Emma Chichester Clark. London: Orchard, 1992.

—— *Greek Gods and Goddesses*. illustrated by Emma Chichester Clark.London: Orchard, 1997

—— *Roman Myths*. Illustrated by Emma Chichester Clark. London: Orchard, 1999.

—— *The Greeks on Stage*. Illustrated by Richard Brassey. Llangrannog: Dolphin, 2002.

Pilling, Ann. *Creation Stories from Around the World*. London: Walker Books, 1997.

Steptoe, John. *Mufaro's Beautiful Daughters*. London: Hodder and Stoughton, 1987/

Ross, Stewart. *The Original Olympics*. London: Wayland 'Ancient Greece', 1996.

—— *Daily Life*. London: Wayland 'Ancient Greece series,' 1999.

Trezise, Percy and Dick Roughsey. *Turramulli the Giant Quinkin*. Sydney: Fontana Picture Lions, 1982.

Verniero, Joan C. et al. *One-Hundred-And-One Read-Aloud Myths and Legends: Ten-minute Readings from the World's best-Loved Literature*. New York: Black Dog and Leventhal Publishers, 1999.

Folktales
Aesop's Fables. London: Bloomsbury Books, 1994.

Bryant, Sara Cone. *The Gingerbread Boy*. In The Fairy Tale Treasury, selected by Virginia Haviland. Illustrated by Raymond Briggs. London; Puffin Books, 1972.

Garner, Alan. *A Bag of Moonshine*. London: Lions, 1992.

Grimm, Jacob and Wilhem Grimm. *Grimms' Fairy Tales*. Reprint. Harmondsworth: Puffin Books, 1976.

Jacobs, Joseph. *English Fairy Tales*. Reprinted. London: Bodley head, 1974.

Picture Books
Ahlberg, Janet and Allen. *Peepo!* London: Viking, 1998.

—— *Each Peach Pear Plum*. London: Picture Lions, 1980.

—— *The Jolly Pocket Postman*. London: Heinemann, 1995.

Alborough, Jez. *Fix-it Duck*. Lion: Picture Lions, 2002.
Baby's World – Baby's First Word and Picture Book. London: Dorling Kindersley, 2002.
Barger, Jan. *Snuggle Nuzzles*. London: Hodder, 2002.
Base, Graeme. *Animalia*. Harmondsworth: Penguin, 1990.
Brown, R. *A Dark Dark Tale*. London: Andersen, 1981.
Burningham, John. *Cloudland*. London: Red Fox,1999.
—— *Whadayamean*. Jonathan Cape, 1999.
Carle, Eric. *The Very Hungry Caterpillar*. London: Hamish Hamilton, 1970.
Cooper. H. *Pumpkin Soup*. London: Transworld Publishers, 1998.
Cousins, Lucy. *Happy Birthday Maisy*. London: Walker Books, 1998.
—— *Maisy at the Farm*. London: Walker Books, 1998.
—— *Maisy Goes Swimming*. London: Walker Books, 1990.
Emberley. *Drummer Hoff*. Illustrated by Emberley. Reprint. London : The Bodley Head, 1984.
Floury, V. and J. Pinkeye. *The Patchwork Quilt*. London: Bodley Head, 1985.
Hutchins, Pat. *You'll Soon Grow Into Them Titch*. London: Bodley Head,. 1983.
Innkeeper, Mica. *Kipper's Box of Books*. London: Hodder, 2002.
Innkeeper and Butterworth. *Jasper's Beanstalk*. Sevenoaks: Hodder and Stoughton, 1992.
Mattingley, Christobel. *The Angel With a Mouth-Organ.* Sydney: Hodder and Stoughton, 1985.
Murphy, Jill. *All in One Piece*. London: Walker Books, 1987.
Ormerod, Jan. *Sunshine*. Harmondsworth: Kestrel, 1981.
—— *Moonlight*. Harmondsworth: Kestrel, 1982.
Parry, Alan and Linda. *Go With Christian: The Pilgrim's Progress for Young Children*. New Alresford: Hunt and Thorpe, 1996.
Platt, Richard. *Pirate Diary: The Journal of Jake Carpenter*. Illustrated by Chris Riddell. London: Walker Books Ltd., 2001.
Price, Matthew. *My Daddy*. Illustrated by Jean Claverie. Templestowe: The Five Mile press, 1986.
Muller, Jorg and Jorg Steiner. *The Sea People*. London: Victor Gollancz Ltd, 1982.
Rosen M. and H. Oxenbury. *We're Going on a Bear Hunt*. London: Walker Books, 1989.
Sutton E. and L. Dodd. *My Cat Likes to Hide in Boxes*. London: Hamish Hamilton, 1973.
Tug Boat. London: Dorling Kindersley, 1998.
Van Fleet, Matthew. *Spotted Yellow Frogs*. Andover: Ragged Bears, 1998.
Vagnozzi, Barbara. *Sleepy Baby*. Slough: Zero to Ten, 2002.
—— *Morning Baby*. Slough: Zero to Ten, 2002.

Wildsmith, Brian. *The Christmas Story*. Oxford: Oxford University Press, 1989.

Wilks, Mikie. *The Ultimate Alphabet*. London: Pavilion, 1987.

Bibliography

Al Aaraj, Kifah. In Pandit Shereen: *Mightier than the Sword*, Books for Keeps, No. 138, January, 2003, 5.

Alderson, Brian. *But are they 'Real' Books?* A Look at Novelty Publishing. In Books for Keeps, November 1998, No. 113, 4–8.

Baddeley, Pam and Chris Eddershaw. *Not so Simple Picture Books*. Stoke-On-Trent: Trentham Books, 1994.

Bettelheim, Bruno. *The Uses of Enchantment: The Meaning and Importance of Fairy Tales*. Harmondsworth: Penguin, 1976.

Berry, J. W. *Cultural Foundations of Behaviour*. In Kazden, A. (ed.) *Encyclopaedia of Psychology*. Washington, DC: American Psychosocial Association and Oxford University Press, 2000; Matsumoto, D. Culture and Psychology. Pacific Grove: Brooks/Cole, 1996.

Blake, Quentin. 'Children's Book Illustration: A Separate Story?' In *Books for Keeps*, No. 121, March 2000, 8–10.

Blanch, David. 'Klaus Baumgart.' In *Carousel*, Issue 13, Autumn/Winter 1999.

Blishen, Edward. 'The Impulse to Story.' In *Through Folklore to Literature*. Maurice Saxby, ed. Sydney: IBBY Australia Publications, 1979, 27–41.

Campbell, Joseph. *The Hero with a Thousand Faces*. 2nd edition, 3rd printing. New York: Princeton University Press, 1973,11.

—— *The Power of Myth*. New York: Doubleday, 1988.

Cox, Marian, Roalfe. *Cinderella: 349 Variants*. London: Nutt, 1893.

Doonan, Jane. *Looking at Pictures in Picture Books*. Stroud: Thimble Press, 1990.

Emberley, Barbara. *Drummer Hoff*. Illustrated by Ed Emberley. Reprinted. London: The Bodley head, 1984.

The Fables of Aesop. Illustrated by Frank Baber. Sydney: Hodder and Stoughton, 1975.

The Famous and Renowned History of Sir Bevies of Southampton. 'Licensed and Entred according to Dider. Printed for W. Thackeray at the Angel in Duck Lane, and F. Deacon at the Angel in Gilt Spur Street, 1689.

Fordham, Freda. *An Introduction to Jung's Psychology*. Harmondsworth: Penguin Books, 1985.

Gough, John. 'Rivalry, Rejection and Recovery. Variations of the Cinderella Story.' In *Children's Literature in Education*, Vol. 21, No. 2, 1990, 99–107.

Graham, Judith and Alison Kelly, eds. Reprint. *Reading Under Control: Teaching Reading in the Primary School*. London: David Fulton Publishers Ltd., 2001, 29–30.

Handford, S. A. *Aesop's Fables*. London: Penguin Books, 1993, 5.

Hooper, Walter. Ed. *They Stand Together*. The Letters of C. S. Lewis to Arthur Greaves (1914–1963). London: Collins, 1979, 10.

Hunt, Peter. (ed) *Understanding Children's Literature*. London: Routledge, 1999.

Jung, C. G. *Collected Works*, (20 vols). Vol. 9, Part 1: The Archetypes and the Collective Unconscious, 2nd edition. London: Routledge and Kegan Paul, 1968.

Lewis, D. 'The Constructedness of Texts: Picture Books and the Metafictive.' In *Signal*, No. 62, 1990, 131–146.

Lynch, P. J. 'On the Use of Photography in Illustration.' In *Books for Keeps*. No. 122, May 2000, 10–11.

McCaughrean, Geraldine. *The Orchard Book of Greek Myths*. Illustrated by Emma Chichester Clark. London: Orchard Books, 1992.

McCloud, Scott. *Understanding Comics*. London: HarperCollins, 1994.

Newberry, Linda. 'I wish I'd written . . .' In *Books for Keeps*, No. 120, January 2000.

Norton, Donna E. *Through the Eyes of a Child*. 3rd edition. New York: Merrill, 1991.

Nodelman, Perry. *Words About Pictures: the Narrative Art of Children's Picture Books*. Athens, Georgia: University of Georgia Press, 1988.

O'Connor, Peter. *Understanding Jung: Understanding Yourself*. North Ryde: Methuen, 1985.

Pullman, Philip. 'Comics.' In *Carousel*, Issue 5, Spring 1997.

Rayner, Shoo. 'Is Computer Art Creative?' In *Books for Keeps*, No. 115, March 1999.

Roger, Mae Durham. 'From Folklore to Children's Literature.' In *Through Folklore to Literature*. Maurice Saxby,(ed.) Sydney: IBBY, 1979, 70.

Rowling, J. K. *Harry Potter and the Philosopher's Stone*. London: Bloomsbury, 1997.

Rose, C. Giants, *Monsters and Dragons – an Encyclopaedia of Folklore, Legend and Myth*. New York: W. W. Norton, 2001.

Sabin, Roger. *Comics, Comix and Graphic Novels*. London: Phaidon, 1996,

Saxby, Maurice. *Through Folklore to Literature*. Sydney: IBBY Australia, 1979, 2.

Schwartz, Joseph H. *Ways of the Illustrator: Visual Communication in Children's Literature*. Chicago: American Library Association, 1982.

Sendak, Maurice. *Caldecott & Co: Notes on Books and Pictures*. New York: Straus and Giroux, 1988.

Shaffer, D. R. *Developmental Psychology: Childhood and Adolescence*. Pacific Grove: Brooks/Cote Publishing Co., 1988.

Stephens, James. *The Crock of Gold*. New York: Macmillan,1956.

Thomson, Pat. 'Meeting Mr Wegner.' In *Books for Keeps*, Issue 24, Summer 2003, 6–7.

Waley, Arthur. 'Chinese Cinderella Story.' *Folk-lore*, Vol. 58, 1947.

Walsh, Jill Paton. 'I thought I'd start with something easy.' In *Books for Keeps*, No. 124, September 2000, 13.

Zipes, J. (ed.) *The Trials and Tribulations of Little Red Riding Hood*, 2nd edition. New York, Routledge, 1993.

CHAPTER THREE

The Child, Growing with Genres

There is in the best children's poetry a sense of the world being seen as for the first time, and of language being plucked from the air to describe it . . . This does not necessarily mean that children's poems are 'simple' in any reductive sense. I would argue that no poem can be called a poem that does not have at its heart some unknowable mystery.

Phillip 1996: xxv

1. Poetry

Not only does poetry express 'some unknowable mystery', but it also speaks to the heart and mind of an individual, expressing insights that seem amazingly new and wonderful. Beatrice Schenk de Regniers captures its essence as she writes:

If you find a little feather, a little white feather,
a soft and tickly feather, it's for you.
A feather is a letter from a bird, and it says,
'Think of me. Do not forget me.
Remember me always. Remember me forever.
Or remember me at least until
the little feather is
lost.'
So . . . if you find a little feather,
a little white feather,

a soft and tickly feather, it's for you.
Pick it up and . . .
Put it in your pocket.

1.1 Selecting Poetry

The selection of poetry for classroom or library should, ideally, be based, on the premise of offering the child the best, the most sensitive and skilfully expressed poems possible – not confined to verse that is just lists of words, merely entertaining, or dressed-up narrative, or rhymes from doggerel-makers of limited insight. The *Signal* journal, by its annual Award to Poetry, has done much in the past to promote poetry of quality for children, but, as categorised by Nancy Chambers, *Signal* editor, it was always strongly on the side of 'heritage' poetry.

In Britain, the National Literacy Strategy provides details to teachers regarding the range and different forms of poetry that children should experience, but they, like teachers world-wide, still have the option to choose specific examples. So what should they choose – heritage poetry from poets of the past and living poets who maintain similar standards? Or should the go with the new wave of verse that began in the 1970s – which makes it already well established by the twenty-first century?

Townsend called it 'urchin verse', adding:

> *In this country, the move from the poetic to the demotic was headed by Michael Rosen, whose* Mind Your Own Business *(1974) was the exemplar. Here was family life in the raw, with its backchat, fury and muddle, and instead of woods and meadows were disused railway lines, building sites and junk heaps. Other collections followed . . .*
>
> *1990, 300.*

Poetry that is true to this familiar background of 'Family life in the raw', and also to contemporary childhood behaviour, is what many twenty-first-century children understand and to which they relate. With Rosen it buzzes along with surprises, energy, humour and cheekiness, using expressions and thoughts that are close to playground language and a child's own inner voice. Yet in sensitivity the 'urchin' poetry does not miss out, because it pulsates with understated emotion and intensely human insight, culminating in recognisable emotions and resolutions. Whether writing about 'Chocolate Cake' or 'Gymnastics', Michael Rosen continually demonstrates poetic grace, which takes his work far beyond mere cleverness and an ear for childtalk, skills that account for his immense popularity. So much about belonging, nostalgia, home and the overall human condition is expressed in the final verse of Rosen's *Mind Your Own Business*:

> *As my shirt falls apart*
> *I'll keep the bits*
> *in a biscuit tin*
> *on the mantelpiece*
> *for years and years and years.*

Other poets of this style are Allan Ahlberg, Roger McGough, Gareth Owen, Valerie Worth, Kit Wright and the *Signal* Poetry Award winner, Jackie Kay. Their work can be readily accessed in anthologies or single author publications.

Also ascending in popularity are the British Black poets who speak out unashamedly with voices that are confident, distinct and different, a true reflection of a vibrant part of the community. See Benjamin Zephaniah's *Talking Turkeys* (1994) *Funky Chickens* (1996) and more recent publications; also Grace Nicholls who appeared with *Come on into my Tropical Garden* in 1988, and James Berry, winner of the Signal Prize in 1988 with *When I Dance*:

> *Only one of me*
> *and nobody can get a second one*
> *from a photocopy machine.*

A Nest Full of Stars, illustrated by Rachel Merriman, is a further collection by James Berry which echoes Caribbean Creole speech and the oral culture of his childhood. At his school performances he recites his poems about ghosts (duppys) in a rap manner:

> *You walk too-too late at night*
> *duppies make your wrong road right.*
> *Around you, they rattle strings of bones.*
> *And duppies dance. Duppies dance.*

An important principle when selecting poetry is to present the work of poets who can open children's eyes in wonder or amusement, make them sparkle with happiness and self-acceptance or because they glimpse a marvellous new way of looking at the world, even if it means they jump along the garden path like Christopher Robin: 'Hoppity, hoppity, hop!' Heritage poetry or Urchin, both have this capacity.

1.2 Poetry Stepping Stones

Tiny feet need stepping stones that are spaced close together, whereon they can tread without slipping or falling. Likewise, infants and young children need simple stepping stones for their first steps to enjoying poetry. On special 'Baby Days' or BookStart functions at the library, librarians may wish to display and share illustrated poems for babies, such as in *Welcome Baby! Baby Rhymes for Baby Times* by Stephanie Calmerson, or *Baby Blessings: Inspiring Poems and Prayers for Every Stage of Babyhood* by June Cotner. Traditional nursery Rhymes, often called *Mother Goose*, which first appeared in England in *Tommy Thumb's Pretty Song Book* in 1744, make an easy beginning in the home and nursery school as they introduce Language patterns, story, characters, humour and opportunity for participation. They also unlock essential elements of poetry: rhythm, rhyme, repetition, and imagery – and they bring immense enjoyment and scope for participation in action and language. Kate Greenaway's *Mother Goose or the Old Nursery Rhymes,* was first published in 1881, yet its appeal continues as it is republished for new generations who hear and act out favourites like "Ring-a-ring-a-roses, a pocket full of posies . . .'

Occasionally the excesses and cruelties of nursery rhymes are criticised by well-meaning adults. Marian Whitehead, in her work regarding the early years, says:

> *The children can sing about terrible behaviour, and even enjoy the shock value of doing so, while also feeling some sense of how unacceptable it really is to slit someone's throat, throw an old man down the stairs or drown a cat in a well.*
>
> *Whitehead 1999, 40.*

She also suggests that:

> *Another dominant theme is, of course, nonsense . . . and play with language and ideas helps children to understand and manage the realities of their lives. By simply turning things 'on their heads' chil-*

dren can test how they work and how far they can be stretched. The far-fetched jokes and nonsense of nursery rhymes are very similar to young children's own humour.

Whitehead, Ibid.

More recent publications like *Lucy Cousins' Big Book of Nursery Rhymes,* use a modern style of illustration, rather than Greenaway's romantic portrayal; while audio books such as the BBC *50 Favourite Nursery Rhymes . . . and More*, offer enthusiastic audio presentations. For pure fun, relished by the modern infant school child who already has an established repertoire of nursery rhymes and is, usually, in control of bladder functions, is Michael Rosen's *Hairy Tales and Nursery Crimes,* especially as 'this little pig' who goes to Sainburys to shop, 'went wee, wee, wee, wee, wee, wee, wee, Oh no, I've wet my pants.'

These early stepping stones can soon be supplemented by poetry from the past that young children enjoy. From Robert Graves comes *Allie,* and one verse is just as loved as four. W. B. Yeats writes *To a Squirrel at Kyle-Na-No;* Walter de la Mare brings delight and wonder with his Some One who 'came knocking at my wee, small door' . . . 'So I know not who came knocking, at all, at all, at all.' D. H. Lawrence's *The Gazelle Calf,* introduces the refrain 'O my children' in an endearing way that seems to hold a biblical ring; mystery is felt in *Roads Go Ever Ever On* by J. R. R. Tolkien, and the riddles, such as *Thirty White Horses* are also enjoyed.

There is magic too good to miss in *The King of China's Daughter* by Edith Sitwell, while Christina Rossetti's short poems, simply expressed, yet rich with feeling and insight, can linger in young minds, coming out in later years in journal references and story writing. Rossetti is one of the few women poets of the past still regularly represented in the canon of children's poetry. Observe children's delight in Rossetti's *The Wind,* or *The Rainbow,* or The *skylark or The Caterpillar* and the evergreen, *The City Mouse and the Garden Mouse.* Unusual but true, one gifted four year-old, entranced by language, loved to be read some of Milton's sonnets, not fully understanding, but awed by the musical flow and inherent power of the words.

These poems of the past reveal poets' feeling for what interests the child while offering surprise and delight. But they do not condescend or speak down to the child, and they allow the child to interpret. The poems also have an established, long 'shelf-life' and are still not quickly tired of. They fulfil the criteria that Norton gives which, in addition to the role of metre, rhythm, selective language and imagery, states:

> *The subject matter should delight children, say something to them, enhance their egos, strike happy recollections, tickle their funny bones, or encourage them to explore.*
>
> Norton 1991, 359.

Other poets of the twentieth and twenty-first century convey the same enchantment to young children in their own ways. Look for exquisite work by Margaret Wise Brown, Eleanor Farjeon, Aileen Fisher, Russell Hobbs, Langston Hughes, Karla Kuskin, Myra Cohn Livingston, A. A. Milne, James Reeves, Kit Wright and Charlotte Zolowtow. Shirley Hughes, classic children's writer and illustrator, reaches the young with *Things I like*. Kaye Umansky and Nick Sharratt have a more pragmatic, fun collection that promotes participation with *Wiggle My Toes*.

Very important is the adult's own pleasure in the poetry s/he shares. Read it aloud in the mood it is written – with nostalgia, cheekily, happily or whatever.

1.3 Stepping Stones for Middle-sized Feet

Key Stage 2 children, 7- 11 years, need middle-sized stepping stones, a little more challengingly spaced though they may still enjoy earlier favourites. Never forget, however, that individual children vary in interests and development. Some children in the primary school years will have big feet, big minds, robust ambitions, and want to stride ahead; others will prefer to linger. This can be one of the problems of the designated educational 'Key Stages' with their prescribed goals. Nevertheless, it sets up a framework that suits the majority. At the same time, it also risks mediocrity of choice as quirky, fun and gimmicky writing sometimes become overused by overextended teachers or librarians who may not have had a grounding in children's literature. Like junk food, it satisfies only briefly, and can be habit forming. Beware! Teacher and librarians need to become discriminating when it comes to poetry selection and to present with genuine appreciation and enthusiasm.

The middle sized stepping stones to the enchantment of poetry will offer poetry of both past and present, which is often collected together well in anthologies, though sometimes perhaps, not so well. Because a work is in a printed collection does not guarantee it has the quality *you* seek, yet it is a form, which by its mere existence, can denote immense power, as Peter Hollindale points out. There are many anthologies available, for every well-known publisher likes to enter the anthology market, but this discussion can mention only a few. Early examples of the best can be found in *The Golden Treasury of Poetry*, (1959) selected by Louis Untermyer, and *The Oxford Book of Poetry for Children* (1985) selected by Edward Blishen. More recent examples are, *The Hutchinson Treasury of Children's Poetry* (1997) which spans all ages and is illustrated by acclaimed artists; *The Puffin Book of Utterly Brilliant Poetry*, (1999) suggested for 8–14 year-olds, includes poems from the popular Spike Milligan, Allan Ahlberg, Michael Rosen, and the charismatic, London performing poet, Benjamin Zephaniah. Anne Fine, the second British Children's Laureate, has compiled a fine collection for 'young readers' and 'middle readers' with *A Shame to Miss*, Books 1 and 2. And they would indeed be 'a shame to miss.'

Some poets of the past who fit into the 'too good to miss' category for the Middle Steps are: the writers of nonsense verse, Lewis Carroll and Edward Lear. For simple but beautiful verse: Isaac Watts, Christina Rossetti, Walter de la Mare and Robert Louis Stevenson whose *Garden of Verses*, over a hundred years after first publication in 1885, still has a magical quality. 'How do you like to go up in a swing?' asks the voice of a child, then, in answer recounts the delights, recalling the sensation of hair flying, legs outstretched, as wind rushes by, flying 'up in the air and down.'

Rudyard Kipling was more than a storyteller and his philosophic poem *If*, still has widespread appeal for school assemblies as it upholds a serious standard of uprightness and self-respect. (Middle Step children are still impressionable and not cynical; nor will they see it as sexist or to be parodied). Hilaire Belloc is another whose work, like Kipling's, spans the nineteenth and early twentieth century. His *Cautionary Tales* have a continuing appeal as they depict laughable, stupid behaviour. See 'There was a Boy whose name was Jim.' Read with expression by an adult, it keeps a class entranced. Likewise does Belloc's *Tarantella* with with its beating melody:

> *Do you remember an inn,*
> *Miranda?*
> *Do you remember an inn?*
> *And the tedding and the spreading*

of the straws for a bedding,
and the fleas that tease in the High Pyrenees,
and the wine that tasted of tar?

A more recent story teller in verse is the Cornish poet, Charles Causley. Through him comes the balladic beat of the past. Hear it, feel it, in much of his poetry as it sings along, often with references to places, traditions and legends of Cornwall. Every teacher should have a copy of his *Selected Poems,* to use in odd moments to bring pleasure and reflective pause in a class. Read about the ghost of 'Miller's End', or 'Annabel-Emily' who would eat nothing but jam, and share the emotions of 'Tavistock Goose Fair', a poignant memory of a young lad's father, killed in battle.

1.4 Many Types of Poems

Teachers report that at this second stage of stepping stones, the child enjoys many forms of poetry:

- *Narrative poems and ballads,* such as Alfred Noyes', The *Highwayman,* or Robert Browning's *Pied Piper of Hamelin;* or the south of England's anonymous minstrel who sang, the *Ballad of the Fox* who went out 'All on a summer's night,O.' *The Forsaken Merman and Other Story Poems*, selected by Berlie Doherty, covers the field of narratives and ballads effectively.
- *Humour* never fails to please the Middle-Step child, including that found in Spike Milligan's verse and Roald Dahl's *Revolting Rhymes.* The latter parodies the nursery rhymes of children's younger years, and have some naughty bits that stir up snickers. At the same time they demonstrate that playing with words and ideas can be great fun.
- *Lyrics,* brief poems that tell of personal feelings and responses to beauty, that are rich in imagery, appeal to many. and young poets enjoy attempting to write them in Literacy Hour. 'The Balloon' by Karla Kuskin is one simple example:

I went to the park
And I bought a balloon.
It sailed through the sky
Like a large orange moon . . .

And then as the day
Started to night
I gave a short jump
And I held the string tight
And home we all sailed
Through the darkening sky,
The orange balloon, the small birds
And I.

- *Shape poems*, written into the shape of the poem's subject, for example a valentine heart, a football, a cross, or a flower, have a brief fascination for some children, though the shape may limit what can be expressed. Share with them Myra Cohn Livingston's *Space Songs* in which 'Moon" is in the shape of a crescent moon and "Meteorites' has a tail.
- *Limericks* and nonsense verse are always fun to read and to write, popularised by Edward Lear and Lewis Carroll in the eighteenth century, but perpetuated today, especially in classroom writing classes because the structure is not difficult to complete or to fill in assigned lines.
- *Free Verse and Haiku* are also markers along the middle road. Free Verse has little or no rhyme and the rhythm used is like that of everyday speech. Haiku is an old form of Japanese poetry, expressed in three lines, simple, yet profound, over which the reader may feel the need to linger to ponder a little. Traditionally there are five syllables in the first line, seven in the second, and five syllables in the last. Topics are frequently linked lyrically to nature. *In a Spring Garden*, edited by Richard Lewis, is one very beautiful collection with examples that Middle-Step children can enjoy, such as:

The chicken
   wants to say something,
The way it's using its feet.
         - Anonymous

or,

Voices
Above the white clouds:
Skylarks.
            - Kyoroku

- Every poetry collection today presents themes, so there are poems about nature, animals, witches and ghosts, maths, moods and feelings, football, seasons, knickers, going to school, dentist or hospital … Selectors should select discriminately, knowing why they have chosen. Should poetry only be 'good for a laugh'?

1.5 For Designer Boots and High Heels

Poetry for the older reader takes the secondary-age student over wider spaced stepping stones to traditional adult poetry and verse. *The Rattle Bag*, coedited by Ted Hughes and Seamus Henry, is one anthology that bulges with treats for young people to discover. Another is The *Walker Book of Classic Poetry and Poets,* edited by Michael Rosen, an example of a collection that looks at many of the 'greats': Blake, Bronte, Shakespeare, Tennyson, Wordsworth … Other poets for this 'Designer Label' stage could well be Byron, as in: 'She walks in beauty'; Samuel Taylor Coleridge with his 'Ancient Mariner'; John Masefield, memorable in Sea Fever' and 'Cargoes'; Thomas Hardy whose metre is masterful, especially in his poems like 'Weathers', frequently selected for children, or in 'Snow in the Suburbs:

> *Every branch big with it,*
> *Bent every twig with it;*
> *Every fork like a white web-foot;*
> *Every street and pavement mute:*
> *Some flakes have lost their way, and grope back*
> *upward, when*
>
> *Meeting those meandering down they turn and descend again …*
> *The steps are a blanched slope,*
> *Up which, with feeble hope,*
> *A black cat comes, wide-eyed and thin:*
> *And we take him in.*

Former Poet Laureate, Ted Hughes, in contrast, uses *free verse* that can touch his audience as his voice speaks persistently, persuasively, using vivid imagery. His nature poetry is never romanticised, but reflects modern societal views toward animals; bitter aspects balanced by the beautiful. He is unsentimentally honest, sometimes sad or funny, always memorable, as in

> *A cowclap is an honest job*
> *A black meringue for the flies.*

Hughes received the Signal Poetry Award in 1995 for *What is the Truth,* and in reference to this recognition, Neil Philip refers to Hughes' 'authority of rhythm, of tone, of observed and felt experience.' In a lyric for older children, Ted Hughes writes about gulls, in *The Mermaids' Purse,* a poem at two levels of interpretation:

> *Gulls are glanced from the lift*
> *Of cliffing air*
> *And left*
> *Loitering in the descending drift,*
> *Or tilt gradient and go*
> *Down steep invisible clefts in the grain*
> *Of air, blading against the blow . . .*

G. K. Chesterton noticed in his lifetime that 'Poets have been mysteriously silent on the subject of cheese.' Late twentieth and twenty-first century poems for teenagers, however, embrace even the formerly taboo, whether it be a teenager's pimple (as in *Get Back, Pimple* by John Agard) or topics of sex, drugs, rock and roll, cancer, AIDS, refugees and child abuse, as in *Poems with Attitude Uncensored* by Andrew and Polly Peters – a real move away from the sublime emphases of the past

Jinx, by the Australian writer, Margaret Wild, is a special for teenagers who respond to poetry about modern society. Short poems, some only two or three lines long, concern adolescence, portrayed in the life of Jen, her family and friends and her deeply disturbed boyfriend, Charlie, who commits suicide. As Peter Hollindale has commented, it is reminiscent of Melvin Burgess' novel, *Junk.* Not melodramatic, it is moving, tender and insightful about relationships. Perhaps the characters can be compared/contrasted with tragic lives of Shakespearian characters whom students study at their Key Stage level 4.

Examination syllabi will largely determine what poetry the young person at this level will experience. Few will read beyond it to seek out their own favourites, but there are always some literary minded ones who do, who have truly acquired the key to the enchanted door and who respond to Shel Silverstein's voice:

> *If you are a dreamer, come in.*
> *If you are a dreamer, a wisher, a liar,*

A hoper, a prayer, a magic bean buyer . . .
If you're a pretender, come sit by my fire
For we have some flax-golden tales to spin.
Come in!
Come in!

This look at possible selections for poetry for older young people has focused largely on British poets, but poets, old and young, of past and present from all over the world, speak with insight. Many are truly too good to miss, and the English teacher who responds to poetry will seek opportunities to present them.

Teachers report that poetry is increasingly listened to, read and written by children of all age groups. The comment 'boring' does not apply, and Benjamin Zephaniah agrees:

WHO'S WHO
*I used to think **nurses***
Were women,
*I used to think **police***
Were men,
*I used to think **poets***
Were boring
*Until **I** became one of **them.***

2. Fiction

The Fiction genre has two subsets. One category is *Fantasy* where characterisation, setting and events that can happen only in the imagination are related as real events. This calls for what Coleridge called 'the willing suspension of disbelief.' The second category is *Realistic Fiction* where the characters, setting and events may be inventions but are true to real life and could possibly happen.

2.1 Fantasy

The Child's Acceptance of the Imaginary

> *There's a cool web of language winds us in,*
> *Retreat from too much joy or too much fear.*
>   *Robert Graves, 1965.*

When young David exclaimed with great excitement, 'I got into my wardrobe, and do you know what? I almost went into the land of *Narnia*,' there was no doubting his belief. He had accepted the magic and wonder of the fantasy world. Margaret Mahy, an award winning and much acclaimed New Zealand writer over more than thirty years, expresses the dream and play world of a child's mind, when she writes of another little boy who said:

> *Mother, there is a big,*
> *roaring, yellow, whiskery lion*
> *in the meadow!*
> *1969,* A Lion in the Meadow

Here, in story, she depicts the child's ability to play with make-believe time, place and characters; to easily accept and to create a change of reality, as well as to shift perspectives and ownership within it. This is demonstrated when Mahy's little boy adjusts to the mother's denials of his imagination and her intrusion into his fantasy. Now the lion hides in a broom cupboard and a dragon is in the meadow! But the lion, symbol of his fears which he can overcome, persists and verbalizes what the little boy feels. Soon they are friends, playing happily in the meadow, with the little boy now riding and directing the lion. It is also interesting to observe that he wants, and is helped by, his mother's emotional assurances, even though he manipulates the situation, which introduces other psychological perspectives, reminiscent of Erickson's second psychosocial stage and Vygotsky's theories (See Chapter 1), while the dream-like images of the fantasy world link with Freud, Jung and modern psychotherapy.

Sendak demonstrates the same use of symbols and the acceptance and relationship between caregiver and child in his classic, *Where the Wild Things Are*, but goes further to show that the child, Max, returns in the end to his familiar, unchanged reality, modified only by his own confrontations in another, dreamlike world. For Max, fantasy is a temporary playground of escape, where ideas and feelings about the self are explored, where role models are copied or invented; where lies consolation to the ego.

Is it reasonable to protect children from fantasy? In *The Cool Web: The Pattern of Children's Reading*, edited by Meek, Warlow and Barton, Chukovsky tells about a little boy whose mother tried to protect him from fairy tales, wanting him to experience only realistic stories. She discovered, however, that without stimulation he created his own fantasies: a red elephant who came to live in his room, a bear named Cora, and make-believe adventures. Early childhood teachers and parents of young children see the same innate ability constantly demonstrated at home or nursery by miniature make-believe space men in jeans, roaring lions and marvellous inventions. Some of these may be influenced by media forms of story, but the child never replays them precisely but with imaginative modifications. As easily as they play, which is fun and natural in their stage of development, they accept, enjoy and cope with stories of the fantasy genre.

2.2 Inner Worlds

Discussion about fantasy and the workings of a child's mind, according to psychoanalytical theory, raise the issue of *Surrealism,* a leading influence in the twentieth century on illustrative style. It is a method featuring more and more in children's picture books of the fantasy genre. The meaning is inherent in the word where

> *The word 'sur' means 'on top of' in French, and 'beyond' when it is used at the beginning of English words ... artists invented the word Sur-realism to describe their work because what they painted was beyond what everyone thought of as being normal reality.*
> *Sturgis 1994, 26.*

Surrealist art attempts to:

- link what initially appear as incongruous images;
- stress detailed realism in order to make incidents believable;
- refer to images already in a viewer's mind;
- stir an intellectual response.

Illustrators of children's books who use Surrealism include Graeme Base, whose book *Animalia* won an Honour Award in the Australian Children's Book of the Year Awards in 1987 as well as Young Australian's Best Book and Kid's Own Australian Literary Award. He admits to not actually writing the books primarily for children, but more to fulfil his own creative desire. Another who uses a highly real-istic style which is similar to Surrealism is Mike Wilks. In *The Ultimate Alphabet are* nearly eight thousand items painted in detail, with juxtaposition of disparate objects, making it a sort of dream world. He believes that:

> *Looking is not the same as seeing ... Children have this ability from a very young age but inevitably the modern environment, the education system and the modes of communication that it utilizes soon reduce this priceless faculty to the level of merely being able to look at things.*
>
> *Wilks 1987, 5.*

Anthony Browne, a highly praised contemporary artist is another protagonist. whose more than thirty picture books since 1976 have aroused much discussion. Doonan believes his illustrations are in a complex and challenging form, using objects as symbols so that symbolic meaanings are there, but accessibility will depend on the interpretive skills appled to them by the reader. Some of his award winning work can be seen in *Gorilla* (1983),illustrations for *Alice's Adventures in Wonderland* (1988), Zoo (*1992*),*Voices in the Park* (1998). In 2000 he received the highly prestigious Hans Andersen Award.

A Master's student, researching the appeal of picture books of the style influenced by Surrealism, reached the conclusion that; (i) children of every age value colour, humour, animals and the excitement they get from searching and discovering things in illustrations. (ii) Despite the juxtaposition of disparate images and detailed 'surreal' illustration, they 'do not appear to understand, or value, Browne's 'cleverness' as adults do, because they cannot view the pictures in the same way.'

The work of theorists confirms the developmental stages of understanding which the researcher notes:

> *Children unconsciously construct a certain degree of meaning from everything they encounter in order to develop their personal map of knowledge and experience, thereby increasing their awareness of reality. They apply logic to whichever world they are in at the time, real or imaginary, and accept situations according to their current beliefs. As a result, younger children react on an emotional level to bizarre illustration because their lack of knowledge and experience, and hence preconceptions, allows them to. As children get older ... they instinctively move towards and intellectual response, although their age still forces them to apply childish logic.*
>
> *Carrington 2002, 83–84.*

2.3 Qualities of Modern Fantasy

Modern fantasy is really an extension of the traditional fairytale form. Vygotsky's analysis of the fable, of the same tradition, is that its acceptance and understanding by a reader depend on willing acceptance and emotional involvement. Bettelheim, in his study of fairytales, says that they are a metaphorical view of society, whereby insights are gained into the world of reality. He sees the *hero* figure as especially meaningful, and he makes the following claim that explains the drug-like effect of fiction:

> *In the course of the story, as we identify with its hero, we gain the ability to live a richer and more meaningful life on a much higher plane than the one on which we found ourselves at the story's beginning, where* **the hero, who is our mirror image,**[1] *was forced to embark on his perilous voyage of self discovery.*
>
> *Story, 27.*

Huck notices an element of universality:

> *Characteristic of most fantasy, like the fairytales of old, is the presentation of a universal truth or a hidden meaning – love overcomes hate, the fools may be wiser than the wise men, the granting of wishes may not bring happiness.*
>
> *1976, 256.*

2.4 Types and Examples

Forms of the fantasy genre vary, but one convenient method for discussion purposes is to divide it into three categories, as John Rowe Townsend does (211), and to which he gives comprehensive coverage up to 1990 in his history of English-language children's literature.

(i) Modern Fantasy Depicts the Anthropomorphic

This means that a rabbit like Beatrix Potter's well-known Peter, or her duck called Jemima, talks, dresses and behaves like humans. Stories

---

[1] Bold is mine.

about bears, mice, rabbits and other animals have been treasured by many children of the past, and the same tradition continues, whether it be in picture book, early reader or novel. One recent example of an anthropomorphic picture book, highly commended for the Kate Greenaway Medal in 2002, was *Fix-It Duck,* by Jez Alborough. 'He's got his tools, he's smart, he's strong. Now what can possibly go wrong?' Of course anything can happen in the realm of fantasy, and does! Another was Terry Pratchett's 2002 Carnegie award, *The Amazing MauRice and his EDUCATED ROdENtS,* an example of a twenty-first century fantasy about an amazing cat; which moves straight into action, in which the characters are defined by what they *do* – a male characteristic. Two contemporary 'Read it again' picture books concern mice, often popular in anthropomorphic fantasy. For the very young, Ruby is a mouse involved with potty training, and that potty gets put to all sorts of creative uses, apart from its real purpose until she gets the idea straight. (*Ruby's Potty* by Paul and Emma Rogers). For the Young, Lilly is a little girl-like mouse who has a precious purple purse, and thereby hangs the tale which is funny, sad and believable. Written rhythmically, with illustrations that catch the eye, it conveys the joy, delights and despair of childhood. (*Lilly's Purple Plastic Purse,* by Kevin Henkes).

Other authors of the Nineteen Nineties who have popularised anthropomorphic fantasy have been Brian Jacques with his Redwall series for the Middle Years – especially his characters Matthias, the bumbling unlikely mouse hero-protagonist, or Tansy the hedgehog or Arven a little squirrel of an enquiring nature. Dick King-Smith has created fanciful pig and sheep heroes and in doing so, fulfils the evaluation criteria for effective fantasy, given above: original, real, controlled style, worthwhile theme.

For competent Older Readers, Philip Pullman, in the first book of his trilogy, *His Dark Materials*, features an armoured bear called Iorek Byrnison who is no sweet teddy bear in human dress. When Lyra, the central character who is on a special quest, meets him, she and her companion hear him speak:

'Iorek Byrinson,' said Farer Corm again. 'May I speak to you?' Lyra's heart was thumping hard, because something in the bear's presence made her feel close to coldness, danger, brutal power, but a power controlled by intelligence . . . Then he reared up massively, ten feet or more high, as if to show how mighty he was . . .

> *"Well? Who are you?'* ... *"What do you want?'*
> *'We want to offer you employment, Iorek Byrnison.'*
> *'I am employed.'* ...
> *'What do you do at the sledge depot? Farder Coram asked.*
> *I mend broken machinery and articles of iron. I lift heavy objects.'*
> *Northern Lights, 179, 180.*

In this short passage Pullman is true to the fantasy setting of the bleak north which he has established, using names and characters that fit; he uses the able animal figure that resembles giants of traditional fairy-tales, and his narrative emphasises the reality of his story. The Bear becomes an heroic, albeit savage and wounded hero, king of all the armoured bears, to whom Lyra turns in compassion, a sympathy that readers can respond to and believe. She says:

> *'Let me help you – I want to make sure you en't too badly hurt, Iorek dear – oh, I wish there was some bandages or something! That's an awful cut on your belly – '*
> *A bear laid a mouthful of some stiff green stuff, thickly frosted, on the ground at Iorek's feet.*
> *'Bloodmoss,' said Iorek. 'Press it in the wounds for me, Lyra. Fold the flesh over it and then hold some snow there till it freezes.'*
> *Northern Lights, 355.*

This demonstration of believable interaction between child and animal is very much in the fairytale tradition, used by Pullman in a unique setting.

Books about talking animals who behave like humans abound, but stories about anthropomorphic *objects* are scarce. The memorable ones include the ever-popular Thomas *the Tank Engine*, and other stories of the railway theme, by Reverend W. Awdry; also Raymond Briggs', *The Snowman*. The Ahlbergs' *Shine a Light* is a more recent example in this category, published by Heinemann in a new extended version. It is the story of two skeletons who set out one night to scare as many as they might meet, taking with them their skeleton dog. Spookyish, but fun, the present edition includes ghostly transparencies that children can project by torchlight, making it a novelty book.

Stories of toys that behave like humans also fit this subdivision of fantasy, one of the best-known being *Pinocchio* by Collodi. Even more popular is the king of all bear characters (and there are SO many), Winnie-the-Pooh, the bear of little brain, with all his delightful companions of the hundred acre wood, where they and Christopher Robin played. Of more recent times, but still an old elephant in storybook years, is the much loved, Elmer, of *Elmer: The Story of a Patchwork Elephant,* by David McKee. A more recent elephant is Ellie, the little elephant whose nose sometimes gets in the way: in *A Hose of A Nose* written by Sue Harris.

Animals and toys can talk about how they feel, be naughty, sad or ecstatically happy, and their behaviour and chatter are quite accepted and understood by children whom the animals and toys resemble. The distance from their immediate reality is bridged easily by symbolism and fantasy together and seem to make these anthropomorphic characters especially loveable and taken to heart.

(ii) Imaginary Worlds and Countries

Lewis Carroll began a new movement in children's literature when he told his story of *Alice's Adventures in Wonderland (*1865) followed by a sequel, *Through the Looking Glass* (1872). Despite being a clergyman – the Reverend Dodgson – he was not instructing or moralising, but entertaining three little girls in an inventive way. (Invention is again revealed in his pseudonym, which is a reversal of the Latin form of his name). The story he told that summer afternoon as they went boating at Oxford together, he first called 'Alice's Adventures Underground' with the child protagonist named after his favourite child friend, Alice Liddell, there present in the boat. The details of Alice and her sister, mentioned at the beginning, were the only true facts, but they serve to place Carroll's story in reality before moving into an adventure, amazing, confused, yet as real as a dream can be, within its own setting and time-frame, all acted out by fantastic characters who, in a bizarre way, reveal back-to-front, copycat behaviours of human behaviour. Down, down Alice falls, down a rabbit hole. Now that would make any Victorian child, used to religious instruction and Sunday stories, sit up and listen, especially as the elements of fantasy grow more and more astounding.

> *'And how many hours a day did you do lessons?' said Alice, in a hurry to change the subject.*
> *'Ten hours the first day,' said the Mock Turtle: 'nine the next, and so on.'*
> *What a curious plan!' exclaimed Alice.*
> *'That's the reason they're called lessons,' the Gryphon remarked:*

> *'because they lessen from day to day.'*
> *...she thought it over a little...* *'Then the eleventh day must have been a holiday?'*
> *'Of course it was,' said the Mock Turtle.*
>
> Carroll 1865/1994, 105.

Lewis Carroll's sequel, *Through the Looking Glass*, also began in the reality of a known, safe environment: the home. There, Alice talks to her mischievous black kitten, while an innocent white kitten is being washed by Dinah, the mother cat, so there is set up an interesting black-white- good-evil symbolic emphasis from the start. Alice talks of the game of chess, about the Red Queen, and her ideas of a room shown in the mirror, probably the nursery, she being a child of the Victorian age. In that looking glass is part reflection of the room, even to its reversed image. The intriguing lack of completeness fires her imagination and moves the story along as she becomes imaginatively involved. She says:

> *'Now, if you'll only attend, Kitty, and not talk so much, I'll tell you all my ideas about Looking-Glass House. First, there's the room you can see through the glass...all but the bit just behind the fireplace. Oh! I do so wish I could see that bit!*
> *... Let's pretend the glass has got all soft like gauze, so that we can get through. Why, it's turning into a sort of mist now, I declare! It'll be easy enough to get through -'*
>
> Carroll 1872/1994, 6, 8.

Thus she enters the dreamlike looking-glass world where there are flowers, insects and animals which talk (anthropomorphics), where fascinating people like Tweedledum, Tweedledee, Humpty Dumpty and others break forth into nonsense rhymes, and importantly – at a level of ego fulfilment – where Alice becomes Queen Alice, though among rival queens (identified later as the two pet kittens).

Five characteristics mark this innovative storytelling by Carroll, matched by subsequent writers: 1. The fantasy is grounded in the safeness of the familiar, to which the traveller returns at the end of the book. 2. There is emphasis on imaginative action by the child hero. 3. The entry point into the fantastic strange worlds and countries could be described like Alice did, as 'curiouser and curiouser.' 4. Use of a journey. 5. Presence of the omnipotent child, believing and courageous despite all difficulties.

Time is not a straight line, it's more of a labyrinth, and if you press close to the wall at the right place you can hear the hurrying steps and voices, you can hear yourself walking past there on the other side.

Tomas Transtromer

(iii) Weird and Mysterious

The third category of fantasy encompasses spells, dragons, wizards, giants, elves and all the other people of the fairy kingdom. It includes the strangely weird, and terror and horror from which the reader can safely retreat by the happy ending that is characteristic of, and important to, children's literature. Some of the best authors who apply it skilfully in long narratives are Susan Cooper, Anne Fine, German writer Cornelia Funke, Alan Garner, Australian author Victor Kelleher, Diana Wynne Jones, Terry Pratchett, J. K. Rowling and J. R. R. Tolkien. Some of these, and others, are discussed in Section Three of this text. Also worth notice is the Australian award winner, Paul Jennings, whose *Thirteen Unpredictable Tales* includes the astounding yet believable fantasy of 'Nails', child of a mermaid., while his *Undone!* includes stories of a boy made of water to another of a mind-reading calf.

Anne Fine attracts proficient younger readers with stories such as *Bad Dreams*. In this story a reader is confronted with a question concerning a dilemma concerning the weird and mysterious:

> *Someone you know has special powers that make her life horribly difficult. Do you:*
> *A. Put a stop to it any way you can?*
> *B. Not interfere, because it's a 'gift' she's been given?*
> *C. Hope things will work out?*

Melanie, called Mel, chooses A, and thereby hangs the absorbing tale of reality interwoven with fantastic powers of the necklace. It also stresses a love for reading, such as shown by Melanie, qualities of friendship and discoveries about self knowledge.

English,Celtic and Welsh superstitions and magic influence Susan Cooper's sequence of five novels that began with *Over Sea, Under Stone.*, in which the Old Ones resist the powers of Darkness. Garner's early work, for older readers, resonates with the same influences and is much too good to miss. *The Weirdstone of Brisingamen*, which has

HARRY
POTTER
and the Order of the Phoenix

J.K.ROWLING

BLOOMSBURY

Illustration 4: An example of the fantasy genre, HARRY POTTER AND THE ORDER OF THE PHOENIX, by J. K. Rowling. Cover illustration by Jason Cockcroft. Published by Bloomsbury. Non-exclusive use granted by Bloomsbury Publishers.

been likened to Tolkien's *The Lord of the Rings,* is bound up with local Cheshire lengendry; in *Elidor,* there is a door which forms a boundary between this world and the fantasy world of Elidor. *The Owl Service,* for which he won both the Guardian Award and the Carnegie medal, overlaps present and past time, sustaining the power of a ancient tragedy in a mysterious way, drawing three young people into its re-enactment.

As well as diminished-size people, *giants* feature in fantasy. They are present in John Bunyan's seventeenth-century *Pilgrim's Progress,* retold for children *in Dangerous Journey* which portrays the great giant Despair pictorially as huge, yet not one to fear, surrounded as he is by the boy heroes and their defender, Great-heart. Another giant, even less fearsome, is Roald Dahl's big friendly giant (*The BFG*) with whom young Sophie becomes friends and has an adventure. In Anthony Browne's *Gorilla*, the gorilla grows more and more giant-like as the story progresses beyond normality. He is not a giant to fear; he is superman, who shrinks back to toy size when normality resumes and Hannah's father fulfils the role she hoped for

2.5 Time-Travel

- *The Charmed Object.* The notion of time passed affecting the present with special significance is addressed by many, including historians, philosophers, poets, writers and artists. It is not surprising, therefore, that writers for children have used, and continue to use, the device of *time-travel* to real and imaginary worlds. At the level of pleasure and escape through story, as well as at the level of personal insight, there is appeal and value to children. Twentieth centuries writers of fantasy for children began as early as 1902 when E. Nesbitt wrote *Five Children and It,* followed by *The Phoenix and the Carpet* and The *Story of the Amulet.* The latter is an example of one type of entry device that opens up time-travel: the motif of a *charmed object.* The Amulet opens the past, whereby children not only explore fictitious societies but have opportunity to discover about themselves on an inner journey. In Anne Fine's *Bad Dreams*, a special necklace connects Imogene to the power of the past, passed down through generations. In Alison Uttley's *A Traveller in Time*, the story teller, Penelope, finds an old mirror wherein she sees herself as another, from the past, and a door transfers her into the sixteenth century. Similarly, a wardrobe door is the entry point to C. S. Lewis's land of Narnia in *The Lion, the Witch and the Wardrobe*. For Tom, Philippa Pearce's hero, it is a clock striking thirteen that leads him into the moonlight of another era, a changed house and a door that leads into a garden where adventure and new friendships await. In *The Forget-Me-Not Clock,* time can be turned back centuries by a child turning the Grandfather clock's hands backwards.

- *Sleep and dreams* seem mingled as other ways of entering time-travel, as young Tolly discovers in Lucy Boston's *The Children of Green Knowe*; when he could hear the rocking horse go creak-croak, creak-croak, as though being ridden; when he hears the running feet of children and the pages of a story book being turned; when he encounters Alexander and Linnet, children of the past. Penelope Farmer in *Charlotte Sometimes,* presents parallel past and present, as Charlotte of 'now- time' and Clare from the past, sleep in their own respective times.

- *A particular location* can also be an entry point to other times and places. Philip Pullman's ambitious trilogy for older readers, *The Dark is Rising,* comprised of *Northern Lights, The Subtle Knife* and *The Amber Spyglass* introduces the journey pattern to an entry point that seems familiar, yet is not, except in place name, Oxford, and moves between three universes: the universe of *Northern Lights,* similar to our own yet different, the universe the reader knows and understands, and a third universe which is different again. In each of these appear the five characteristics noted earlier. In Susan Cooper's, *King of Shadows* (1999), the location to enter the fantasy time travel, is London, via the reconstructed Globe Theatre on the south bank of the Thames. To this place comes Nathan Field from a Youth Theatre Production at Atlanta where he had played the small part of the Boy in Shakespeare's *Henry V*. He enters Elizabethan England through the persona of the sixteenth-century Nat Field, a boy actor borrowed by William Shakespeare to play before the queen. Twentieth-century Nathan rejoices that 'It wasn't a dream, it wasn't a dream, it wasn't a dream.' (152). Perhaps the only possible weakness in this fantasy is that perhaps Cooper tries too hard to explain rationally how and why the time travel took place. When plot, setting and characterisation are persuasively real enough, and the experienced traveller is ready and ripe for fantasy harvest, belief is easily suspended.

2.6 Size in Fantasies

Not only can time change in the genre of Fantasy, but *size* also. Alice became only ten inches tall when she first entered Wonderland, the result of having drunk from the bottle that was not marked 'poison' but tasted of cherry-tart, custard, pineapple, roast turkey, toffee and hot buttered toast. She does not stay tiny for long, soon becoming nine feet tall, but in the world of Mary Norton's *The Borrowers*, the cast is forever small, living in another example of an imaginary world, persuasively told and believable. Hidden away behind the clock in the hall under the kitchen live the Clock family, last of the borrowers who borrow from the 'human beans, who live above them. Also memorable are the tiny people of Swift's Lilliputia, in *Gulliver's travels*, or the little hobbits, created by Tolkien, who live in the world of Hobbiton.

2.7 Science fiction

grips the imaginations of many children. Before the genre was popular on television, many readers felt drawn into Madeleine L'Engle's fantasy trilogy: *A Wrinkle in Time; A Wind in the Door; A Swiftly Tilting Planet*. The principal child characters are highly intelligent, so unusually so that some people in their neighbourhood regarded them as not 'all there' or 'oddballs'. The youngest of the Murry family, Charles Wallace, has a kind of sixth sense which his older sister, Meg, observed on many occasions as he appeared to probe her mind. It is this special knowing and intelligence that make them vulnerable to the 'tesseract' experience – a wrinkle in time.

The Star Wars theme is one that some Upper Primary School and High School readers now enjoy. Work by Jude Watson and Dave Wolverton provides, for some, compulsive reading, as in the popular *The Rising Force (Star Wars: Jedi Apprentice)*, and *Jedi Apprentice – The Fight for Truth*. Other readers enjoy Patricia Wrede's *Searching for Dragons (Enchanted Forrest Chronicles)*. The writing may not be of the highest quality but has its own skills and standards, so that the Jedi series and others of the science fiction genre have a committed following of readers whom teachers and librarians should recognise.

2.8　Some guidelines for evaluation of fantasy

Look for:

(i)　an original plot, constructed well and believable;
(ii)　details of characters and setting that an audience can accept as real;
(iii)　a style that is controlled and suits the story;
(iv)　a worthwhile theme.

3.　Realistic Fiction

The Perilous Realm of Realism, a Window on the World

3.1　Realism and the Young

When the 'Wendy House' at Nursery becomes a place where 'mother' cooks and gives instructions; where dolls become babies, soothed, fed, bathed, dressed and prepared for walks; when a little boy with a policeman's hat and a notebook arrests or cautions his playmate on a tricycle, these children are acting out realistic fiction. They are playing a part that symbolically represents real life, though to them it is all a game.

In the play-like world of picture book realism, everyday people and common occurrences can be easily recognised. Here are the true faces of babies and older children, as for example in *Baby Faces* by Margaret Miller. Here are depicted children's true-to-life activities and their challenging situations in a family or neighbourhood, acted out by characters who behave like real boys and girls, and real mummies, daddies and others, as seen in any of Shirley Hughes work.

Animal characters, always act like animals in realistic fiction, (even if dressed up by child playmates, as happens) but they are not anthropomorphics who go shopping, cook etc. Examples are Lion *in the Long grass,* by Ruth and Ken Brown, which tells of the self-sacrificial care of a mother lioness and the grand-parent-like old lion to a cub, and *Doggies* by Sandra Boynton.

Accessible and colourful, the realistic fiction of the picture book is a window on the world for the audience of the young. It reflects the intimacies and habits of every child's home, goes into other people's houses, to other lands and customs or times. It deals with many areas, even the perhaps yet untried, such as going to the doctor, hospital, dentist or pre-school. It is unafraid to deal sympathetically with even a subject like death, as does Michael Rosen in his *Lovely Old Roly,* story of a family pet which dies. And it can (i) *assure* the child: ' you are just like other boys and girls' – yet you are special, too; or (ii) *suggest,* even *challenge* : ' you could do *that,* easy-peasy, if you tried'; or (iii) *comfort*:: 'you will feel better soon; you, too, can be sad and brave;' or (iv) *model:* dogs, cats, horses … how clever, special and helpful animals are. We must look after them!'

The recognition of the look-alike self in true-to-life settings is one of the reasons why picture books of the realism genre, and there are many, have such appeal. The best of them are shortlisted annually for the Sainsbury Baby Book Award and the Kate Greenaway Medal. Their affirmation of the animal or child is a reason why babies, the Foundation Stage child and the young school age child, 5 -7 years love a realistic picture story. It is very recognisable, safe, often predictable and the child of ther story always achieves.

3.2 Realism for 7–11 year olds

Readers in Key Stage 2 continue to enjoy realistic fiction. Anne Fine never fails to please with her stories that reflect society. For the younger, early reader in this middle group, *Stranger Danger?* begins with the visit of a policeman to Joe's class at school. He shows a film, establishes some rules. "Never go with a stranger!' everyone chants on his instruction – behaviour that is mirrored by the baby daddy-long-legs that Joe has been coaxing on to the palm of his hand. But then some strangers visit Joe's school . . . challenging the new ground rules. *Goggle Eyes* is about Kitty's mother and her new boyfriend. Kitty is determined to break up their friendship, and tries several ways … It is situation that some children in the twenty-first century easily relate to, and they can appreciate the loving support of Kitty's Nan. Also for this group of children, from the Australian author, Gwenda Turner, comes The *Tree Witches,* one example that mirrors children's own games and clubs:

> *Their hide-out was in a tree*
> *at Shirley's place.*
> *It was a wonderful tree-house,*
> *very strong and steady.*
>   *1983, n.p.g.*

There is an element of fantasy in this work of realistic fiction, but because it is just a game and neither believed in by the girls, nor by their new friend (who calls himself 'Addi addi, chickeri, chickeri, oony, pooney om pom alari, alla balla whisky, Chinese salt!') they tell him,

> "We're REALLY witches in disguise.'
> The boy laughed.
> They all laughed.

Ibid.

So the reader laughs, too, grounded in the reality, perhaps inspired to try out his/her variation of this game with friends.

An English author with appeal to middle primary school readers is Jacqueline Wilson who is unafraid to address the details of family life that many children must face in a society where one in four children are affected by divorce before the age of 16. *The Suitcase Kid* addresses contemporary family breakdown, placing ten- years-old Andy in the middle. Adjusting to being a suitcase kid, torn between two parents with all the emotional trauma involved, is supposed to be 'as easy as ABC.' Not so, initially, but the notion of the alphabet leads into the clever device of organising the book alphabetically. Wilson handles it all lightly, yet realistically and with sensitivity, so essential to readers caught in a similar dilemma. *The Mum-Minder* is another modern story, one chaotic week in Sadie's life which she writes as a diary in the school holidays.

Judy Blume's still popular books portray life as lived in America, yet there is a recognisable similarity to life in other Western cultures. Her work has been sought-after since the Nineteen-Seventies; such as *Tales of a Fourth Grade Nothing, Blubber,* and the stories about Fudge: *Superfudge* and *Fudge-a-mania.* Now there is a new, modern sequel, *Double Fudge,* which is funny because of Blume's skill at characterisation and dialogue and also because Fudge is like many boys, superb at causing chaos. The dialogue and interaction between the Hatcher family and their cousins is true-to-life. This family of five includes twins who, like most twelve- year-old girls, are becoming very interested in personal beauty. Added to all this recognisable realism is a focus on family life, loving and sharing.

3.3 Books for the Older Reader

explore situations which directly affect most young people in some way: sibling, peer and other rivalries, bullying, insecurity and self-doubt. They also move more deeply into issues of modern society: disentigrating families, sexism, tensions of race and colour, sexuality and gender, male/female relationships, AIDS, violence, drink, dress, drugs, war, land mines and a 'green' environment. Profanity is not uncommon. But they are not all serious, as shown by *Not Dressed Like that, You Don't!* by Yvonne Coppard. Readers hear their own parents' voices in the book title, and two diaries, of teenager Jenny and her mother, portray opposite points of view from the adult and child perspective, all told with hilarious effect.

Literature is a veritable wide-open window on the world for adolescent readers, and also for those pubescents who want t to 'find out.' Now is the time that their bodies are growing and changing, along with their sense of self-worth and personal identity. Now they are questioning, arguing, asserting their rights, conforming to peer rituals, breaking rules, are captivated by idealism, often obsessed with diaries and the self, and asking 'Does s/he like me? Will we go out together?' Obsession is common for fashion, pop or football stars or a cd collection. They experiment with the mannerisms, dress and habits of their society, which may include models on stage, screen, and, yes, the printed page. (Likewise, many grandmothers of today grew up seeing themselves as an Anne of Green Gables look-and-act-alike, or one of the Secret Seven.)

Judy Blume's books for young adults experimenting with relationships still move off library shelves: *Tiger Eyes* starts with a funeral and Davy, a distressed, isolated teenager. *Forever* is graphic and explicit about sex; about idyllic young love that cannot last. Jacqueline Wilson also understands teenager's lives, but is never didactic and allows her characters to live and speak for themselves, sounding like real people. Her *Secrets* mirrors a home where a step-dad reigns and how the central character, Treasure, copes with the problem of him beating her. It is neither without pathos, nor humour and excitement. Another recent work is Wilson's *Girls in Tears (2003)* a mirror on friendship and what happens when Ellie, one of a special threesome of girls falls in love with a boy, Russell, and the girls' special togetherness is challenged; who start to change and grow up somewhat. *Tenderness,* by American Robert Cormier, lacks the delicate touch and humour of Blume and Wilson. It focuses on two teenagers from dysfunctional families, Lori and Eric, kindred spirits, starved of love and emotional security, and In Cormier's usual style portrays the darker side of life.

More and more war stories are being published. *Stones in Water* by Donna Jo Napoli is one recent example of war fiction, about the son of a Venetian gondolier, taken into a Nazi slave-labour camp, who eventually emerges into a Europe devastated by war. It is stark and truthful, fast moving yet not at the expense of restraining insight and growth of character. In the tradition of the best realistic fiction the reader, too, has the challenge of growth and change, along with the story hero. From the Swedish author, Henning Mankell, comes *Secrets in the Fire*, about Sophia, victim to a landline in Mozambique by which she loses both legs and a sister. Its sequel, *Playing with Fire*, sees the family's tragedy compounded when Sophia's older sister is diagnosed with AIDS. True stories, they have a poignancy that can draw readers in and extend their horizons

4. Historical Fiction

A Living Past

Books about the past can bring former times and people to life so that they seem to live again. Historical Stories that appeal to children demand:

(i) strong writing with characters whose settings, language, actions, conflicts and resolutions are true to the time period described.

(ii) a worthwhile theme that comes through the style, mood and all-over 'togetherness' of the writing, making it truly believable.

Katherine Paterson, twice a winner of both the National Book Award for Children's Books and the Newberry Medal, affirms the place of truth and honesty in the writing of historical books:

> *Being true to the facts of history has certain limitations for a writer, But I must confess a rather obvious advantage. Historical facts offer all kinds of help in that devilish task of plotting a story. In* The Master Puppeteer, *for example, the story is stretched between the plague of 1773 (during which 200,000 are said to have died) and the great famine of Tokugawa times, which began in 1783 and lasted until 1787 . . . a thirteen-to fourteen-year period, the entire lifetime of a young adolescent . . . In choosing to tell such a story I saw that a certain honesty was demanded by history.*
>
> Paterson 1981, 73–74.

This too-good-to-miss author demonstrates truth and honesty in another historical novel: *Jip: His Story*, child of a slave and white master. Likewise, Gary Paulsen picks up the theme of slavery in America in the 1850s in two books, *Nightjohn* and *Sarny*, both told with integrity regarding brutality and inhumanity, yet also demonstrating the determination and courage of child protagonists who are enabled by receiving love and ways into knowledge and self fulfilment.

It is interesting to note Paterson's appraisal of how historical fiction was regarded in the past:

> When I first began to write historical fiction, I had no idea that it was a sort of bastard child of letters – respectable neither as history nor nor as fiction. Twelfth-century Japan, torn apart by wasteful wars and civil strife, didn't seem very far away from Washington, D.C., in late 1960s. It never occurred to me that I was writing romantic literature. It seemed not only realistic but terrifyingly current.
>
> *Paterson 1981, 72.*

In this statement, Paterson has touched on the essence of the continuing appeal of historical fiction, for not only is there the fascination of a story that involves past lives and ways of living, but there is also the awareness that girls, boys, grown-ups and general society have not changed very much. This awareness is conveyed to some extent because the writer uses modern eyes and coinage of speech, but the options, decisions and outcomes are based in history and are therefore basically true. Writers show different ways of approaching their historical themes, different periods and settings, but all reveal strength in their child characters who determine to be true to themselves and what they have been taught; who have a will to survive despite injustice, persecution or difficulty.

Historical fiction for children covers from the Bronze Age to the second World War and immediately afterwards. It can begin with the story of a boy whose experience portrays what it could have been like to live on the South Downs of England nine hundred years before the birth of Christ. The book which portrays this scene is *Warrior Scarlet* by Rosemary Sutcliff, throbbing with life and truth. The first chapter introduces nine- years-old Drem, half naked except for a kilt of rough wool dyed with red-brown crotal dye, who identifies the landscape of his day while fondling a dog's ears as he gazes out

> southward where the chalk fell in long, slow turf slopes and ridges between willow and hazel choked combes, into the forest and the

> *March Country far below, and the Marshes spread away and away*
> *to the shining bar of the Great Water on the edge of the world.*
> *Below him the turf . . . was laced with criss-cross sheep-tracks . . .*
> Sutcliff, 1958, 10.

So Drem's role as a shepherd boy is introduced, yet he longs to be a warrior, despite having only one good arm. How could such a disabled boy ever kill a wolf – foe of sheep and people – and deserve to wear the warrior's scarlet? Challenge, determination, effort and near defeat all combine to bring the story to life.

Another story by Sutcliff makes the medieval period meaningful, centred on the legends of King Arthur and his knights, heroes all in their time as much as any modern achiever, such as football and athletic stars of today whom the developing child emulates. Here are courage, rivalries, ambition, splendours and destinies, set in the mystery of magical Celtic myth. In *Knight's Fee,* Sutcliff moves on to turbulent Norman England. For the child of English ancestry it magnifies a picture of his/her cultural past, for others there is the portrayal of how a boy can grow within the opportunities that life brings, as Hugh rises from the lowly status of dog-boy to knight.

Just as Sutcliff focuses on heroic children, so does Geoffrey Trease in his story set in sixteenth century England, *Cue for Treason.* Here the element of conflict, an integral part of story, is Peter's forced leave from his home in Cumbria after a demonstration against the enclosure of common land, showing that demonstrations are no modern phenomenon. Involved with a group of travelling players, typical of the period, he meets Kit, a girl in disguise as a boy, who proves to be a wonderful actor: the child achiever, again. Geraldine McCaughrean also moves into the theme of travelling players in her *A Little Lower than the Angels.*

Trease's more recent work is *A Cloak for a Spy,* published in 1997, set as in his previous work in sixteenth-century England before the famous Spanish Armada. Also set in the time of expectancy of the Armada, when the British fleet is preparing at Plymouth, is Anne Turnbull's *Gunner's Boy.* Twelve-year-old John Emery whose father was killed by Spaniards, walks to Plymouth to enlist and there joins the *Fortune.* Turnbull's narrative makes seaboard life for a young lad painfully real, as is the well researched, vivid account of the campaign, recounted through John's eyes. But it is not just a thrilling war story that is true to its period, for it tells of the boy's growth in understanding of a jealous peer who tormented him, and of a deepening compassion for a defeated enemy.

Frederick Marryat's *Children of the New Forest*, an historical classic, highlights the effect of the English civil war in the 1640s, on a family of four children who are orphaned but support each other and stay together. The seventeenth century comes to life further through the pen of Jill Paton Walsh as a girl called Mall tells of *A Parcel of Patterns,* brought to the Derbyshire village of Eyam with disastrous effect. As the Great Plague spreads through the village, the human's propensity for self-sacrifice, rivalry, suffering, death, hope and bonding love, all appear. Finally the ultimate resolution to conflict and pain come as Mall tells that

> *There came time when the silence of the street, and the stillness of my quiet house, was suddenly broken by bells. A great clamour of bells, ringing round all the slopes of Eyam, with brazen voices, Shouting joy. The first and third and fourth of the Eyam bells are marked 'Jesu be our speed.' The second says 'God save the church. And now all four clanged together out of order, sang that the Plague was gone, gone, gone, gone, gone!*
>
> Jill Paton Walsh 1988, 131–2.

The story concludes with plans to leave Eyam for New England, showing how love and faith in God transfer to the American continent.

A more recent writer of historical fiction, Celia Rees, shows a link between England and the new world of the seventeenth-century American colonies in her books *Witch Child* and its sequel, *Sorceress.* As with Rees' other publications, these two books are grounded in historical research, the first starting with the witch-hunts of the mid 1660s, in England and then Salem, America, and the second reverting to life among the Mohawk Indians in the same period when the 'witch child' becomes a healer among the native people. What adds to the believability of the total story is the unique way a modern-day researcher uses an e-mail address to find information about the secret journal kept by the child, 'Daughter of the Erl King and the Elfin Queen' whose grandmother hangs as a witch. The portrayal of the Puritan bigots in their black coats and hats as tall as steeples, the female witch pricker who stabbed at grandmother, and the test to see if she would float – the conclusive test – make it gripping reading.

Philip Pullman, another contemporary writer, looks into the past of Victorian England in *The Ruby in the Smoke.* The central heroic figure is sixteen years old Sally Lockhart, an uncommonly pretty girl who responds to the challenge of orphanhood and takes on running a business. Greed, intrigue, murder are part of the dark, smoggy London scene which extends to the Far East, but Sally can use a pistol and kills a man, which makes her unusual for a young female hero of her times. As a thriller and as a gripping character portrayal it becomes a compulsive read!

An important issue of the years before the first World War was Women's Suffrage, a cause taken up by Marjorie Darke in *A Question of Courage*, strangely introduced to its hero, seventeen-year-old Emily, as the outcome of being knocked off her bicycle by a car. Although many of the women committed to this cause were from the upper classes, Emily comes from a working class family and works as a seamstress. The story demonstrates the cost and emotions of conviction involved in allegiance to a cause, one in which Emily, with all the idealism of the young adult, faces difficult decisions about her political activity. Although the book was first published in 1975, but reissued in 2002, and the focus is now nearly one hundred years in the past, the unrest and change that characterises the world of the twenty-first century makes this historical fiction meaningful to other young people on the cusp of adulthood.

The Great War of 1914–18 is made real through *Some Other War* by Linda Newberry, telling the story of seventeen-year-old twins, Jack who joins the army and Alice who becomes a VAD nurse, both serving in France. Seen through their eyes and actions, it is a realistic, dramatic story that highlights fear and hope, suffering and love, warfare and pacifism, but never in a saccharine or over-gruesome way. It affirms that young people still seek similar ideals and ask the same questions in times of war.

Stories about the period of the second World War bring this more recent history to life for young readers whose great grandparents would have then been living. *Carrie's War*, the classic by Nina Bawden, features three friends from London, two boys and a girl, whose lives intertwine with the people of the Welsh village to which they are evacuated. Jill Paton Walsh portrays the war from another perspective – through two adolescent boys who take part in the evacuation of Dunkirk in *The Dolphin Crossing*. Robert Swindells explores it in *Blitzed* through World War II enthusiast George who discovers that along with the miracles of Dunkirk, the blitz has a down side and that there are those who will even steal from the dead. Swindells takes up another theme in his *Brother in the Land*, resulting from his commitment to the Peace Movement, Greenpeace and anti-nuclear campaigns.

A grim and chilling tale, honestly told, it tells of the impact on a town of nuclear holocaust.

For young children, and older ones to Key Stage 2 who enjoy picture stories, the issue of war and how it separates and traumatises families, who nevertheless never give up hope, is told in the sensitive narration and beautiful illustrations of, *The Angel with a Mouth-Organ*, by the Australian author, Christobel Mattingly: 'After the planes the soldiers came. They took away fathers, brothers, sons . . .' It is a timeless picture of war though based on war in the twentieth century, presumably World War II. The ending is positive and reassuring to children, who need love and support in their growing years as part of their emotional and personality development, according to Maslow's theory. At the end of Mattingly's endearing, not over-sentamentalised tale, the family are reunited:

> *My sister said, "Can we go home now?" And our mother asked it with her eyes.*
> *But our father shook his head. "There's no home to go to. And other people have taken our land."*
> *My sister said, "It's not fair. After everything . . ."*
> *But our father put his mouth-organ to her lips and her words turned into funny sounds. And we all laughed.*
> *"We'll find another home," our father said. "You'll see.'*
> *And we did. Though it took a long while . . ."*
>
> *Mattingly 1985, n.p.g.*

Walking through Europe by children affected by war is also the theme of books for the Middle Years, 7–11, readers: *I am David* by Anne Holm, told in persuasive first-person narrative as are many books of historical fiction, and *The Silver Sword* by Ian Serailler, both relating the resilience of children who trekked through Europe following World War II.

Beyond Europe, similar effects of war are brought to life more starkly for Older Readers In *Empire of the Sun* by J. G. Ballard. It is the powerful story of twelve years old Jamie, separated from his parents, forced to change from privileged child to prisoner of the Japanese. The raw details of internment and the honest, sometimes shocking and ugly portrayal of a boy's struggle over four years to survive the horrors of separation, starvation, illness, situations of bloodshed, death and the white flash of the atom bomb, all involve tremendous emotional trauma. But 'Jim' becomes a survivor in a sort of 'coming of age' experience. Whew!

There is one other work of more recent events that draws the reader in a similar way, though there are less blood and guts. *The Other Side of Truth* by Beverley Naidoo begins in the civil strife of Nigeria in the mid 1990s, with the child characters of twelve-years-old Sade and her ten-years-old brother, Femi. Separation from parents is again in focus as the pair are smuggled out of their homeland after their mother's murder, only to be abandoned in London, which is to them a foreign culture. Can they survive the numbing pain of separation from any family members, foster homes, new school and powerful school gangs? They can and do, for family love with its precious memories and letters add strength.

In conclusion

it should be noted that the genres of Poetry, Fantasy and Realistic Fiction of an historical past or contemporary present time have their own distinct characteristics and should be selected as essentials to tempt the taste buds of every child. As has been shown, each category, presents the heroic child or another role model at the centre, frequently as a flawed hero, but one who will struggle and face the challenges that life throws at them, for conflict is true to life and lies at the heart of every good story plot. Sometimes the protagonists will be abundantly happy and laugh, sometimes they will suffer and cry, but they are always recognisable children in a process of development – similar to, or models for, their audience who assume a vicarious position as they read.

Like Alice, falling into adventures in Wonderland, child readers may as a result of entering imaginatively into Fantasy and Realistic Fiction perhaps shrink in some way, or they may grow taller, metaphorically speaking. Like Alice when she came to the three-legged table, having tumbled down the well, it is very possible that they will find a golden key to enchantment.

Children's Sayings

"My father read me a long poem called "The Ancient Mariner". I really liked it. I want to be a poet." Jenny, 12 years.

"I think *Watership Down* is a wonderful book even though I have not quite finished it yet. It's about rabbits who sense danger and have horrible and nice journeys." Andy, 9 years.

"*The Extra-Terrestrial Storybook* is a very good book although in some parts I didn't understand it. One of my favourite bits is when Elliott puts a lot of M&Ms on the floor, and E.T. thinks that they are the tablets he takes to keep him alive so he starts to eat them all!" Jack, 9 years.

'I liked *The Personality Potion* because Danny faced up to the biggest bully in the school." Nat, 9 years.

"My favourite authors are Terry Pratchett and Paul Jennings. I like *The Unstoppable*. It's on my bedside table right now!" Martin, 13.

Tutorial Topics

1. Find examples of poetry for children as in (i) a humorous poem (ii) a story poem or ballad (iii) a lyric. Read these aloud several times and decide what is special about that poem, then read the same poems to two children and observe and comparer their responses.
2. Buy yourself a good anthology of children's poetry. Read it and select your favourites. Plan to share these in some way and also to reread them in the future.
3. Identify the important characteristics of the fantasy genre within any of the following: *Harry Potter* series; *The Ropemaker* by Peter Dickinson; *Northern Lights* by Philip Pullman; *The Hobbit* by J. R. R. Tolkien.
4. Discuss why books for children in the genres of Fantasy or Realistic Fiction genres should/or need not, have a happy ending. Give examples from children's literature to assist you as you prove your case. If you can see any relevance to child development theories, use these also.
5. Read one sample of realistic fiction by Anne Fine or Jacqueline Wilson. Then read an example of historical realism written by Rosemary Sutcliff, Robert Swindells, Geoffrey Trease or Celia Rees. Compare these works and identify, with specific examples, what they share in common.
6. Read through the Children's Sayings (above and in previous chapters). What do they tell you about children and their reading?

Further Reading

Poetry

Causley, Charles. *Selected Poems for Children*. Illustrated by John Lawrence. London: Macmillan Children's Books, 1997.

Hollindale, Peter. 'Recent Poetry for Children.' In *Books for Keeps*, No. 137, November 2002, 10–13.

Styles, Morag. *From the Garden to the Street*. London: Cassell, 1998.

WWW sites
<www.poetryzone.co.uk>
<www.poetrysociety.org.uk>
<www.poetrybooks.co.uk>

Fiction: Fantasy and Realism

Kuznets, L. R. *When Toys Come Alive: Narratives of Animation, Metamorphosis and Development*. New Haven, CT: Yale University Press, 1994.

Egoff, Sheila A. *Worlds Within: Children's Fantasy from the Middle Ages to Today*. Chicago: American Library Association, 1988.

Hunt, Peter and Millicent Lenz. *Alternative Worlds in Fantasy Fiction: Contemporary Studies in Children's Literature*. London: Continuum International Publishing group, 2002.

Leeson, Robert. *Reading and Righting: the Past, Present and Future of Fiction for the Young*. London: Collins, 1985.

Odean, Kathleen. 'The Story Master.' Interview with Philip Pullman. *School Library Journal*. (USA). October 2000.

Townsend, John Rowe. *Written for Children*. 5th edition. London: The Bodley Head, 1990, 211–245.

——— *Ibid*, 246–260.

Historical Fiction

Blos, Joan. 'The Overstuffed Sentence and Other Means for Assessing Historical Fiction for Children.' In *School Library Journal* (USA), November 1985: 38–39.

Stephenson, Chris. 'Celia Rees: e-mailing the 17th century.' In *Carousel*, Issue 21, Summer 2002, 34.

Children's Books Cited

Poetry

Agard, John. *Get Back Pimple*. London: Puffin Books, 1997.

Agard, John and Grace Nichols. *A Caribbean Dozen*. London: Walker Books, 1994.

Belloc, Hilaire. 'Tarantella'. Quoted in *The Oxford Treasury of Classic Poems*. Ed. M. Harrison and C. Stuart-Clarke. Oxford: O.U.P., 1996.

Benjamin, Floella. *Skip Across the Ocean*. Illustrated by Sheila Moxley. London: Frances Lincoln, 1998.

Bennett, Jill, ed. *Seaside Poems*. Illustrated by Nick Sharratt. Oxford: Oxford University Press, 1998.

Berry, James. *A Nest Full of Stars*. London: HarperCollins, 2003.

Blishen, Edward. *The Oxford Book of Poetry for Children.* Illustrated by Brian Wildsmith. London: Oxford University Press, 1982.

Bradman, Tony, ed. *Off to School. Poems for the Playground.* London: Hodder Wayland, 1998.

Calmerson, Stephanie. *Welcome Baby! Baby Rhymes for Baby Times.* London: HarperCollins, 2002.

Causley, Charles. *Selected Poems for Children*. Illustrated by John Lawrence. London: Macmillan Children's Books, 1997.

Cotner, June. *Baby Blessings: Inspiring Poems and Prayers for Every Stage of Babyhood.* New York: Harmony Books, 2002.

Cousins, Lucy, illustrator. *Lucy Cousins' Big Book of Nursery Rhymes*. London: Macmillan, 1998.

Dahl, Roald. *Revolting Rhymes*. Illustrated by Quentin Blake. London: Puffin Books, 2001.

de Regniers, Beatrice, Schenk. 'If You Find A Little Feather.' Quoted in *When a Goose Meets a Moose*. Clare Scott-Mitchell, ed.Sydney: Methuen, 1980.

Doherty, Berlie, ed. *The Forsaken Merman, and Other Story Poems*. Illustrated by Nick Malard. London: Hodder Children's Books, 1998.

Fine, Anne. *A Shame to Miss Poetry Collection.* Books 1 and 2. London: Corgi Children's Books, 2002.

Foster, John, ed. *Dragons, Dinosaurs, Monster Poems*. Illustrated by Korky Paul. Oxford: Oxford University Press, 1998.

Graves, Robert. *Collected Poems.* London: Doubleday & Co., 1961.

Greenaway, Kate. *Kate Greenaway's Mother Goose or the Old Nursery Rhymes.* New York: Gramercy Publishing Company, 1978.

Hardy, Thomas. *The Illustrated Poets: Thomas Hardy*. London: Aurum Press, 1990, 53.

Hughes, Shirley. *Things I like.* London; Walker Books, 2001.

Hughes, Ted. *What is the Truth?* London: Faber, 1984.

—— *The Iron Wolf*. London: Faber, 1995.

—— *Poetry in the Making*. London: Faber and Faber, 1997.

—— ed. *By Heart: 101 Poems to Remember.* Faber and Faber, 1997.

—— *The Mermaid's Purse*. Faber and Faber, 1999.

Hughes, Ted and Seamus Henry. *The Rattle Bag: An Anthology of Poetry.* London: Faber and Faber, 1982.

The Hutchinson Treasury of Children's Poetry. London: Hutchinson Children's Books, 1997.

Kuskin, Karla. 'The Balloon' from *In the Middle of the Trees*, quoted in *When a Goose Meets a Moose*, poems chosen by Claire Scott-Mitchell. Sydney: Methuen Australia, 1980.

Lawrence, D. H. *The Complete Poems of D. H. Lawrence.* London: William Heinemann Ltd., 1964.

Lewis Richard, Ed. Illustrated by Ezra Jack Keats. *In a Spring Garden.* New York: The Dial Press, 1965.

Livingston, Myra Cohn. *Space Songs.* New York: Holiday House, 1988.

Noyes, Albert. 'The Highwayman'. Quoted in *The Golden Treasury of Poetry.* Selected by Louis Untermeyer. New York: Golden Press, 1959.

Opie, Iona *My Very First Mother Goose.* London: Walker Books, 1996.

The Oxford Treasury of Classic Poems. (Oxford Treasury Classics). Oxford: Oxford University Press,1997.

Patten, Brian. *Mouse Poems.* London: Hippo, Scholastic, 1998.

—— , ed. *The Puffin Book of Utterly brilliant Poetry.* London: Puffin Books, 1999.

Peters, Andrew and Polly. *Poems with Attitude Uncensored.* London: Hodder Wayland, 2002.

Playtime Rhymes. London: Dorling Kindersley, 2000.

Rosen, Michael. *Mind Your Own Business. London:* Deutsch, 1974; London: Scholastic, 1996.

—— 'This Little Pig.' In *Hairy Tales and Nursery Crimes.* London: Andre Deutsch, 1985.

—— *We're Going on a Bear Hunt.* London: Walker Books, 1989.

—— , ed. *The Kingfisher Book of Children's Poetry.* Illustrated by Alice Englander. London: Kingfisher Publications, 1985

—— ed. *The Walker Book of Classic Poetry and Poets.* Illustrated by Paul Howard, 2001.

Silverstein, Shel. 'Invitation.' In *Where the Sidewalk Ends.* Harper and Row, 1974.

Sitwell, Edith. *The King of China's Daughter.* In *Early Poems.* Oxford: Basil Blackwell & Mott Ltd. In *When a Goose Meets a Moose.* ~Claire Scott-Mitchell, Ed. *Poems for Young Children.* Sydney: Methuen, 1980.

Stevenson, Robert Louis. *A Child's Garden of Verses.* Illustrated by Susan Bonners. New York: Golden Press, 1978.

Tolkien, J. R. R. 'Roads go ever on an on.' *The Hobbit.* Reprint. London: Unwin Paperbacks, 1983, 281.

Umansky, Kaye. Illustrated by Nick Sharratt. *Wiggle my Toes.* London: Puffin Books, 2002.

Untermyer, Louis, ed. *The Golden Treasury of Poetry.* 17th printing. New York: Golden Press, 1974.

Wild, Margaret. *Jinx. London:* Walker and Company, 2002.

Yeats, W. B. *Collected Poems of W. B. Yeats.* Macmillan Publishing Co., Inc. 1919. Quoted in *When a Goose Meets a Moose,* Claire Scott-Mitchell, ed. Sydney: Methuen Australia, 1980, 72.

Zephaniah, Benjamin. *Talking Turkeys*. London: Puffin, 1995.
—— *Propa Propaganda*. Newcastle: Bloodaxe Books, 1997.
—— *Who's Who*. Quoted in BOOX. Issue No.1., 8.

Fiction: Fantasy
Adams, Richard. *Watership Down*. Reprint. London: Penguin, 1978.
Awdry, W. *Thomas the Tank Engine: the Complete Collection*. London: Heinemann Young Books, 1996.
Alborough, Jez. *Fix it Duck*. London: Picture Lions, 2001.
Boston, Lucy. *Children of Green Knowe*. Reprint. London: Puffin Books, 1986.
Briggs, Raymond. *The Snowman*. London: Picture Puffin, 1980.
Bunyan, John. *The Pilgrim's Progress*. Retold as *Dangerous Journey*. Ed. Oliver Hunkin. Aytesbury: Candle Books/Eerdmans, 1994.
Carroll, Lewis. *Alice's Adventures in Wonderland*. Reprint. London: Puffin Books, 1994.
—— *Through the Looking Glass*. Reprint. London: Puffin Books, 1994.
Cooper, Susan. *King of Shadows*. London: The Bodley Head, 1999.
Collodi et al. *Pinocchio*. London: Penguin Classics, 2002.
Dahl, Roald. *The BFG*. Illustrated by Quentin Blake. London: Puffin Books, 1982.
Farmer, Charlotte. *Charlotte Sometimes*. London: Chatto and Windus, 1969.
Fine, Anne. *Bad Dreams*. London: Corgi Yearling, 2001.
Garner, Alan. *The Weirdstone of Brisingamen*. (1961). Reprint. London:Collins Voyager, 2002.
—— *Elidor*. London: Collins, 1965.
—— *The Owl Service*. London: Collins, 1967.
Lily's Purple Plastic Purse. Illustrated by H. Henkes. Translated by Teresa Mlawer. Everest Publications, 1998.
Jacques, Brian. *The Pearls of Lutra. A Tale of Redwall*. London: Red Fox, 1996.
Jennings, Paul. *Thirteen Unpredictable Tales*. London: Puffin 1996.
—— *Undone! More Mad Endings*. London: Puffin Books, 1994.
King-Smith, Dick. *The Sheep-Pig*. London: Puffin Books, 1999.
Kotzwinkle, William. *The Extra-Terrestrial Storybook*. Illustrated by Melissa Matheson, photographer. London: Putnam Publishing Group, 1982.
L'Engle, Madeleine. *A Wrinkle in Time*. New York: Laurel Leaf, 1976.
Lewis, C. S. *The Complete Chronicles of Narnia*. Illustrated by Pauline Baynes. London: Picture Lions, 2000.
Mahy, Margaret. A *Lion in the meadow*. Reprint. London: Picture Puffins, 1976.
McKee, David. *Elmer: The Story of a Patchwork Elephant. London:* Red Fox, 2000.
Milne, A. A. *The Christopher Robin Story Book*. Reprint. London: Methuen & Co. Ltd., 1966.

Nesbitt, E. *The Story of the Amulet.* London: T. Fisher Unwin, 1906. London: Puffin, 1959.

Nix, Garth. *Calling on Dragons.* Scholastic US, 1994.

Norton, Mary *The Borrowers.* Reprint. London*: Dent, 1992.*

Pearce, Philippa. *Tom's Midnight Garden.* London: Puffin Books, 1993.

Potter, Beatrix. *The Tale of Peter Rabbit.* F. Warne & Co., 1902. Harmondsworth: Penguin, 1986.

—— *The Tale of Jemima Puddle-Duck.* F. Warne & Co., 1908. Harmondsworth: Penguin, 1987.

Pratchett Terry. *The Amazing MauRice and his Educated ROdEnts.* London: Doubleday, 2001.

Pullman Philip. *Northern Lights.* London: Scholastic Ltd., 1996.

Rogers, Paul and Edwina. *Ruby's Potty.* Sudbury:Dalton Children's Books, 2001.

Sendak, Maurice. *Where the Wild Things Are.* Reprint.London: Puffin Books, 1977.

Swift, Jonathan. *Gulliver's Travels.* London*: Penguin Popular Classic s, 1994.*

Tolkien, J. R. R. *The Hobbit.* Fourth edition. Reprint. London: Unwin Paperbacks, 1983.

Uttley, Alison. *A Traveller in Time.* Illustrated by Phyllis Bray. London: Reprint. Faber and Faber, 1973.

Watson, Jude, and David Wolverton. *The Rising Force: Star Wars – Jedi Apprentice: The Deadly Hunter.* Schmidt, 2000.

—— *Jedi Apprentice – The Fight for Truth.* Schmidt, 2000.

Wrede, Patricia. *Searching for Dragons.* Nevada: Magic Carpet Books, 2002.

Realism

Blume, Judy. *Double Fudge.* London: Macmillan, 2002.

—— *Forever.* London: Macmillan Children's Bookls, 2001.

Boynton, Sandra. *Doggies.* MagicCarpet Books, 2002.

Brown, Ruth and Ken. *Lion in the Long Grass.* London: Andersen, 2002.

Coppard, Yvonne. *Not Dressed Like That You Don't!: Diaries of a Teenager and of Her Mother.* London: Piccadilly press, 2000.

Cormier, Robert. *Tenderness.* London: Puffin, 1997.

Fine, Anne. *Stranger Danger?* London: Puffin Books, 1991.

—— *Goggle Eyes.* London: Puffin, 1990.

MacDonald, Alan. *The Personality Potion.* Illustrated by John Eastwood. Oxford Reading Tree: Treetops. Oxford: Oxford University Press, 1997.

Mankell, Henning. *Secrets in the Fire. Sydney:* Allen and Unwin.

—— *Playing with Fire.* Allen and Unwin.

Miller, Margaret. *Baby Faces.* New York: Little Simon, 1998.

Napoli, Donna Jo. *Stones in Water.* Penguin Putnam Inc. USA, 2001.

Rosen, Michael. *Lovely Old Roly.* Illustrated by Priscilla Lamont. London: Frances Lincoln, 2002.

Turner, Gwenda. *The Tree Witches. London:* Puffin Books, 1985.
Wilson, Jacqueline. *The Suitcase Kid. London:* Corgi Yearling Books, 1992.
—— *The Mum-Minder.* London: Corgi Yearling, 1993.
—— *Secrets.* Illustrated by Nick Sharratt. London: Corgi, 2003.
—— *Girls in Tears.* New York: Delacorte Press, 2003.

Historical Realism
Ballard, J. G. *Empire of the Sun.* Sydney: Buccaneer Books, 1997.
Bawden, Nina. *Carrie's War. Reprint.* London: Puffin Books, 1977.
Darke, Marjorie. *A Question of Courage.* Reissue. London: Frances Lincoln
    Barn Owl Books, 2002.
Holm, Anne. *I am David.* Reprint. London: Methuen, 1980.
Marryat, Frederick. *Children of the New Forest.* London: Hodder and
    Stoughton, 1999.
Mattingly, Christobel. *The Angel with a Mouth-Organ.* London: Hodder &
    Stoughton, 1985.
McCaughrean, Geraldine. *A Little Lower than the Angels.* Oxford: Oxfrod
    University Press, 2003.
Naidoo, Beverley. *The Other Side of Truth.* London: Harper Trophy, 2002.
Newberry, Linda. *Some Other War.* London: Frances Lincoln Barn Owl
    Books, 2002.
Paulsen, Gary. *Nightjohn.* London: Macmillan Children's Books, 1993.
—— *Sarny.* London: Macmillan Children's Books, 1997.
Pullman, Philip. *The Ruby in the Smoke.* London: Puffin, 1985.
Rees, Celia. *Witch Child.* Cambridge MA: Candlewick Press, 2002.
—— *Sorceress.* Cambridge MA: Candlewick, 2002.
Serailler, Ian. *The Silver Sword. London: Red Fox, 2003.*
Sutcliff, Rosemary. *Knight's Fee.* Illustrated by Charles Keeping. Oxford:
    Oxford University Press, 1973.
—— *Warrior Scarlet.* London: Puffin Books, 1976.
—— *The Sword and the Circle.* London: Red Fox, 1988.
Swindells, Robert. *Brother in the Land.* New York: Holiday House, 1985.
—— *Blitzed.* London: Corgi/Transworld inc., 2003.
Turnbull, Anne. *Gunner's Boy.* London: A. & C. Black Flashback, 2002.
Walsh, Jill Paton. *A Parcel of Patterns.* Reprint. London: Penguin Books, 1988.

Bibliography

Bettelheim, Bruno. *The Uses of Enchantment.* London: Penguin Books,1978.
—— 'The Psychological Role of Story.' In *Story in the Child's Changing
    World.* IBBY, 1982.
Carrington, Rebecca. *The Emperor's New Clothes: Questioning the Value
    of Surrealism in Picture Book Illustration.* An unpublished Master's
    Dissertation, Loughborough University, 2002.

Chambers, Nancy. *Signal* 59, 1989, 94–97.

Doonan, Jane. 'Hans Christian Andersen Award 2000 to Anthony Browne.' In *Signal* 92, May 2000, 19.

—— 'Drawing Out Ideas: A Second Decade of the Work of Anthony Browne.' In *The Lion and the Unicorn*, 23 (1), 1999.

Fisher, Carol J. and Margaret A. Natarella. 'Young Children's Preferences in Poetry: a national survey of first, second, and third graders.' In *Research in the Teaching of English*, 16. December, 1982, 339–54.

Godden, Rumer. 'Shining Popocatapetil: Poetry for Children. In *The Horn Book,* May/June 1988. Also quoted in Donna E. Norton, *Through the Eyes of a Child*. New York: Merrill, 1991.

Graves, Robert. 'The Cool Web' from *Collected Poems.* London: Cassell, 1992.

Hardy, Thomas. *The Illustrated Poets*. London: Aurum Press, 1990.

Hollindale, Peter. 'Recent Poetry for Children.' In *Books for Keeps*, No. 137, November 2002, 10–13.

Huck, Charlotte. *Children's Literature in the Elementary School*. 3rd edition. New York: Holt, Rinehart and Winston, 1976.

Locherbie-Cameron, M. A. L. 'Journeys through the Amulet: Time travel in Children's Fiction.' In *Signal* 79, January 1996, 45–61.

Meek, Margaret, Aidan Warlow and Griselda Barton. *The Cool Web: the Pattern of* Children's Reading. London: The Bodley head, 1978.

Norton, Donna E. *Through the Eyes of a Child*. New York: Merrill, 1991.

Paterson, Katherine. *Gates of Excellence.: On Reading and Writing Books for Children.* New York: Elsevier/Nelson Books, 1981.

Philip, Neil. The Signal Poetry Award, 47, May 1995, 71.

Sturgis, Alexander. *Magic in Art*. London: Belitha, 1994, 26.

Styles, Morag. 'Ted Hughes 1930–1998. In *Books for Keeps*, No. 114, January 1999.

Terry Ann. *Children's Poetry Preferences*: A National Survey of the Upper Elementary Grades. Urbana, Ill. National Council of Teachers of English, 1974.

Thomson, Susanna. Poetry. 'What do Children Like?' In *Carousel*, Issue 10, Winter 1998, 24.

Townsend, John Rowe. *Written for Children*. 5th edition. London: The Bodley Head, 1990.

Transtromer, Tomas. *Collected Poems*. Newcastle: Bloodaxe Books Ltd., 1989.

Wilks, Mike. *The Ultimate Alphabet*. London: Pavilon, 1987, 5.

Whitehead, Marian. *Supporting Language and Literacy Development in the Early Years*. Reprint 2001. Buckingham: Open University Press, 1999.

Zephaniah, Benjamin. Interview in BOOX, Issue No. 1, 8.

CHAPTER FOUR

Every Child Deserves the Best

The best stories are like extended lyrical images of unchanging human predicaments and strong, unchanging hopes and fears, loves and hatreds.

Cook 1969, 2.

There are many elements that compose an outstanding piece of writing for children. Professional evaluators, authors and child readers each have their own perspectives:

- *Authors:* Helen Dunmore sees an essential essence as 'a flash of recognition' that story brings a child. Katherine Paterson seeks excellence and to make it possible for children to make 'miraculous leaps of imagination'. Tim Bowler applies Ernest Hemingway: 'Hone your writing until it's like a bullfighter's sword.' Philip Ardagh wants to make a 'personal connection' to his audience.
- *Writers and Critics:* Aidan Chambers stresses literature as 'the best expression of the human imagination'; he also identifies essential qualities like fun yet subversive, refreshing and a source of comfort. Jack Zipes emphasises the subversive strengths of storytelling, showing how the 'ordinary can become extraordinary.'
- *Children*[1] whose sayings contribute to this book, in their evaluation of fiction saw from the viewpoint of their ages, experience and maturity. *8–9 year-olds* referred to humour, jokes, holding their

---

[1] 35 primary school children; 10 secondary.

interest, books that 'helped me', excitement and imagination. *The 11–13 year-olds* probed more deeply, although 'fun to read' surfaced frequently. They identified suspense, fantasy, exciting plots, intriguing and clever storylines, also stories that stir deep emotions as they tell of racism, relationships or other issues of concern.

1. Book Awards

Book awards for children's literature seek to recognise the sort of standards already mentioned in the best work available, usually published in the year preceding the award. Book awards in the countries of their origin not only mirror their immediate culture, but also reflect a universality of the human spirit while embracing the principles set out above. Winning books are written in such a way that the reader cannot put the book down and forget about it, for it resonates on and on in the mind, sometimes forever. Topic, theme, characterisation, plot with its inevitable conflicts, and the music and imagery of language, work together harmoniously to form an impactful, superior work. This can be said of any of the selections made by the following countries, for world-wide writing for children is scaling new mountain peaks.

1.1 Britain

Current book awards vary in their criteria for selection, but books which stand apart from others in uniqueness and distinctly special qualities are sought.

- The *Carnegie Medal* is the most prestigious award, conferred by CILIP and chosen by librarians for an outstanding work of fiction for children and young people.
- The *Kate Greenaway Medal* is also awarded by CILIP, selected by librarians for distinguished illustration. These awards are made annually in the midsummer following the books' year of publication.

In addition to other awards, made by county libraries, the Scottish Arts Council and the *Times Education Supplement,* further nation-wide British awards are:

- *The Guardian Award for Children's Fiction,* conferred by the *Guardian* newspaper.
- *The Whitbread Children's Book of the Year.* This award comes from a UK leisure company and is decided by a panel of three adults and two child judges from a shortlist compiled by children.
- *Smarties Book Prize,* given by the firm, Nestle, and administered by Booktrust, for books in three categories: ages 5 and under, 6–8, 9–11 years.
- *Sainsbury's Baby Book Award* for the best book for a baby under one year.
- *Blue Peter Awards,* conferred by the BBC children's programme, began in 2000. There are two sections: *The Judges' Awards*, selected by a celebrity judging panel, selecting from paperback titles published in the UK in the previous year, then read by Blue Peter child judges. These select (i) The best book to keep forever (ii) The Book I couldn't put down (iii) The best book to read aloud. From these the Book of the Year is chosen. The Blue Peter *Voters' Awards* are voted for by children throughout the UK through their local library. In 2001 there were two categories: The Best Storybook and the Best Book of Knowledge.
- *The British Book Awards.* Commonly referred to as the 'Nibbies', these are awarded annually and are chosen by over 150 representatives of the book industry, rather than by librarians, teachers and children.

1.2 International

- *Hans Christian Andersen Medals* are awarded by the International Board on Books for Young People (IBBY). These are awarded in alternate years, even-numbered, to authors and illustrators in recognition of entire *oevres*.
- *Phoenix Awards* from the Children's Literature Association, awarded to a book written in English, published 20 years previously.
- *Mythopoeic Awards* are given for fantasy for children and for adults and in recognition of scholarly work in Myth and Fantasy studies.
- UNESCO Prize for Children's and Young People's Literature in the Service of Tolerance.

1.3 Australia

Awards are made by the very active Australian Children's Book Council. The categories are *Book of the Year*: for Older Readers; for Younger Readers; for Picture Book of the Year, including those for mature readers; the Eve Pownall Award for Information Books.

1.4 Canada

promotes many awards for excellence in children's literature. Possibly the most prestigious are: the Canadian Library Association's Book of the Year, and the Governor General's Literary Award in Children's Literature.

1.5 New Zealand

has a high literacy rate and level of reading interest. Its awards for children's literacy are conferred by the Library and and Information Association of New Zealand Aoteroa. The Children's Literature Foundation of New Zealand composes an annual list of 'Notable Books' in Junior and Senior Fiction, Non-Fiction and Picture Book categories.

1.6 South Africa

Awards for excellence in children's literature are made for books in Afrikaans, English and South African languages. Three categories cover books for pre-kindergarten, children aged 7–11 years and youth aged 11–16 years.

2. Winners: Too Good to Miss

Since 1936 when the first *Carnegie Medal Winner* was selected by the Library Association, some truly memorable books have been chosen as outstanding books of the year. Different readers select favourites for different reasons, but all books selected reach a standard of excellence in the view of the selective panel. Even to comment on one 'special' book, of but one award of a decade in an overview, is difficult, for all the winners hold laudable qualities, as the following selection shows, yet they exemplify the characteristics that go to make a winner. Because the award has been given for almost 70 years, it is possible to identify the development of books for children during this period.

2.1 The Pre-War Thirties

Pigeon Post by Arthur Ransome was the first recipient. It was sixth in the 'Swallows and Amazons' series of ten adventure books, immensely popular for fifty years or more, available still as a reprint edition. Why was it so special, so much so that there is an active Arthur Ransome Society in Britain? No doubt characterisation and dialogue contributed through distinct, believable personalities, especially the four children who are the 'Swallows' and the four who are 'Amazons;' who live an idyllic, pre-war, golden setting of freedom. Children of nine years upwards always revel in secret clubs, are energetic, imaginative, explorative, impetuous, seek adventures, with often a little knowledge that may be a dangerous thing, and this is what Ransome conveys so plausibly. The winning book might be identified as 'wholesome' yet it is not stuffy, just the portrayal of believable kids with a minimum of adults to get in their way. As well as characterisation, the action that keeps moving on is an important ingredient.

2.2 The Post-War Forties

During the 1940s the Carnegie prize was withheld in the war years 1943 and 1945 when no book was considered suitable. The year 1946, however, was the year of Elizabeth Goudge's enchanting fantasy, *The Little White Horse*. Its popularity has soared again since Joanna Rowling identified it as a book she 'absolutely adored' as a child, but it was a great favourite earlier, in 1946. The ambience was Victorian, historical even in its award year, and its romantic fairy tale, scary feel continues to give it distance in time, place, mood, message and style. The persuasion of its setting – Moonacre Manor in the idyllic valley of Silverdew – and its cast of characters: a red headed, feisty orphan named Maria Merryweather, along with her animal allies and friend Robin, and always the haunting memory of the Moon Princess and the mysterious little white horse, set this book apart.

2.3 The Developmental Fifties

The 1950s began with ambition everywhere in the Western world as post-war recovery exploded. It was also depicted in Kit who wanted to be a singer, hero of *The Lark on the Wing* (winner in 1950), but although competently written by the talented Elfrida Vipont Foulds, who later wrote the memorable *Elephant and the Bad Baby* (1969), ambition of childhood was not a new theme but one which Noel Streatfield had focused on in the 1930s. Certainly the 1950s emerged as a decade of strong development for children's literature and contributed some award winners that are already regarded as classics, particularly C. S. Lewis's *The Last Battle* in 1956 and two years later, Philippa Pearce's *Tom's Midnight Garden.*

It was *The Borrowers* by Mary Norton that was quite astounding in its creative imagination, making it the out front winner in 1952. For the first time, young readers discovered the 'truth' about quiet old houses: that tiny people – parents and children, with interesting names like Overmantel and Rainpipe – live their own busy lives lives in secret places, for instance below the floor boards, behind oak panelling or under a grandfather clock, as do the Clocks family. Pod is the father borrower who can open the gates to an upstairs world; who takes his daughter, Arriety, with him to borrow some brush fibre from the doormat in the hall upstairs -and thereby hangs the tale! Fully believable characters, only inches high, yet reflections of humans, they borrow every thing from 'human beans' who do not realise such little people exist. It began a series of six stories for which children soon developed unsatiable appetites, and when the BBC made a film version in the 1990s, the rapture was renewed, seemingly to have faded little since.

The decade of Fifties growth ended with an award in contrast to *The Borrowers*, to historical realism, yet equally well crafted and believable. It recognised the research and imaginative prowess of *The lantern Bearers*, by Rosemary Sutcliffe.

2.4 The Restructured Sixties

The 1960s were highlighted by the appearance of Alan Garner's *The Owl Service,* original, imaginative, a weird and haunting mix of Welsh myth and reality, written in Garner's masterly style with scholarly overtones. Today It is frequently studied as a GCSE text. For younger readers (Stage 2), the 1961 medal went to a fantasy from Lucy Boston's *Green Knowe* series, *A Stranger at Green Knowe.* in a house that echoes with memories of Norman, Tudor and Georgian times, where past and present live side by side, the story features a gorilla of all creatures. Writing in her autobiography, she tells how she spent many hours in the front of the cage of Guy, a great gorilla at the London zoo. She watched his grief and witnessed his tragic dance as he tried to tear down his prison, a rare sight but one which she was able to vividly and movingly portray in her award winning book, conveyed with the force of her belief that all life must have respect. The fact that all the Green Knowe stories centre in Boston's own home, the Manor House at Hemingford Grey, Cambridgeshire, where a rocking horse and birdcage mentioned in her stories are still in an attic bedroom, seems to add its own persuasive veracity. In her autobiography, Boston also describes the farce of the award ceremony, in a time when the recipient was not expected to make a speech and a medal for children's literature appeared to be held in far less esteem than forty years on.

Some medal winners are highly praised and discussed in literary journals at the time of their award, then disappear from the limelight as if they were never-ever centrestage. The 1968 winner, a work of fantasy by Rosemary Harris, *The Moon in the Cloud*, is an example.[2] Based on the biblical story of the flood, which Harris sets at the time of the Egyptian Old Kingdom, the protagonist is Reuben, a young animal tamer, who embarks on a dangerous journey into Egypt to obtain animals for the Ark. Several ingredients are clearly important at the outset: the notion of *journey,* an important theme of all literature; a youth faced with challenge; myth and historical detail woven together by fantasy into a cohesive whole. The use of a biblical story as starting point is in itself unusual, although Norse and Celtic myths have inspired such authors as C. C. Lewis, J. R. R. Tolkien and Alan Garner, and Lewis's *Narnia* series conveys biblical allusions in its imagery. Harris explained her choice:

> *It is a marvellous story, and the fact that every toy shop, thousands of years after it was written, stocks a Noah's Ark, shows its extraordinary power over the human heart. It is also an extremely magical story, with its Ark as a place of safety in a turbulent, evil*

---

[2] See P.H. 'Review – The Moon in the Cloud.' *The Horn Book Magazine,* April, 1970, 46 (2).

world; its animals, symbolising perhaps the various powers and instincts of man, and ending with God's moving covenant with Noah by the setting of a rainbow in the sky. Perhaps the story has always had a hold on my imagination, without my altogether realising it till I wrote The Moon in the Cloud.

Harris 1969, 224.

There is much to praise in this book. There is the way that Egypt of the past with its fascinating mummies, pyramids and animal-headed gods becomes real, even with humour. For example, the High Priest of Sekhmet does his work with amusing, mortal detail:

Now he made a round of his dwelling, paying attention to a god in an alcove here, or that one in a shrine there, then in a panic returning to the first one three times three ... it was very exhausting, and he feared to leave anyone out ... he was looking under his couch to see if any minor deity had taken up residence during the night when Kenamut's messenger arrived.

Harris 1977, 90–92.

There is, additionally, rich language to describe the opulence of Egypt: 'fruits of all kinds, sweetmeats, waterfowl spiced and saladed, red wine, golden wine, white wine, sparkling wine ...' There is also the formal language of the Court with its honorifics, elaborate titles and ritual. The author knows the historical detail but never makes it heavy, rather she weaves it into the fabric of the fantasy.

Characterisation in *The Moon and the Cloud* is outstanding, with fully rounded and believable characters, yet even very minor ones are brought to life with deft strokes: Ham's young wife is 'clumsy, because he made her nervous with his cruelty.' Reuben is a hero with human frailties; Ham is a superb villain, a little over-painted for emphasis, who uses his sensitivity for evil purposes. The animals develop as characters most of all, acquiring lessons about co-operating together and growing in loyalty. It is a gentle portrayal of a child's own development which children can accept because, as Donna Norton states:

young children are drawn to the strong feelings of loyalty that the animals in modern fantasies express as they help each other out of dangerous predicaments, stay with friends when they might choose other actions, or protect their human owners while risking their own lives. The memorable animals characters ... show a wide range of recognisable traits. Children often see themselves in the actions of their animal friends.

Norton 1999, 367.

The climax is exciting: the appearance of the moving golden statue of Sekhmet, under the secret control of a wily priest who is hidden inside. Amidst the crowd's panic, Reuben and the tomb robber escape, yet small incidents throughout the story have foreshadowed all that happens, so that Reuben can ultimately take his place aboard the Ark.

This was a layered, cinematic work, with special delight to be found in its animal characters. Nevertheless its day appears to have past, yet it was a link in the process of literature which is renewal and restruction, especially in Harris's synthesis of the past allied with child insight.

2.5 *The Stimulated Seventies*

The outstanding work of 1970, *The God Beneath the Sea*, written by Leon Garfield and Edward Blishen, was another look at the past, but not through the eyes of Christian faith, which some felt had let them down during World War II, so that they restructured their lives without it. Many adults will remember the 1970 impact of the story of the Greek gods, omnipotent, sometimes vindictive, and their interaction with humankind.

The Seventies saw other remarkable winners. No-one who has read it can forget the ending to *The Turbulent Term of Tyke Tiler?* (1977) by Gene Kemp, or the special abilities of *Josh,* (1971) written by the Australian author, Ivan Southall, or the wonder of Peter Dickinson's *Tulku* (1979), Penelope Lively's *Ghost of Thomas Kempe*(1973) or Mollie Hunter's *Stronghold* (1974). In total it was a splendid decade for children's literature.

Richard Adam's gripping and imaginative *Watership Down* (1972) was possibly the most unusual winner, for its characters are rabbits, unforgettable rabbits who see the English countryside through rabbits' eyes and make a tremendous journey. In an ever rabbit way, they reflect human superstitions, struggles, hope and determination to survive against destructive elements. The characters are memorable: sensitive and clairvoyant Fiver, strong and aggressive Bigwig, witty Bluebell, hateful Black Rabbit who causes sickness and death, and the ever authoritative Hazel.

2.6 *The Exciting Eighties*

The 1980s began with an unusual medal selection, again authored by Peter Dickinson who had won in the preceding year. This time it was a collection of stories from the Old Testament of the Bible, *City of Gold,* told creatively from an inside feel of the situation, whether it concerned 'In the Beginning' and the fall of man, 'The Promise to the Fathers' with a marvellous rendition of the story of the remarkable Joseph and his brothers, and so on, until the fall of the city, Jerusalem, which seems to strangely link 1980 to the location of suicide bombings in beyond 2000.

The winning authors of the exciting Eighties are established, highly respected writers whose work continues to flourish. They opened up new themes and emphases in society, as by Margaret Mahy with her *The Haunting* (1984) and *The Changeover* (1984), and Berlie Doherty's bringing to life of disability in *Granny was a Buffer Girl* (1986). The accomplished Geraldine McCaughrean made her debut on the Carnegie winners' list with *A Pack of Lies* (1988), while Anne Fine showed her indisputable skill with *Goggle Eyes* (1989). The originality and timeliness of the subject matter, the after effects of divorce and the way in which Fine treats these contemporary issues, can be identified as contributing to the book's overall superiority, being realistic fiction with all the essential components of the genre. As Stephanie Nettel observes, the potentially bleak subject of divorce and a parent's new partner, viewed from the child's perspective, is handled in a bright and funny manner by Fine. She also brings sympathy for all concerned.

The central character, Kitty, is a well defined teenager with typical action and language – 'Why me?' Her tirades and unpleasantness toward Gerald, the interloping boyfriend, are revelations of her deep hurt and anger about a situation she did not cause and cannot change. The issue of nuclear disarmament adds another layer and is a useful plot device. The presence of humour helps to carry the topic, and, as Peter Hunt observes, the comedy does not detract from the issue of divorce. On the contrary, it enables a reader to laugh and find light relief.

Perhaps, as some suggest, the contemporary nature of the book will date *Goggle Eyes* in time, if it has not already done so. It may also be that an underlying didacticism may cause the book to become anachronistic though important in its decade.

2.7 The Wow Factor Nineties

The Eighties opened the way, and the Nineties went on boldly to explore the now largely Humanist society. In the 1991, *Dear Nobody*, by second-time winner, Berlie Doherty, dwelt on unplanned, teen pregnancy, a topic that fitted with the UK status of having the highest rate of underage teen pregnancies in Western Europe. Her character, Helen, expresses denial: 'I'm not pregnant. You don't exist. You are nobody.' The reaction of her boyfriend, Chris, on the brink of going to university, shows horror at the prospect of fatherhood, and for them both, their story becomes a journey in personhood. They still need to develop communication skills with each other; it is only through reading her letters to the unborn that he knows her true feelings and he he tells her his love through Yeats, and indirectly. "How many words is it?' Helen asks as cocky as a sparrow. 'Three' he replies, to which she laughs and says, 'Three back.' It is a vivid portrayal of teenage sexuality and romantic love wherein Chris realises, 'I'm not yet ready for myself.'

Anne Fine received the accolade for the second time in 1992, but thereafter, except for Theresa Breslin in 1994, the winning authors were male[3] for six years until the end of the decade. They wrote powerfully on themes that reflect issues of death and bereavement, sexuality, addiction, isolation within a family, bittersweet memories and the morality of war. Philip Pullman's Book 1, *Northern Lights*, winner in 1995, began the trilogy, *His Dark Materials* which introduced a new depth of literary reference and imagination into children's literature.

2.8 The Progressive Post Modern 2000s

Beverley Naidoo broke the pattern of male author domination with *The Other Side of Truth* in the year 2000. Now the problems that prompt political asylum and the difficulties that non-white children face when coming to England as refugees are depicted in the story of a sister and brother, Sade and Femi. This common scene of the year 2000 and beyond was thereby thrust right at centre stage of children's literature.

[3] These were Robert Swindells, Philip Pullman, Melvin Burgess, Tim Bowler, David Almond, Aidan Chambers, 1993–1999.

Pullman went on to become Author of the Year for Children's Book of the Year, 2000 in recognition of the third book of his *Dark Materials* sequence: *The Amber Spyglass.* Particularly in this trilogy, Pullman has contributed to and renewed a high level of scholarship in British children's literature, seen as far back as fifty years previously in C. S. Lewis J. R. R. Tolkien, so it attracts a more select body of readers. His use of parallel worlds, the daemon, or other self, which each character takes with him/her, as by Will, or by Lyra, is an amazing and forceful image. The entire imaginative scope, the Miltonic literary allusions, the cosmic vision and the cyclic way it begins and ends with the same hero – all this and the continuing saga of journey and destiny is compelling and unforgettable storytelling.

In amazing contrast, the winning book of the following year, 2001, concerned rats. Rats! What a con-man is Maurice the cat, with his perfect money-making scam and his use of educated rats whom he cannot eat for lunch! Yet this same creature does have an 'inner cat' that acts like a conscience and monitors his behaviour. It is a most unusual book in execution and presentation, highly original yet resonant with echoes of Dick Whittington, Dickens, Beatrice Potter, Dick King Smith and Brian Jacques. Coming from the innovative Discworld Universe, it broke new ground, was highly imaginative and offered respite from the *angst* of some previous winners

2.9 Conclusions About Winners

The winners described have common attributes: paramount is an imaginative topic or freshness of approach with characters who 'live' and continue to do so in readers' minds. Other elements include the timeliness of theme in relationship to children's interests, ambitions and current issues, conveyed in a persuasive writing style. In all, relating Zipes' words, 'the ordinary becomes extraordinary!'

Many books which were past award winners are still available, either still published or on library shelves. Librarians and teachers should keep these titles in mind as they make their selections.

2.10 Different Criteria by Different Evaluators

prompt different awards. Winners of the many other awards listed, too numerous for discussion in this work, should also be noted and selected, remembering that the Whitbread Award for a Children's Book,[4] by which children air their own views, is a balance for the Carnegie award and others. The Whitbread and Smarties prizes were the only significant British awards ever gained by Roald Dahl,[5] despite much acclaim overseas: *The Witches* (Whitbread, 1983); *Esio Trot* (Nestle Smarties, 1990). Following his death in 1990, *Matilda* was voted by children to be 'the Nation's Favourite Children's Book in a BBC Bookworm poll in 1998 (before the Blue Peter awards began). He also won the Millennium Children's Book Award and Blue Peter Book Award in 2000 for *Charlie and the Chocolate Factory*.

J. K. Rowling's similarity in writing style to Dahl was noted early on by adult critics, as Eccleshare points out. Like Dahl, an international superstar, she has not won a Carnegie medal in the years preceding 2004, but she has won other awards, such as the Nestle Smarties Prize twice: in 1997 for *Harry Potter and the Philosophers Stone* and with *Harry Potter and the Chamber of Secrets* in 1997, plus the Children's Book of the Year in 2000. For *Harry Potter and the Prisoner of Azkabah* she received the Whitbread Award in 1999. In effect, however, Rowling is really **world-winner** by popular sales and adulation of Harry Potter. Selling 200,000,000 copies of her work in 200 countries in 50 languages by 2003, plus all sorts of imaginable and unimaginable merchandise, is a world phenomenon. Book 5, *The Order of the Phoenix* is expected to reach the greatest print run in history.

3. Books that Live: Classics

A story is a special thing.
The ones that I have read,
They do not stay inside the book,
They stay inside my head.
                    Marchette Chute

---

[4] The 2003 winner was Hilary McKay's *Saffy's Angel*. *Sorceress* by popular author, Celia Rees was short-listed, sequel to Witch Child which was short-listed for the Guardian Children's Fiction Prize in 2001.
[5] He also won the Surrey School Award for *Charlie and the Chocolate Factory* in 1973 and for *Charlie and the Great Glass Elevator* in 1975.

3.1   Classics

Classics are extraordinary books which have perpetuity because of distinction and quality of writing, rather than a short period of popularity. Some will have been designed for children, others have been taken over and 'adopted' by children themselves. Margery Fisher suggests they offer

> *universal truths, universal values, to one generation after another, impermeable to the erosion of time.*
>
> Fisher 1986, 1.

When one asks for readers' favourite books – as was done by the BBC in 2003 in a nation-wide search for the most highly regarded – some readers like *this* book, others adore that, but children's classics are always mentioned. Over a wide sampling, certain books that have taken on long life emerge over and over again, having captured the hearts of generations of readers. It is not possible to make a definitive list, although publishers attempt to do so: the Hodder Classic book-list suggests titles and authors from 1678; Puffins' Ancient and Modern list gives more than one hundred titles from the nineteenth century on, described by them as 'the essential collection.' Collins publishes a Modern Classics series which dates from 1925; Oxford Modern Classics series brings back old favourites from 1939. Faber, Red Fox and Scholastic also publish classic selections. There is not complete agreement, yet there certainly is a 'canon' of highly respected work of books that live, many having gone beyond a life confined to story to influencing language and symbolism in society.

3.2   Seventeenth Century Prototype

The Hodder list of classics begins with the seventeenth century *The Pilgrim's Progress,* which may be regarded as a prototype of children's literature. It became a best seller right from the start, with an enormous readership which extended over the next two hundred years, published in many lands and languages. Its popularity only began to fade, like an heirloom daguerreotype, during the twentieth century, cynicism being a by-product of societal change and diminished interest in the Christian Church. As Collmer pointed out in 1989, the work had more editions and had been published in more foreign languages than any other book written in English. It was a forerunner of the Harry Potter phenomenon.

There is considerable evidence from tributes to Bunyan that *The Pilgrim's Progress* influenced many English authors of the past who contributed to Britain's literary greatness. They included Browning, Burns, Coleridge, Johnson, Lamb, Pope, Richardson, Ruskin, Southey, Swift, Macaulay, and twentieth-century children's writers Boston, C. S. Lewis and Ardizzone. It also influenced public figures and social reformers. But it especially influenced children who quickly made the book their own, as historians of children's literature recognise. Field, in the late nineteenth century said that of course the work was not written for children but

> *successive generations of children have so fastened upon it and made it their own that we cannot exclude the book from their literature ... expresses itself in a directness and simplicity of diction which goes straight to the heart of a child.*
> Field 1892, 202.

Townsend says that it was 'children's literature by adoption.' Haviland wrote of its 'joy and delight' for 'English speaking children for more than 300 years.' Its influence in North America, like that in Britain, was extensive, as shown by MacDonald who argues persuasively for Bunyan's place in the children's canon of literature. Like Harry Potter, the influence extended beyond books, in the nineteenth century especially, to include jig saw puzzles, board games, cut-out figures, colouring books, movable books called Harlequinades and other items for nursery and school.

Who were the early child readers of *The Pilgrim's Progress*? No names or records survive to identify the seventeenth-century readers, but it can be reasonably assumed that the first of them were children in Non-conformist and Dissenting homes, sons and daughters of merchants, shopkeepers and clothiers. These young readers probably included Bunyan's own grandchildren and the children of his immediate friends and parishioners.

Why was *The Pilgrim's Progress* special? What are the elements that set it apart and make it the prototype? Firstly, exciting reading for children was rare in the seventeenth century and books of religious instruction and good advice abounded. In contrast, Bunyan's vigourous writing style must have been amazing, even shocking at times, because of its cast of unfamiliar, smooth-tongued, vacillating or evil characters. Here was a book that resembled popular romances, ballads and fairy tales, which Bunyan himself had read as a youth in chapbook form, sold by pedlars, prior to his conversion to Christian faith. Adults accepted it as a religious book with biblical texts in the margins, but children discovered the thrill of a well-told tale that included giants, dragons, monsters, persecution and the skulls of victims in the Valley of the Shadow.

Secondly, it was the gripping story of dangerous pilgrimage and a quest, one that moved along at a rollicking pac – if the didactic parts were left out, as children would discover. It was not the pilgrimage of a saint, an idolised folk hero or superman, but of one who felt confused, forgot, went to sleep at the wrong time and place, depended on loyal friends, yet despite his weaknesses pursued his journey to a triumphant end: Christian, ordinary yet with a tender conscience, wanting to flee from evil and destruction, who travels through the mountain trails and winding paths fraught with danger and temptation, all the way from the City of Destruction to the Celestial City; story of a hero.

Thirdly, The spirit of Part II, written six years after Part 1 because of popular demand, is typical of children past and present who set out to reach a goal. The child heroes, four boys and a girl, demonstrate real behaviour, not the idealised, as was common in seventeenth century literature which was often about pious children who died young. In contrast, here are boys who disregard their mother's warning about picking and eating plums that overhang a wall on their pathway, so that subsequently she has to call the doctor. They grow hot and sweaty after an uphill climb and need fruit and a rest to recover; they are full of questions – what, why, where, may we ... ? They are scared and cry on encountering a giant, Giant Maul, yet they later fight against Giant Despair with courage, and then cheer and celebrate their victory. The four brothers are well-rounded, distinct character types, resembling children of centuries in the future: Ransome's four Swallows and Amazons or Lewis's four children in *The Lion, the Witch and the Wardrobe.*

Fourthly, its fresh and unique way of writing was what may be termed pastiche, whereby different devices, motifs, unlikely characters and ideas from different philosophies combine together, as Lewis, Tolkien and Pullman have done latterly. Indeed Pullman admits 'I have stolen ideas from every book I have ever read.' Bunyan uses giants, monsters, hobgoblins, dragons, fiends and a witch, as well as Pope and Pagan, Adam the First, Moses and Demas and the Shining Ones, plus a mix of tableaux and artefacts. Two strains of writing converge: a serious, didactic voice of a preacher-prisoner, and that of a story teller who has children of his own and knows they like action, adventure, riddles, puns and jokes. It makes a syncretic, harmonious whole.

It is also interesting to note: (i) the entry point to story of a dream, used as a device for time travel and built on by later writers (ii) the mix of narrative from the characters' points of view, plus use of rhymed verses or splendid poetry. Bunyan's pilgrim poem, often sung as a hymn at school assemblies, in churches, or as a choral piece, seems immortalised and is frequently used today:

> *Who would true valour see,*
> *Let him come hither;*
> *One here will constant be,*
> *Come wind, come weather.*
> *There's no discouragement*
> *Shall make him once relent*
> *His first avowed intent*
> *To be a pilgrim*

Fifthly, the characters grow as a community and in self knowledge, becoming active decision makers along the journey, set against the changing backdrop of England in political and social upheaval. Yet they seek a greater power than themselves, putting their trust in the Lamb, while with Lewis's characters, Aslan the lion is the saviour, and for Will and Lyra, the witch-queen, Serafina Pekkala, is one source of rescue.

Finally, at the heart of the allegoric *Pilgrim's Progress* the ages-old conflict of good versus evil and its resolution is enacted, as it is within the work of later classics and award winners. As Duriez says, 'Parable, allegory and fiction is the closest we can come to speaking of Heaven'. In Lewis's *Last Battle,* the Shadowlands disappear as the conflict, as far as Narnia is concerned, is finally resolved. Although a liar, Lyra – a name that carries with it a sound of sweet music – is the unlikely hero whose vision of the brilliant city that lies beyond the Northern Lights draws her on throughout her journey and its conflicts.

> *Behind them lay pain and death and fear; ahead of them lay doubt and danger, and fathomless mysteries. But they weren't alone. So Lyra and her daemon turned away from the world they were born in, and looked towards the sun, and walked into the sky.*
> *Pullman 1996, 398–399.*

Retellings for children of The *Pilgrim's Progress* abounded in the nineteenth and early twentieth century, including Enid Blyton's deconstruction, *The Land of Far Beyond*. For children of the late twentieth and the twenty-first centuries there are Bunyanesque versions in contemporary design, appearance and writing style. For young children, *Go with Christian,* by Alan and Linda Parry is a pop-up version, with tabs to pull, a maze to pursue and a board game to play.

The same authors have adapted Bunyan's work in *The Evergreen Wood.* Beautifully illustrated in colour, all the characters are now animals, with Christopher Mouse taking on Christian's role and the White Mouse that of Evangelist. The Dark Wood becomes the City of Destruction from which the animals must flee from annihilation. The Evergreen Wood, place of peace and safety, equates with Bunyan's Celestial City; in Badger's House lives Badger, who fulfils the role of Interpreter, while rabbits called Stickle and Fickle represent Obstinate and Pliable. Other characters, rounding out the story, are an array of other English animals: toad, owl, field mice, weasels, lamb, hawks, squirrels, mole, cat, rats, fox, frog, all portrayed true to to their natural instincts in an enchanting style that is reminiscent of Beatrix Potter and Kenneth Grahame.

The Evergreen Wood is, yet at the same time, is not *The Pilgrim's Progress.* It is the progress of a small rodent that belongs to an established tradition of the mouse in literature.[6] Christopher is a brave but unlikely hero who goes out in armour provided by others; who says at the last, believing that his wife and children will soon join him in the Evergreen Wood: 'My happiness . . . is almost complete.' It is a type of deconstruction, though it is more of a reduction, whereby locus and personae have different names but similar attributes. To a large degree it fulfils Demers' criteria for the success of Bunyan's allegory: weakness and strength in the hero; use of personified abstractions; and symbolic typography.

Where is the sovereignty of a saviour figure? It is present in the Lamb. Where is the support throughout the journey? It is present in the physical intervention of the Lamb himself in the form of the White Mouse, and in the encouragement of friends like Ginger, Flame and Honey Squirrel who give the mouse a helmet, shield and sword, like Christian received from the maidens at the House Beautiful. It is present in the Stream of Living Waters that sustain several times; that heals after the little mouse encounters a huge wild cat – equivalent of

[6] See Mary Trim: 'Viva Hunca Munca: what every children's librarian should know about mice in children's literature.' *The New Review of Children's Literature and Librarianship*, 2, 1996, 95–102.

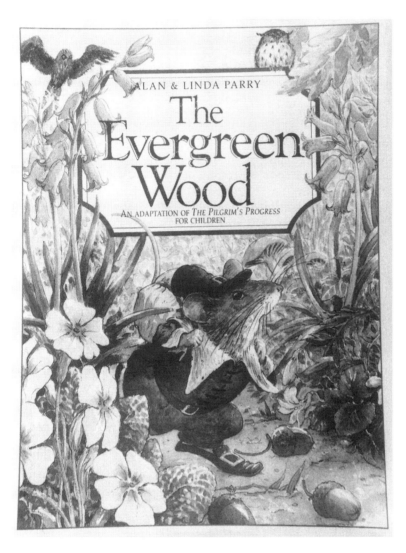

Illustration 5: *The Evergreen Wood by Alan and Linda Parry* adapts the story of *The Pilgrim's Progress* to picture book format. Cover reproduced by permission of John Hunt Publishing.

a giant in Bunyan's story; present again in a letter from his wife and children, telling of their decision to set out on the same journey.

These late twentieth century writers not only build on Bunyan but they also depict a familiarity with a tradition in children's literature to which other classics have contributed, such as the anthropomorphised animals of Beatrix Potter and Kenneth Grahame.

Dangerous Journey is for capable readers of Key Stages 2 and beyond. This version was prepared for a television series, 'Dangerous Journeys', in the 1980s, and it uses the original words of John Bunyan, selected by Oliver Hunkin. Dramatic, vividly illustrated, it is a memorable picture book for older readers that will perpetuate the classic for other generations.

More recent again in publication is *John Bunyan's A Pilgrim's Progress*, admirably retold by the accomplished Geraldine McCaughrean; it received the Blue Peter Book Award in 2000. Making its point for a new generation, it concludes with Christian speaking:

> *I am on a pilgrimage . . .*
> *Everyone is.*
>   *McCaughrean 1999, 102.*

Margery Fisher points out its probable continuing place within the national consciousness, the exciting nature of the journey, its emblematic narrative and its reflection of the mid-seventeenth century. Regarding morality she bases its relevance as dependent on certain conditions which she sets out:

> **if**[7] *warnings against the temptations of covetousness, lust, vanity, hypocrisy, deceit and intolerance are still relevant.*
>   *Fisher 1988, 13.*

3.3 Eighteenth Century

Two books also 'adopted' by children, though not written specifically for them as Townsend observes, are *The Life and Strange Surprising Adventure of Robinson Crusoe of York, Mariner* (1719) by Daniel Defoe and *Gulliver's Travels* (1726) by Jonathan Swift. Both picked up the theme of a journey which sat comfortably within a century of sea travel and empire expansion; both were imaginative adventures; both were popular through subsequent centuries, though lagged behind *The*

---

[7] Bold is mine – M. Trim.

Pilgrim's Progress, despite Swift's aspirations for it to be as successful. Both picked up certain aspects of Bunyan's style, notably religious faith, travel, wit and fantasy. Several publishers include both books in their lists today, for example, in Penguin Classics for older readers. Picture book versions for the young, are published by Oxford University Press, Usborne and Longman.

As a character, Robinson Crusoe easily captures the imagination, for here is the story of a rebel, sole survivor from a storm-wrecked ship who is washed ashore where he has the challenge of making shelter for himself and surviving for over twenty-five years. This basic theme lends itself to picture story format; in full versions there is more to cope with: satire, emotional and historical details. It is considered the first English novel and has sired a dynasty of adventure stories in which protagonists meet the challenges of land, sea and the elements, meeting the unexpected and all the ambiguities of life. The theme continues to surface in different guises in junior fiction, as for example in Wyss's *Swiss Family Robinson* (1812–13), Stevenson's *Treasure Island,* (1883) and, more recently in *Kensuke's Kingdom* by Michael Morpugo, in which a modern-day Robinson is washed up on an island in the Pacific. Winner of the Children's Book Award 2000, it was also shortlisted for the Blue Peter prize.

Another shipwrecked traveller, Lemuel Gulliver, has amazing adventures, beginning with meeting the tiny people of Lilliiput, over whose 15 centimetre/six inch heights he towers like a giant in a miniscule world (and this, over two hundred years before *The Borrowers*). Then he sequentially finds himself a pigmy among the giants of Brodningnag, encountering the noble race of horses called the the Houyhnhnms, then among the animals of human form but brutish instincts, the Yahoos. At its face value it is a remarkable tale, amazingly inventive, while at another level it is serious satire, an allegory of different aspects of the human condition.

3.4 Nineteenth Century

In this century, literature for children really accelerated in production. *Alice's Adventures in Wonderland* (1865) is a high-water mark, a story designed just to amuse, rather than to teach; a completely new trend. What an astounding, imaginative adventure comes to one sleepy little girl who falls down, down, down a hole, following a white rabbit with a watch in his waistcoat pocket! In its sequel, *Through the Looking-Glass and What Alice Found There* (1871), Lewis Carroll's unpredictable, hilarious, mad world of fantasy that behaves divergently from reality with rules turned upside down, continues to entertain. Alice shares with her kitten her ideas about the reflective world she can glimpse -'all but that bit just behind the fireplace'- and asks the kitten how she would like to go there. True to the childish practice of explorative climbing, she is soon up above the fireplace over which the mirror hangs. It begins to melt away, and thus the entry-point into story is made. Both books pre-empt the riotous settings created by Roald Dahl and continue the pattern of Bunyan of providing an entry into a dreamlike world where rhymes and verse abound.

3.5 Twentieth Century

Many marvellous classics are treasured from the pre World War II years. One of these, *The Hobbit,* (1937) by J. R. R. Tolkien, is a journey with a difference for it is peopled, not by humans, but by a fantasy race previously unencountered in children's literature. They are the Hobbits, smaller than dwarfs but bigger than Swift's Lilliputians, of whom Bilbo Baggins is the hero – another unlikely, reluctant hero – who sets out to share in an adventure arranged by the wizard, Gandalf. In contrast to seventeenth-century Christian, he is comfortable in his home in the hill and has no desire to leave. Another difference lies in the quest: that of regaining a treasure previously belonging to Dwarves, but stolen by Smaug, the dragon. Thirteen dwarves are his travelling companions whom Trolls – soon encountered on the journey over the Misty Mountains – plan to roast and eat.

The story has memorable moments and characters as the non-stop action progresses chapter by chapter. Beorn is unforgettable for some readers. He is sometimes a huge black bear and sometimes, by transformation, a vigorously strong black-haired man with mighty limbs and a great beard. Bilbo, and thereby the reader, sense him eerily shadowing the travellers in an enchanted bear form as they depart to pursue their quest. Small, slimy Gollum is another 'unforgettable', especially by his individualistic expressions, constantly referring to 'my preciouss' and also by his use of riddles – which links Tolkien with both Bunyan and Carroll.

3.6 Time Travel

Many themes emerge in twentieth-century classics. Time travel is one of these, beginning with E. Nesbit's *Story of the Amulet* and Kipling's

Puck of Pook's Hill, both published in 1906. One outstanding book of twentieth-century children's literature which suggests a parallel existence of past and present is *A Traveller in Time* by Alison Uttley (1939). The story is narrated in the first person by Penelope Taberner Cameron around whom time shifts back and forth between the twentieth and sixteenth centuries. Thus she becomes observer to life and intrigue in the past as Francis Babington plots to rescue Mary, Queen of Scots, via a secret underground passage, from her imprisonment in Wingfield Manor, Derbyshire.

Townsend believes that *Tom's Midnight Garden* by Philippa Pearce (1958) is a masterpiece, stating in 1971 that it was the best book to ever have won the Carnegie Medal up to that time. Not only does it emphasise a garden setting – an image of childhood growth which is popular in children's books – but also uses the device of time shifts to focus on the main action which largely concerns beyond the rooms of the house. Like Bunyan, the author uses the device of dreaming. In this case, while Mrs Bartholomew dreams of her childhood, the grandfather clock strikes thirteen (indicating time that is extraordinary) so the way can open for Tom to find the marvellous garden that is suspended in the past, where he makes his new friend, Hatty, and the adventure unfolds with its many revelations. Pearce's expression flows like a melody with evocative description and detail:

> *They skated on, and the thin, brilliant sun was beginning to set, and Hatty's black shadow flitted along at their right hand, across the dazzle of the ice. Sometimes they skated on the main river; sometimes they skated along the flooded washes. Only the willows along the bank watched them; and the ice hissed with their passage.*

3.7 Power to the Child

Another focus of both twentieth century award winners and classics has been the emphasis on the child: loved and permitted freedom that leads to adventure, exploration, leadership, decision making and achieving.

The Secret Garden by Frances Hodgson Burnett (1911) depicts Edwardian England when the British Empire held sway throughout the world. Brought up in India, always cared for by an Ayah and other native servants who indulged her every whim, nine years-old Mary Lennox enters the story as a disagreeable child in appearance and behaviour. The freedom she claims for herself, the creativity that compassion unlocks within her and her unstoppable spirit make this the classic it has become.

Milly-Molly-Mandy, much loved by young children growing up in the 1930s and 1940s, was another such a character, invented by Joyce Lankester Brisley. Milly-Molly-Mandy was not the loud and horrible child of an increasingly permissive society that Dahl later described (loved by his readers), but far more gentle; loved and guided by her family in a small, idyllic English village of the 1920s. The everydayness of her life, going errands, blackberrying, climbing trees, playing tricks . . . became adventures as she and her friends, Little-Friend-Susan and Billy Blunt explored their neighbourhood. (The books included wonderful maps set out clearly for children to follow). The series retains old fashioned charm about a golden time, when children could play freely and life was safe from molestation.

Little Tim, a small boy in a red jersey, stole many reader's hearts as he showed how to stow away on a steamboat and to survive storms and shipwreck. *Little Tim and the Brave Sea Captain*, (1936), first in a series, was written and illustrated by Edward Ardizzone. Tim is a no-frills hero, straightforward, unassuming, bold, who has fantastic adventures. Oh the thrill – to a young reader- of seeing your role-model-hero-peer standing alone with the captain on the bridge as a ship is sinking! It is thought that Ardizzone's Little Tim series

> *mark for the very young a kind of watershed on the move from infancy to independence . . . The authority, the humour in line and composition, the controlled exuberance of visual fancy and the gentle nudge of adult realism, have never been matched in the sphere of children's picture books.*
>
> Fisher 1986, 59–60.

Enid Blyton was a prolific author who published over six hundred books in her lifetime (1897–1968). She won no awards, however, although she became the first children's author to be published in paperback, was published in several languages other than English and some of her stories were developed for television. The secret of her success may lie in the fact that her stories emphasise freedom of the child, without the constraints of grown-ups.

Children loved Blyton's stories, and they still sell millions of copies annually and are currently published by such publishers as Hodder Children's Books, Egmont Books and Mammoth. For many years from the 1950s on, however, they were disapproved of by librarians and teachers who feared that, by reading Blyton, children would never learn to read the great works of literature. Her writing has been accused of such things as a formulaic writing style, simplicity and superficiality, an attitude of discrimination toward non-middle class characters, racism, sexism, with little to offer a child intellectually or developmentally. Nevertheless, despite the protestations of grown-ups who sought more scholarly, literary writing, children wanted to read about the secret seven, the famous five, about Noddy with his wizard cap, his yellow car and array of friends, including a black gollywog (such as many children cherished among their toys in the days preceding political correctness – PC). It is alleged that Blyton shrugged off attacks and stated that criticism from those over the age of 12 did not really count.

Her adventure series were immensely popular. *The Castle of Adventure* is a typical action packed story of children free to sail off alone for an island adventure filled with mystery, excitement and great food – a dream- 'I wish' world. Books about the Secret Seven Society and their dog, Scamper, are equally adventurous. Some sample chapter headings indicate content: *Secret Seven Meeting; A New Password; What Fun to Belong to a Secret Society; A Surprising Discovery; Underground Happenings.* The final chapter announces resolution, the mystery solved by child-power: 'The jigsaw is Finished'. No-one can 'bamboozle' the Secret Seven.

David Rudd, who has written a scholarly work entitled *Enid Blyton and the Mystery of Children's Literature*, comments

> *I suggest that Blyton's books are loved chiefly because they cele-*
> *brate childhood: being a child and enjoying holidays, food,*
> *adventures, friendships etc. They glory in this space. So they offer*
> *a more emotional, existential satisfaction, which is time out from*
> *the everyday world of growth, of development.*
>
> *Rudd 2003.*

Of recent years 'urchin verse' has become part of the poetry scene, meaning poetry of an easily accessible style that represents the voice and real language of ordinary people, in contrast to the less accessible style appreciated by a more elitist, literature facile audience. Perhaps 'urchin prose' suits Blyton and other popular, simplistic writers who fulfil children's emotional/psychological need for an easy escape from reality through story. The term is not suggested in a derogatory sense to make it divisive, but as recognition of another valid dimension of children's literature. Whatever is said or done, children of the past, now adults, – some of whom are members of the Enid Blyton Society

– as well as children of the present, still cherish the imaginative stories by Blyton that give all power to the child.

3.8 Conclusion

Books that live, whether they are winners, classics, or other works that children love because they 'speak' to them, shape the adult that the child becomes. A simplistic example is that J. K. Rowling who loved *The Little White Horse,* has become a writer of fantasy for children. Many other writers tell how books impressed them as children. C. S. Lewis's autobiographical work, *Surprised by Joy*, relates how his child-hood home had 'endless books': in the study, drawing room, cloakroom, two-deep in a great bookcase on the landing, books in bedrooms, piled high in an attic, books of all kinds and none forbidden. In his first stories, written as a child, he combined 'dressed animals' and 'knights-in-armour' – shades of *Narnia.* He also mentions Nesbit's trilogy, especially loving *The Amulet* (with its time travel, a device he employed in the *Narnia* series. *Gulliver* was another favourite, as were the Beatrix Potter books and Longfellow's poem, *Saga of King Olaf.* To Alison Uttley, fairy tales by Hans Andersen filled her imagination as a child, tales she retold to her friends as they walked home from school. In turns, over and over again, she also devoured the great classics, *Robinson Crusoe, Swiss Family Robinson* and *Nicholas Nickleby.*

A more recent publication, *The Child that Books Built,* (2002) by Francis Spufford, considers his personal journey in literature. Among a number of books that he vividly recalls are Laura Ingalls Wilder's *Long Winter* and Tolkien's *The Hobbit.* Other authors and illustrators whose work he loved from the 1960s-1970s were Joan Aitken, Errol Le Cain, Shirley Hughes, Leon Garfield, Rosemary Sutcliff, Ursula Le Guin and C. S. Lewis *Narnia* series, each of which captures the energy of the period. He especially celebrates *Where the Wild Things Are*, by Maurice Sendak. Spufford's literature experience is linked with family tragedy, and raises provocative questions about *why* an individual selects what genres s/he does.

What adults read aloud to children in their formative years, and which children request for over and over again, will become part of the fabric of their being. Sarah Johnson advises parents to never let a book into the house unless they can bear it a thousand readings aloud later! Picture books she recommends as distance-stayers are by Eric Carle, Beatrix Potter, Jill Murphy, DrSeuss and Laurent de Brunhoff. Of

Judith Kerr's *The Tiger Who Came to Tea*, and Alan Ahlberg's *Burglar Bill,* she speaks with high praise: 'Every line is perfection.' She suggests that Allan and Janet Ahlberg's classic *Peepo!* and *Each Peach, Pear, Plum*, should be under every child's bed.

For older children, Johnson recommends reading a chapter each night from books with much dialogue, such as about Winnie the Pooh, or T. H. White's *The Sword in the Stone,* which introduces King Arthur and the sword, Excalibur, or the classics: *Charlotte's Web,* by E. B. White, *The Wind in the Willows* by Kenneth Graham, some of Arthur Ransome, Tolkien's *The Hobbit*, and C. S. Lewis's Narnia stories.

Of course parents, librarians and teachers will have their own favourites too, which they will want to share, sometimes telling why, thereby sharing ones-self as well as a beloved book. Reading and loving go together to contribute to growing and knowing.

There are numerous sources of information regarding award winners and classics, in critical works, such as by Hunt (2001), or by Thacker and Webb (2002), while journals, literary supplements to newspapers and www. sites will inform and update, and colleagues will collaborate and advise. As a professional who works with books and respects the interests and needs of children, read many of the books for yourself, listen to children's own comments, watch which titles they choose when in the library or note journal accounts of their preferences. This way you will discover facts like the popularity of Irish author Eoin Colfer's Artemis Fowl. A sneaky and deceitful protagonist, but popular with boys aged 9–13 years who enjoy Harry Potter, he ranks in a survey of the 'Top Ten Fiction Titles' in one English school, published in 2003 by Books for Keeps.

3.9 Before Selection

Keep in mind two things:

- You have the privilege of being guardian of the best literature available to children. Winners and Classics are a rightful part of their literary inheritance. Place them where they can be seen. Select a book for a child and you are helping to select the future.
- Remember that children may judge books differently from adults, yet their responses are as valid for them as in-depth, adult critical analysis. They see from a quite different level of development and experience. Number one on a Parent's list for children in 1998 was

Matilda by Roald Dahl. In contrast, children placed the Goosebump series in first place.

- Children get reading fads sometimes and a fixation on one author or genre. Do not become alarmed – but keep on selecting the best and making the library a welcoming place and the classroom book-focused. Have fun!

Children's Sayings

"Pullman's series, *His Dark Materials* is amazing. I couldn't wait to get the second and third books." Vicky, 14 years.

I like books with animal characters and thrilling adventures, especially if they're funny too." Jo, 10 years.

"I agree with Jo about books." Phil 10 years.

"*Look Out for the Elephant* by Enid Blyton is good because I like the bit where this little girl feeds an elephant that escaped from the zoo." Giles, 8 1/2.

"I like *The Treasure Seekers* by E. Nesbit because it is exciting and brilliant.". Kathryn, 8.

"I'm 17 and I've just finished AS level. We studied Margaret Attwood's *Alias Grace* and I found it gripping. I also learnt a lot about the nineteenth century. But, you know, I have great memories of the William books. I still enjoy them!" – David.

Tutorial Topics

1. Discuss the opinion of author/illustrator, Maurice Sendak:

    Children don't give a damn about awards. Why should they? We should let children choose their own books. What they don't like they will toss aside. What disturbs them too much they will not look at. And if they look at the wrong book, it isn't going to do them that much damage. We treat children in a very peculiar way, I think. We don't treat them like the strong creatures they really are.

2. Read and compare two books: the latest award winner of the Carnegie Medal or Guardian prize and the Whitbread Award. What similarities and/or dissimilarities do you identify? What is your overall impression of the work?
3. If you choose to focus on books for young children, read the latest award winners for the Greenaway and Nestle Smarties awards. What features make them special?
4. Read any classic listed for children. Discuss the attributes that commend it for the contemporary child's reading.
5. Discuss: 'Just as a rich dessert is not to grow on and offers empty calories, so may a book that passes time and is then forgotten have its place in the diet of children's reading.'
6. Read and analyse a work by Blyton, Dahl or Rowling.

Further Reading

Hunt, Peter. 'Tread Softly For You Tread On My Dreams: Academicising Arthur Ransome.' In *International Review of Children's Literature and Librarianship*. Vol. 7, No 1, 1992.
—— *Children's Literature*. London: Blackwell Publishers, 2001.
Fisher, Margery. *Classics for Children and Young People*. Stroud: Signal Book Guide; Thimble Press, 1986.
Nikolajeva, M. *Children's Literature Comes of Age*. Toward a New Aesthetic. New York: Garland, 1996.
Rudd, David. *Enid Blyton and the Mystery of Children's Literature*. Palgrave, 2000.
Thacker, Deborah Cogan. and Jean Webb. *Introducing Children's Literature: From Romanticism to Postmodernism*. London: Routledge, 2002.
Watson, Victor. *Reading Series Fiction*. London: RoutledgeFalmer, 2000.

Children's Books Cited

Winners

Books marked * are not winners but are cited in the section.
Adams, Richard. *Watership Down*. Reprint. London: Penguin Books, 1978.
Boston, Lucy. *A Stranger at Green Knowe*. London: Faber, 1961.
*Colfer, Eoin. *Artemis Fowl*. London: Puffin Books, 2002.
Dahl, Roald. *Charlie and the Chocolate Factory*. London: Puffin, 2001
—— *Charlie and the Great Glass Elevator*. London: Puffin, 2001.
—— *The Witches*. London: Puffin, 2001.
—— *Esio Trot*. Illustrated by Quentin Blake. London: Puffin, 2001.

—— *Matilda*. Illustrated by Quentin Blake. Puffin Books, 2001.
Dickinson, Peter. *Tulku*. London: Gollancz, 1979.
—— *City of Gold*. New York: Pantheon Books, 1980.
Doherty, Berlie. *Granny was a Buffer Girl*. London: Methuen, 1986.
—— *Dear Nobody*. London: Hamish Hamilton, 1991.
Fine, Anne. *Goggle Eyes*. London: Hamish Hamilton, 1989.
Foulds, Elfrida Vipont. *The Lark on the Wing*. Oxford: oxford University Press, 1950.
Garfield Leon and Edward Blishen. *The God Beneath the Sea*. London: Longman, 1970.
Goudge, Elizabeth. *The Little White Horse*. London: Puffin, 2001.
Harris, Rosemary Harris. *The Moon in the Cloud*. London: Faber, 1968.
Hunter, Mollie. *The Stronghold*. London: Hamish Hamilton, 1974.
Kemp, Gene. *The Turbulent Term of Tyke Tyler*. London: Faber, 1977.
Lewis, C. S. *The Last Battle*. London: Bodley Head, 1956.
Lively, Penelope. *The Ghost of Thomas Kempe*. London: Heinemann, 1973.
Mahy, Margaret. *The Haunting*. London: Dent, 1982.
—— *The Changeover*. London: Dent, 1984.
McCaughrean, Geraldine. *A Pack of Lie*s. Oxford: Oxford University Press, 1988.
McKay, Hilary. *Saffy's Angel*. London: Hodder Children's Books, 2002.
Naidoo, Beverley. *The Other Side of Truth*. London: Puffin, 2000.
Norton, Mary. *The Borrowers*. Illustrated by Sian Bailey. London: Puffin Modern Classics. Puffin Books, 1993.
Pullman, Philip. *Northern Lights*. London: Scholastic, 1995.
—— *The Subtle Knife*. London: Scholastic, 1998.
—— *The Amber Spyglass*. London: Scholastic, 2000.
Pratchett, Terry. *The Amazing Maurice and His Educated Rodents*. London: Doubleday, 2001.
Pearce, Phillipa. *Tom's Midnight Garden*. Oxford: Oxford University Press, 1958.
Ransome, Arthur. *Pigeon Post*. London: Cape, 1936.
Rees, Celia. *Sorceress*. London: Bloomsbury Children's Books, 2002.
Rowling, J. K. *Harry Potter and the Philosopher's Stone*. London: Bloomsbury, 1997.
—— *Harry Potter and the Chamber of Secrets*. London: Bloomsbury, 1998.
—— *Harry Potter and the Prisoner of Azkaban*. London, Bloomsbury, 1999.
—— *Harry Potter and the Goblet of Fire*. London: Bloomsbury, 2000.
Southall, Ivan. *Josh*. Sydney: Angus and Robertson, 1971.
Sutcliffe, Rosemary. *The Lantern Bearers*. Oxford: Oxford University Press, 1959.

Classics
Books marked * are not classics but are mentioned in this section.
Ahlberg, Janet and Alan. *Burglar Bill*. London: Puffin Books, 1979.

—— *Peepo!* London: Viking Kestrel Board Book, 1997.

—— *Each Peach, Pear, Plum.* London: Viking Kestrel Picture Books, 1999.

Ardizzone, Edward. *Little Tim and the Brave Sea Captain.* London: Scholastic, 2002.

Brisley, Joyce Lankester. *Milly-Molly-Mandy Stories.* Reprint. London: George G. Harrap and Company Ltd., 1937. Also in Young Puffin Read-Alouds. London: Puffin Books, 1992

Bunyan, John. *The Pilgrim's Progress.* New York: Signet, 1964.

*—— *Dangerous Journey.* Hunkin, Oliver, Ed. Reprint. UK: Candle Books/Eerdmans, 1997.

Burnett, Frances Hodgson. *The Secret Garden.* Illustrated by Shirley Hughes. London: Victor Gollancz, 1988.

Blyton, Enid. *Go Ahead Secret Seven.* Leicester: Brockhampton Press, 1953.

—— *The Land of Far Beyond.* Reprint. London: Dragon Books, 1986.

—— *Two Books in One*: The Island of Adventure/The Castle of Adventure. Macmillan Children's Books, 2002.

—— *The New Big Noddy Book.* Bristol: Purnell Books, 1984.

Carroll, Lewis. *Alice's Adventures in Wonderland.* Reissue. London: Puffin Classics, 1994.

—— *Through the Looking Glass.* London: Puffin Classics, 1994.

Defoe, Daniel. *Robinson Crusoe.* John Richetti. Ed. London: Penguin Classics, 2003.

—— *Robinson Crusoe.* D. F. Swan. Ed. London: Longman Picture Classics, 1995.

Grahame, Kenneth. *The Wind in the Willows.* 21st edition. Reprint. London: Methuen, 1972.

Kerr, Judith. *The Tiger Who Came to Tea.* Reprint. Collins Educational. London: 1998.

Kipling, Rudyard. *Puck of Pook's Hill.* Ware: Wordsworth Education Ltd., 1994.

Lewis, C. S. *The Lion, the Witch and the Wardrobe.*

Longfellow, Henry Wadsworth. 'The Saga of King Olaf.' In *Complete Poetical Works of Henry Wadsworth Longfellow.* Amereon Ltd., 2000.

*McCaughrean, Geraldine. *John Bunyan's A Pilgrim's Progress.* London: Hodder Children's Books, 1999.

*Morpurgo, Michael. *Kensuke's Kingdom.* Reading: Heinemann, 1999.

Nesbitt, E. *The Story of the Amulet.* London: Puffin Classics, 1996.

*Parry, Alan and Linda. *Go with Christian.* New Arelsford: Hunt and Thorpe Ltd., 1996.

*—— *The Evergreen Wood.* Reprint. Alresford: Hunt and Thorpe, 1994.

Pearce, Philippa. *Tom's Midnight Garden.* London: Puffin, 1993.

Sendak, Maurice. *Where the Wild Things Are.* Reprint. London: Picture Puffins, 1977.

Stevenson, Robert Louis. *Treasure Island.* London: Ward, Lock and Co. Ltd., 1958.

Swift, Jonathan. *Gulliver's Travels*. London: Penguin Classics, 2003.

Tolkien, J. R. R. *The Hobbit*. 4th edition, reprint, London: Unwin, 1983.

Uttley, Alison. *The Country Child*. London: Puffin, 1984.

—— *A Traveller In Time*. Reprint. London: Faber, 1973.

White, E. B. *Charlotte's Web*. Reprint. London: Puffin Books, 1977.

*White, T. H. *The Sword in the Stone*. Reprint. London: Collins, 1968.

Wyss, Johann. *The Swiss Family Robinson*. Everyman's Library Children's Classics. London: Everyman, 1994.

Bibliography

Boston, Lucy. *Memories: incorporating Perverse and Foolish and Memory In A House*. Cambridge: Colt Books Ltd with Diana Boston, Hemingford Grey, 1992.

Bowler, Tim. 'Honed to Perfection.' In *Carousel*, Issue 22, Autumn-Winter 2002, 38.

Butler, Jan. 'St Martin's Top Ten Fiction Titles.' In *Books for Keeps*, No. 139, March 2003.

Carpenter, Humphrey, and Mari Prichard, eds. *The Oxford Companion to Children's Literature*. Oxford: Oxford University Press, 1984.

Chambers, Aidan. *Booktalk: Occasional Writing on Literature and Children*. London: The Bodley Head, 1985.

'Children's Authors More Popular than Ever in Libraries.' *Stockton-on-Tees: Registrar of Public Lending Right*, 2000.

Chute, Marchette. *The Children's Book of Poems, Prayers and Meditations*. London: HarperCollins, 1998.

Cook, Elizabeth. *The Ordinary and the Fabulous: an Introduction to Myths, Legends and Fairy tales for Teachers and Storytellers*. London: Cambridge University Press, 1969, 2.

Colmer, Robert G., ed. *Bunyan in Our Time*. Kent, Ohio: The Kent State University Press, 1989.

Demers, Patricia. *Heaven Upon Earth: The Form of Moral and Religious Children's Literature to 1850*. Knoxville: The University of Tennessee Press, 1993.

'Does it matter what they read?' *BBC Bookworm and Waterstone's Poll*, Parents' List. Children's List: Best-sellers at School Book Fairs, fo 1997.

Dunmore, Helen. 'I Thought I'd Start with Something Easy . . .' in *Books for Keeps*, No. 124, September 2000, 13.

Duriez, Colin. *The C. S. Lewis Handbook*. Eastbourne: Monarch, 1990, 81.

Eccleshare, Julia. *A Guide to the Harry Potter Novels*. London: Continuum, 2002.

Field, E. M. *The Child and His Book: Some Accounts of the History and Progress of Children's Literature*. London: Wells Gardner, Darton and Cp., 1892.

Fisher, Margery. *Classics for Children and Young People*. Reprint. Stroud: Thimble Press, 1988.

Gray, Keith. 'The Fact and Fiction of Philip Ardagh.' In *Carousel*, Issue 22, Autumn-Winter 2002, 24.

Harris, Rosemary. 'The Moon in the Cloud.' In *The Junior Bookshelf,* August 1969, 224.

Haviland, Virginia. *Children and Literature: Views and Reviews*. London: The Bodley Head, 1973.

Heins, Paul, ed. 'Out on a Limb with the Critics.' In *Crosscurrents of Criticism: Horn Book Essays* 1968–77. Paul Heins, ed. Boston: Horn Book, 1977.

Hunt, Peter. *Children's Literature: an Illustrated History*. Oxford: Oxford University Press, 1995, 304.

Johnson, Sarah. 'Books you may be forced to read 1,000 times.' London: *The Times*, November 2, 2000, News 13.

Lewis, C. S. *Surprised by Joy*. 18th Impression London: Collins, 1978.

Locherbie-Cameron, M. A. L. 'Journeys through the Amulet: Time-travel in Children's Fiction.' In *Signal* 79. January 1996.

MacDonald, Ruth, K. *Christian's Children. The Influence of John Bunyan's Pilgrim's Progress on American Children's Literature*. New York: Peter lang, 1989.

—— 'The Case for The Pilgrim's Progress.' In *CLAQ*, 10/1, 1985, 29–30.

Nettel, S. 'The Guardian Award.' In *Books for Keeps*, No. 62, May 1990, 31.

Meek, Margaret. Adults Reading Books. In *Books for Keeps*, No. 125, November 2000, 10–12.

Nettel, S. 'The Guardian Award.' *In Books for Keeps*, No. 62, May 1990, 31.

Norton, Donna E. *Through the Eyes of a Child*. 3rd edition. New York: Macmillan, 1991. 308.

Page, Benedicte. 'Finding Out What Children Think.' In *The Bookseller,* 15 December, 2000, 29.

Paterson, Katherine. *Gates of Excellence: On Reading and Writing Books for Children*. New York: Elsevier/Nelson Books, 1981.

Pullman, Philip. *The Amber Spyglass*. London: David Fickling Books/ Scholastic, 2000, 549.

Rudd, David. From a personal letter to Mary Trim, February 28, 2003.

Spufford, Francis. *The Child that Books Built*. London: Faber and Faber, 2002.

Tibbutt, H. G. *What They Said About John Bunyan*. Bedford: Bedfordshire County Council, 1981.

Townsend, John Rowe. *Written for Children*. 5th edition, London: Bodley Head, 1990.

Trim, Mary. *A Changing Hero: The Relevance of Bunyan's Pilgrim and The Pilgrim's Progress Through Three Centuries of Children's Literature*. An unpublished PHD thesis. Loughborough University, 1998.

Walsh, Jill Paton. 'I Thought I'd Start with Something Easy . . . In *Books for Keeps*, No. 124, September 2000, 13.

Zipes, J. *Storytelling. Building Community. Changing Lives*. New York: Routledge, 1995, 6.

CHAPTER FIVE

The Exploring Child

I like books that have interesting facts and information your teacher never tells you.

Genni, 12 years

1. Information Books

Implicit in the United Nations Declaration of the Rights of the Child is the right to know and understand. This experience comes through all types of literature but a knowledge of facts relates particularly to the information genre.

Information Books, as Norton suggests, contribute a number of values to a child's development:

(i) to answer a child's curiosity and to inform;

(ii) to impart knowledge about the world;

(iii) to supplement on timely subjects aired on television, radio or via newspapers;

(iv) to introduce the child to the scientific method which shows how scientists reach conclusions, using observation, comparison, formulation and testing of hypotheses.

(v) Information books encourage critical reading and thinking skills;

(vi) they encourage self-reliance yet creativity also.

Once children, like Genni, have discovered the mine of information that is stored in information books, they seek them out on library shelves for themselves and *enjoy* what they discover.

1.1 Topics

Children will find material if it is *organised* efficiently. Librarians are trained in this skill, but some mothers and teachers are not, and they may want to do a little organising of books at home, or to encourage the child to organise his/her books. Tidy shelves and tidy minds often go together! Some possible topic areas and titles which interest children are:

(i) Animals and Nature

For example:
Great Apes by Claire Llewellyn
Fossil Fish Found Alive by Sally M. Walker
The Wayland Book of Common British Trees by Theresa Greenaway
Journey Into the Desert by John Brown (photographer)

(ii) Reference Material

Oxford First Dictionary	For the beginner reader and writer.
Oxford First Thesaurus	Bright illustrations; a complete page and sentence example for each definition
Oxford Student's Dictionary	For the secondary school student
My Very First Oxford Atlas	Intended for 4–7 year olds
DK Children's Picture Encyclopaedia.	This is a reference book for young children

(iii) Other popular topics include:

Science, as with, Our Solar System by Jon Kirkwood
Countries and People of the World for example, *Vietnam; The Usborne Book of Peoples of the World: Internet -linked*
Racism as in *Racism* by Jen Green in the *What do we think about . . .* series.
Cars and Trucks: *Ben's Big Book of Cars: Big Trucks,* by Ben Blathwayt
Vegetarianism: *Why are People Vegetarian?* by A. Brownlie
The list of topics can obviously go on and on, but what the librarian or teacher selects and promotes will depend on current project emphases in schools, timely events in society, or interests expressed by students who 'want to know.'

1. 2 Chronological Method

A *chronological method* of time periods categorises them as books about Yesterday, Today and Tomorrow, for young children to Key Stage 1–2. By centuries for older children: upper Key Stage 2, 3, 4.
   Examples: titles indicating content:

(i) Yesterday

The Young Oxford History of Britain and Ireland, by Mike Corbishly et al
Kitchens through the Ages, by Richard Wood
The Great Depression, by Marion Yass
All About the Second World War, by Pam Robson

(ii) Today

Computers Unlimited, by Lisa Hughes
Hidden Under the Ground, by Peter Kent. This book does exactly what the title suggests, dealing with the out of sight lives of cave dwellers, underground creatures, ancient tomb makers, minerals, tunnels and the development off mechanical digging/excavating machinery.

(iii) Tomorrow

Lasers Now and in the Future, by Steve Parker
Designer Genes, by Phil Gates
Eyewitness Guides: Future, by Michael Tambini

1.3 Narrative Type

Margaret Mallett points out that children's books tend to be organised under topic headings but can also be effectively communicated through *narrative*. She suggests such categories of (i) life cycles (ii) journeys and (iii) historical stories. She also sets journals, biography and autobiography in a time sequence. Her examples of Information books of the *Life Cycle* topic area, told as stories for children to about 7–8 years, come in the series, *Animal Lives*, and include *The Otter* by Sandy Ransford, and *The Barn Owl, b*y Sally Tagholm. For *Journeys,* try *Walk with a Wolf* by Janni Howker, about the journey of wolves to the wild, far north.

1.4 Evaluating and Selecting Information Books

Some pertinent questions can be asked when evaluating books in the information genre:

- *Are the facts and illustrations accurate, up-to-date, and distinguished from theory or speculation?*
- *Are stereotypes eliminated?*
- *Are different points of view presented in controversial subjects?*
- *Is the writing style interesting and suit its target audience?*
- *Are children challenged to become analytically involved in some way, conducting their own research, experimenting or collecting and reporting their own data?*

2. Biographies

Autobiographies and biographies for children are published in less numbers than works of fiction. Yet true stories can be inspirational, especially if written well and depict great lives, such as those of explorers, scientists, sporting heroes, or children who have suffered and lived through tumultuous times and experiences. They go beyond inspiring a child to determinedly seek a goal; they depict real life and underline the possible strength and endurance of the human spirit, as seen in Anne Frank's diary.

Some recent publications are examples of the range of biographic material available. Scientists feature in the Hodder Wayland series, *Scientists Who Made History.* Small volumes of about 48 pages tell the lives of 'greats', such people as Marie Curie, Edison, Galileo, Einstein and Darwin, whose research and discoveries contribute to the comfort of contemporary life and to extending understanding of humankind's life on Planet Earth. Others concern John Logie Baird, the Scot who pioneered television, fibre optics, radar and developed video recording; the multi-gifted Italian, Leonardo da Vinci, painter, sculptor, architect, engineer and scientist; Michael Faraday, notable English chemist and physicist, and Guglielmo Marconi, Italian electrical engineer, a pioneer in the invention of radio.

These characters come alive for child readers because the authors highlight interests and relationships in childhood. For instance they can discover that, when just a boy, Baird installed a hydroelectric plant in the kitchen sink waste pipe of his manse home, thus providing electric light; that Marconi's father did not like his young son's interest in science, and it was his mother who encouraged him the Faraday, son of a blacksmith, started work as a bookbinder at a young age but, fascinated by electromagnetism, went on to discover the induction of electric currents and made the first dynamo, subsequently exploring the magnetic field further and also electrolysis. Young da Vinci could sing well as a child, but he developed his other talents, for which the world remembers him, when the family moved to Florence.

Women scientists are recognised in two other booklets: Rosalind Franklin who did foundation work on the structure of DNA, and Dian Fossey whose observation and study of mountain gorillas illuminates the family structure, language and habits of what are believed to be humankind's closest primate relatives. It also affirmed the need to protect their environment and that of other threatened wildlife, thus allying with the Green movement.

Former Spice Girl, Victoria Beckham, 'Posh Spice', is the subject of *Learning to Fly*. The story of her shyness, of bullying in her childhood, her belief in herself that one day she would 'fly' – not in the sky but on the stage and in public life – and the difficulties she had to get there, must warm the hearts of 'Posh' fans and young 'wannabes.' It certainly did for one Year 9 girl, who wrote,

> *I would recommend this book to people aged 11+ because this was an enjoyable book to read – it gave me dreams, tears and edge of the seat tension.*
>
> Samantha, 2002, 20.

I Have Lived a Thousand Years. an autobiographic story by Livia Bitton-Jackson opens the way for discussion of the consequences of dictatorship and inhuman behaviour toward political, social and other minorities. Ten years old Ellike escapes being a victim of one of the four gas chambers that each could exterminate 6,000 people; she survives the terror and evil of the notorious Nazi concentration camp at Auschwitz during World War II. Hers is a story that demonstrates courage and the will to live.

For twelve years old Teddi, suffering from brain cancer, *Camp Good Days*, is a special, happy place, an oasis springing with love. This true story is told in *For the Love of Teddi* ... by Lou Buttino. It shows another dimension of human interaction, that of caring and compassion.

2.1 *True letters*

are a type of autobiographical writing. They can certainly bring real lives into focus as is shown in *Dear Daniel: Letters from Antarctica*. At the time of writing, Daniel is the nine-year-old godson of travel writer Sara Wheeler who writes him letters during her summer in Antarctica. With diagrams, maps and illustrated fact boxes, it gives fascinating factual information but, beyond the learning involved, shows how people stretch themselves to respond to challenge and adventure, in this case in the ice-covered continent surrounding the South Pole where, for least one night during the southern summer, the sun never sets.

Letters are also the basis of *Letters to Henrietta*. The author, Neil Marshall, is a family relative who used the Jefferson family diary of 1850–1950 to depict a family living through those years. Letters that Henrietta wrote to, and received from, her brothers who fought in the First World War are a convincing way of telling what people experienced and how they felt in grim times and places.

3. Series Publishing

The Series type of publishing, which fits schools' need to record measurable results in reading, as is required by the National Literacy programme in Britain, has become an integral part of publishing in the twenty-first century. The librarian should be familiar with the popular characters of both Information and fictional series and be prepared to promote the works or direct young readers to the books' location on the shelves. The teacher should be equally familiar, or moreso, with what is available for various stages of development in the Key Stages of reading,[1] even if not totally depending on the series option.

---

[1] See Introduction

3.1 Informational Picture Books (Series)

Many books which emphasise concepts come in abundance for babies and pre-schoolers, such as in the Ladybird series, *First Discovery*. Suited to Key Stage 1 at about 4–6 years are the *Max-Fax* series and *The Past in Pictures* (Hodder Wayland). For the developing reader and Middle Years child approaching or at Key Stage 2, there are the informative activity books, such as *Festivals* in the *Copy and Cut'* series from publishers A. and C. Black. Hodder Wayland offer excellent factual material, often with superb photographs, in their series, *The Age of Castles.* and *What do we think about . . .,* which deals with issues such as Adoption, Alcohol, Bullying, Racism, Hospitalisation, Death and Disability, while Happy Cat's 'Talking it Through series' offers information on such topics as food and allergies, asthma and hearing difficulties.

Serious informational series such as *Future Tech* (Belitha Press), *Talking Point* (Scholastic), *Eyewitness Guides* (Dorling Kindersley) and *Activators* (Hodder) are designed for 10 years plus, established readers. *World Organisations* looks at important international organisations for 14 years plus readers at Key Stages 3- 4. Similarly, Hodder Wayland's series, *Lives in crisis* explains such crisis experiences as *The Great Depression.*

3.2 Fiction with the same characters throughout (Series)

Examples of this category are the *Animal Ark* series by Lucy Daniels, the 'Meg and Mog' books by Helen Nicoll and Jan Pienkowski and the *Julian Stories* by Ann Cameron. At Key Stage 2, the child may soon discover for him/herself Enid Blyton's 'Famous Five' and other characters of her 'Secret Seven' with their many adventures which, despite all adult criticism in the past regarding racism and stereotypical characters, won children's popularity stakes and continue to do so. The *Swallows and Amazons* series, written by Arthur Ransome were also past favourites, while J. K. Rowling's *Harry Potter* series dominates fictional series in the years beyond 2000. With stories about the same characters, the child grows to know them like special friends and to enjoy, act out and predict their antics, as well as becoming familiar and comfortable with the author's writing style, all of which can give reassurance to the emerging reader. As Judith Graham and Alison Kelly point out:

The child knows what to expect; it is easier to enter a 'secondary world' when you've been there before. This idea of a 'secondary world comes from Tolkien (1964) who explains that readers are 'sub-creators' who suspend disbelief as they read.

Graham and Kelly 2000, 32.

3.3 Similar in Appearance (Series)

Books are of about the same length but may be written by different authors and are 'real books.' For the nursery child there is the 'I Can Read' series which includes long-time favourites like *Little Bear's Visit* of the *Little Bear* books, written by Else Minarik and illustrated by Maurice Sendak. Newly fluent readers can enjoy books in the progressive series that ranges from Banana level to Superchamp (Heinemann) by such acclaimed authors as Jacqueline Wilson, Dick King-Smith and Penelope Lively. For other young readers, Puffin offers three kinds of bridging books, including the 'Happy Families' series in which author Allan Ahlberg excels. Other series are marketed as 'Roaring Good Reads' (Collins), 'Jets' (Harper Collins), 'Take Part' series (Ward Lock) 'The Babysitters' Club' (Hippo/Scholastic) and 'Spirals' (Stanley Thornes).

   Popular with Key Stages 2 and 3 are the 'Point Horror' series and 'Point crime'. *The Beat: Losers* by David Belbin is an example in the Point Crime series, an example of the easy reading style that is typical of this genre: just straight narrative about real life – a scratch card win, a seedy Nottingham estate, love and dreams, poverty, covetousness, deception, conflict and the challenge to police and and to young people themselves in this environment. Absent are any lyrical, literary passages, alliteration, simile, metaphor, flashback; it is just a story in chronological order, yet even that has value, as many readers' addiction testifies.

4. The 'Horribles' series and Their Kin

The Horribles series (Scholastic) are frequently devoured by established readers of Key Stage 2. These are in the Informational genre, told and illustrated in an innovative way – a mix of fact, colloquialisms, humour and elements designed to grab the reader's interest and attention – so that they stand up very nicely, thank you, alongside fiction series. Eleven years-old Elisabeth has her bookcase packed with many of her favourites. She owns many of the *Horrible Histories*, with such tantalising titles as *Rowdy Revolutions, The Terrible Tudors, The Awesome Egyptians, The Blitzed Brits, The Angry Aztecs, The Groovy Greeks, The Measley Middle Ages, The Cut-Throat Celts, The Woeful Second World War, The Balmy British Empire* and *The Incredible Incas,* all written by Terry Deary. Alongside these are a collection of *Horrible Science books*: *Bulging Brains,* with a colourful cover illustration to match the title, shows signs of wear and possible circulation among friends. Pushed against these are a selection from the *Dead Famous series: Cleopatra and her Asp, Mary Queen of Scots and her Hopeless Husbands, Oliver Cromwell and his Warts.* It is no wonder that Elisabeth talks confidently about famous people from history, as if she knows them well. As a Key Stage 2 reader she is a typical female enthusiast of Series.[2]

Middle Years readers, of about Key Stage 2 who contributed their book reviews to this text, enjoy the Knowledge series, for example, *Triffic Chocolate* and *Awesome Archaeology*, plus the Horrible *Geography* and *Murderous Maths* series. Except for brightly coloured covers, these books are in black and white, but they have humorous illustrations breaking up text; they have the magnetism of the cheeky comic book yet the authority of the academic. They clearly appeal to their audience because, given the opportunity to write a book report on any book of their choice read recently, some nine and ten year olds chose to write about titles that reflect the Horribles: *Blood, Bones and Body Bits, Stormy Weather, Deadly Diseases* and *Disgusting Digestion* are, all of which they strongly approved, not just for the blood and gore but for the knowledge they could boast afterwards.

5. Crossovers

The world-wide popularity of J. K. Rowling's *Harry Potter* sequence, J. R. R. Tolkien's *Lord of the Rings* and Philip Pullman's *series, His Dark Materials* among both children and adult readers, indicates the place of the 'crossover' type of book in the fiction market – the 'crossover' label being a recent term to designate books that do not belong exclusively to either juvenile, young adult or adult market They

---

[2] The NCRCL study, Young people's Reading at the End of the Century, identifies that series books are more favoured by KS2 girls.

are sometime published with covers exclusive to each group but are books which all can enjoy, such as Antoine de Saint-Exupery's classic, *The Little Prince,* appealed in the past. Of course young people have always read adult novels, some children with a high reading age starting to do so at ten years of age, just getting on with growing and knowing without any fuss. On the other hand, many adults read children's books for pleasure, but the Crossover is not written with a narrative style or topic that specifically suits one age group. Its imagination, narrative skill and theme will suit any able reader.

Published as an adult book, yet intended for any reader over the age of twelve, *Across the Nightingale Floor* by Lian Hearn is considered of the crossover type by its publishers, Macmillan. Certainly it can be enjoyed by a wide age range as it uses the theme of youth growing to maturity in an epic adventure, passing through scenes of sex and horrific violence. The protagonists are Takeo and Kaede, Japanese young people in medieval Japan who fall in love in the Romeo and Juliet mode, whose story is told by Takeo in the first person, while Kaede's is narrated in the third person.

Another recent example of work that suits the crossover market is the trilogy by Joan O'Neill, firstly *Daisy Chain War*, followed by *Bread and Sugar*, then by *Daisy Chain Dream,* much acclaimed in Ireland where it was first published. This affirmation of family life as it overcomes adversity is a story one can warm to as time, place and characterisation resonate with life,even in its bleak moments such as when pregnant Biddy is confined to the Magdalen Convent and must work in the convent laundry.

Another crossover novel is a graceful retelling of a traditional story: *Beauty: A Retelling of the Story of Beauty and the Beast.* by Robin McKinley. Its theme of the transforming power of love, resonates throughout literature and cannot help and holds timeless appeal, for, as Maslow theorised, love is a basic need for personality balance and fulfilment.

6. Book Mates: Encouraging Boys to Read

Look up 'Dads and Lads' or "Lads and Dads' on the Internet and you will discover many references. Some are focused largely on physical activities, as conducted by the YMCA, while libraries also include activities but especially encourage fathers and their sons to enjoy books together. This is in recognition of the fact that males lag behind females in reading interest and skill; that girls outperform boys at every age, up to and including the British GCSEs.

6.1 Reasons

Reasons why many boys do not read well and do not like to read, according to an ERIC report, written by Wendy Schwartz, is accounted for by several reasons: biological and cognitive aspects, ineffective teaching strategies and materials, lack of motivation, and family life that does not include reading models and participation. According to studies by Simpson (1996) and Smith and Wilhelm (2002), boys value reading less than girls, regard it as merely a way to retrieve information but not as pleasurable recreation. In England, the 1995 reading survey, *Young People Reading at the End of the Century,* conducted by the National Centre for Research in Children's Literature, (NCRCL) found a similar response by males, particularly after age 11. By Key Stages 3 and 4, a divergence in male/female interest in information books appears, showing that more boys than girls read widely in this genre.

6.2 Responses

In recognition of a challenging need, the Hampshire Country Library, UK in conjunction with the School Library Service and the Public Library Service, has been successful in implementing recreational reading programmes which achieve the interest of 'dads 'n lads'. Moreover, the Hampshire report reading reports offer illuminating comments about the books and authors that males enjoy. The most popular individual title, according to librarian Anne Marley's report on a reading group of about 10 pairs of fathers and sons, is *Adrian Mole: the Wilderness Years*, by Sue Townsend, fourth in the humorous yet touchingly real Adrian Mole series about males growing to and attaining manhood. It is interesting to note that the most popular author is Bill Bryson, travel writer.

   Other reports from different locations in Britain indicate that author Anthony Horowitz is eminently popular with his *Diamond Brothers Mysteries*, also with *South by South East:* a Diamond Brothers trilogy, and the *Stormbreaker* series which features the reluctant teenage superstar, Alex Rider. Likewise, Terry Pratchett gets the thumbs-up for fantasy with such works as *Johnny and the Dead* and *The Colour of Magic,* and Philip Pullman for *Northern Lights,* as does Terry Deary with his imaginative *Horrible Histories: Dark Knight and Dingy Castles* and *Savage Stoneage.,* Other favourites were Paul Jennings' *Unmentionable,* humorous and odd stories about boys' experiences, Robert Swindell's 1993 Carnegie Award winner, *Stone Cold,* which concerns the plight of homeless teenagers, and Frederick Forsyth's *No Comeback,* ten stories of deception, blackmail, revenge and murder. Stories that feature football, as by Neil Arksey, and the ten science fiction/fantasy *Wheel of Time* series, by Robert Jordan, were also popular, as was Gary Paulsen's *Hatchet,* about a teenage hero who struggles to stay alive when alone in the Canadian wilderness. Books that make 'library lads' laugh out loud are frequently mentioned, as with Michael Lawrence's, *The Poltergoose.* On the serious side, Nelson Mandela's biography of many pages is commended, as is Bryson's tongue-in-cheek Notes *from a Small Island.*

Teenage boys also recommended some titles shortlisted for the 2003 Carnegie Award, books which contain aspects found in the previous books listed. For example, *Martyn Pig,* by Kevin Brooks, is a murder mystery, yet with bizarre humour, unfolding with surprising twists, turns and moral ambiguity. Its cover is certainly designed to catch a young man's eye with its depiction of a black-coated teenager sprawled on the pavement. Boys largely commented on *Martyn Pig's* exciting nature. while reviews by girls – shown on the Carnegie Internet site – indicate that girls, in contrast, notice *characterisation,* such as Martyn's troubled nature,and *relationships,* as in Martyn's paucity of friends, a drunken father and no mother.

6.3 *A pattern of preference*

emerges through these selections. Teenage boys are interested in books that concern (i) Books about other male teenagers growing up (ii) Mysteries (iii) Spy stories (iv) Fantasy (v) Weird and funny tales (vi) Books that are exciting, often with a dark, cruel, sinister element. (vi) Humour. (vii) They will even tackle biography when the character is a male hero. Again these findings agree with the 1995 NCRCL findings in their far greater sampling,[3] which points out the importance of humour and horror to male teenage readers.

---

[3] Their report covers 4172 Key Stage 3: pupils aged between 11 and 14 years; 1819 Key Stage 4 pupils aged between 14 and 16 years.

Given that many boys are reluctant readers, any scheme that encourages males to bond together in friendship and the common interest of books they prefer, must achieve positive results, as the Hampshire sample, though not a large one, indicates. Any home environment where books abound, where they are used and accepted by the family as important components of everyday life, often referred to by parents and children, sets up for young people an ongoing *immersion* in literature, a principle of growth in literacy advocated by Cambourne and Turbill.[4] The success of the 'Dads 'n' Lads 'type programmes even motivates teenage male readers to happily participate in Teenage Book Festivals.

6.4 Further Observations

(i) The Hampshire reports are anecdotal rather than empirical, as they do not set out to be a scientific study or questionnaire based, as by the NCRCL, yet they offer some interesting data. The groups began from the premise of offering reading opportunities of teen males and their fathers together.

(ii) All the books referred to in the Hampshire study and ongoing reviews demand reading competency, so this was not a group of dyslexics or readers with a low reading age, although some books, were recommended by publishers for younger readers, as with *The Poltergoose*, while Horrible Histories are usually read by Key Stage 2 students.

(iii) Except for Sue Townsend, all the authors are male, writing about topics that interest male teenagers.

(iv) Some 'lads' appeared to prefer books they could 'pick up and put down' easily, that were easy to get into, and they often select short stories.

(v) Imaginative tales still appeal to teenage males.

(vi) The library scene and librarian host must have influenced, to some extent, the books subsequently chosen and enjoyed.

6.5

David Almond, author of the Whitbread Award winning *Skellig*, addresses the issue of 'Writing for boys'? when commenting on his

---

[4] See Section 1, Chapter 1.

Illustration 6: Book Mates: Father and son enjoy books together (Black and white photo, by Len Eastwood).

work, *Kit's Wilderness*. Popular with male readers, it concerns danger, threats of violence, ghosts, a demonic lead character, the Game of Death and powers of darkness. The author says,

> *It is a book, I suppose, that may appeal particularly to boys ... deals with the problems that boys face in places like the wilderness where the old industries have died.*

Knowing that boys and girls read his books, because he receives letters from both groups, he then addresses the issue of writing addressed directly to males:

> *But it isn't a book written for boys, and I must admit that I'm rather sceptical about over-deliberate, over-formulaic attempts to entice boy readers.*
>
> Almond, 1999, 29.

On the other hand, Robert Swindells' hard-hitting novels which usually carry a message, focus on teenagers and on males in particular, their challenges and conflicts they will meet in contemporary society – post nuclear bomb threat, child abuse, exploitation, right wing political groups, homelessness – but his work cannot be categorised as 'over-formulaic.' As well as *Stone Cold's* appeal to male teenagers, it seems that Swindells' *Dosh* and other titles hold their interest similarly.

Teenage males do not want to be 'messed about with'; they really do want to know and understand, and books that meet their need and interest do have a following, especially when it is attached to male bonding. *The Reading Champions* nationwide scheme which aims to find positive male models for reading may help.

Special Situations

7. The Dyslexic Reader

The dyslexic reader has special needs to be met and understood. Professionals know that there are two true types of dyslexia, according to American studies. The first of these is *Biologically Determined Dyslexia,* according to Harris and Hodges (1981). The second type is *Acquired Dyslexia* which causes difficulty in reading as the after-effect of a brain injury. Estimates of the prevalence of the biological form range from 20% of the population, according to Shaywitz (1996), down to 1%, with most estimates not rising above 5% of the population, according to Hynd and Hynd (1984).

In Britain, the first official recognition of the condition in education came in the Code of Practice (DfE 1994) and is understood *broadly,* often coming within the term 'Specific Learning Difficulty', with precise problems pinpointed. Gavin Reid's definition is an accepted one:

> *patterns of difficulties relating to the processing of information within a continuum from very mild to extremely severe which result in restrictions in literacy development and discrepancies in performances within the curriculum.*
>
> Reid, 1998, 2

There are, of course, specific diagnostic assessments, but the librarian and teacher will not be involved in administering these. Studies such as that of Vellutino *et al* (1996) show that when given intensive tutoring and encouragement, children can develop interest in reading and overcome their difficulties. The librarian and teacher's role is to select and promote books that will encourage dyslexic children to read and also to enable them to find on the shelves the books they want to read.

7.1 Encouragement to dyslexics

can come through how. when and where a book is displayed. A book's format is also important, including the following characteristics: an eye-catching cover and title, a chronological sequence of events, clarity of meaning and writing style without convoluted sentences, vocabulary that is within the dyslexic reader's range of decoding or prediction, and especially action by the protagonists, not off-putting long descriptive paragraphs. Many teachers observe the popularity of the Harry Potter series with dyslexic – how they almost gobble them up – and with other reluctant readers. This is because J. K. Rowling's work uses this formula so that each chapter offers active progression of the plot. As Julia Eccleshare says:

> *The Harry Potter books are accessible stories which cross all divides: They are neither too literary nor too popular, too difficult nor too easy, neither too young nor too old. Rowling's clear and predictable structured prose style is particularly praised by those working with dyslexic readers who can read and enjoy these seemingly difficult books.*
>
> *Eccleshare, 2002, 106*

Any children with reading difficulties can enjoy rhyming texts because they are easily memorised, also the humour of such author/illustrators as the Ahlbergs and Quentin Blake; also familiar traditional tales, and the secrets hidden in picture books by Anthony Browne and Pat Hutchins. Picture books need not be restricted to young children. Along with individual encouragement and tuition, however, it is important that books for dyslexic readers are not 'misaligned'[5] with the reader's interest and age, or other contributing factors such as class and culture. For lists of stories about dyslexic child heroes, the Book Trust provides appropriate bibliography, which can also inform and inspire general readers. Some examples of suggested titles are *Skulduggery: A*

[5] Margaret Meek's term in reference to books and the struggling reader (1991).

Detective Story by Anne Adeney, an adventure with mystery and much humour. Another dyslexic hero is Brian, whose nickname is Brain, a star at football, told in *Football Daft* by Rob Childs. It is interesting to note that all the central characters appear to be males in the Book Trust selection of seventeen books, which reflects the preponderance of male dyslexics in society.

Information books can not only meet the needs of dyslexic children but also explain what dyslexia is to others. In an example, *Dyslexia*, Althea writes about the experiences of six children, one of the *Talking it Through series*. Well researched and vetted by dyslexic pupils, their parents and teachers, it begins, 'We have dyslexia. We want you to know what it is like.' For Key Stages 3 and 4, *Dyslexia* is an informational book in the *Health Issues* series. Not only does it consider myths about the condition, explain its complexity and report on research, but it also suggests that among other 'greats', the writers, Hans Andersen and Agatha Christie, may have been dyslexic.

8. Books for the Visually Impaired

Like the reluctant reader and dyslexic, visually impaired children have special biologically induced needs that should be met to enable them to experience and reap the benefits of literature. Over half of all visually impaired children are in mainstream schools in Britain and every librarian and teacher who is involved recognises the value of auditory story tapes/discs and the assistance of one-to-one aides when necessary.

The Feel Happy project, run by Living Paintings Trust, a registered charity, offers a support scheme: a free postal library. Their catalogue, for example, includes popular picture books for young children, such as John Burningham's *Mr Gumpy's Motor Car* or the *Little Kipper stories*. On a three month loan, for home or school use, they come in Touch and Sound packs which include a book, supplemented with additional pages that the child can feel to 'meet' the characters through bright, raised images. They include Braille text and a cassette which describes the illustrations; resources for older children link with the National Curriculum. A story for general readers, is Tangerine, by Edward Bloor. Set in Florida, it tells of Paul, a legally blind seventh-grader and the competitiveness between him and his vicious and amoral brother, both football heroes. At his first school Paul is labelled 'handicapped' so at his second school he keeps his legally blind status a secret and is able to play the soccer he loves and grow in self esteem.

9. Books for the Disabled

Fiction which has a disabled central character can be pleasurable reading as well as informative and inspirational to a general audience, as well as to those with similar afflictions. Jessy, of *Best Friends* who has Down's Syndrome, shows she is just like any other child and can feel anger and jealousy, especially when her sister brings her special friend home for tea ... Ben of the exciting *Blue Bottle Mystery* has Asperger's Syndrome; Joey, in *Joey Pigza Swallowed the Key,* has Attention Deficit Hyperactivity Disorder (ADHD), and what a pain he can be, as he recognises himself, thinking that perhaps his brain is full of bees in this funny and exciting story, told in the first person with good effect. *Joey Pigza* ... won the Children's Books category of the American Nasen Special Educational Needs Awards in 2001. Another special, illuminating book, reminiscent of *Annie's Coming Out* is *Me and My Electric*, scribed for several wheelchair users who could not write, or barely speak which shares these disabled young people's interests and dreams.

10. Reflections of Society

> *Children's literature, utopian or Arcadian by definition, has come to its own antithesis. Basically, there are no restrictions any longer to what subjects can be treated in children's literature; the question is how they are treated.*
>
> Maria Nikolajeva, 1998, 223.

Literature always mirrors the society of its day. It is therefore no surprise to find topics like child abuse, sex, drug addiction, food denial, variant forms of sexuality and the dysfunctional family all in the settings of today's children's literature, often with uneasy disclosures and endings, although conventional plot closures were traditionally affirmative and safe.

10.1 Dysfunctional Families

Dysfunctional implies a malfunction and this term applies to the family unit when it is operating in an imbalanced way. There are various possible causes of the imbalance, such as parental or siblings' diminished health, economic deprivation, parental low intelligence or lack of education, parental selfishness, poor self control or ugly tempers and societal pressure. The three award winning books, *Matilda, Junk* and *Skellig,* demonstrate different dimensions and ways of portraying dysfunction. The storytellers may not have consciously intended them to be read in this light, but the elements are identifiable. On the other hand, Jacqueline Wilson makes her focus very evident in The *Suitcase Kid* as she writes lightly yet sensitively of the story of ten years old Andy who is caught in the middle of family breakdown. With a similar skill *The Ogre Downstairs*, by Diana Wynne Jones, portrays a step family disturbed by a new step-father. It takes some magic to bring the assurance of ultimate healing that every child in a dysfunctional family needs.

Matilda, by Roald Dahl, deconstructs in a colourful and over-the-top way the concept of harmonious relationships in the family. In his own inimitable style – distasteful to some adults – he presents a succession of repulsive characters who are eventually defeated by the exceptionally gifted Matilda, child of the misguided ineffective parents, Mr and Mrs Wormwood. At school she suffers at the hands of her sadistic headmistress, Miss Trunchbull, but is befriended by Miss Honey who is, herself, a victim of adult injustice. Dahl's biographer, reports that

> *no book of Dahl's ever sold so fast. In Britain alone, half a million copies went across the counter within six months.*
>
> Treglown, 1994, 245

The key to *Matilda*'s popularity is perhaps the all-powerful child at the heart of this story, one who can overcome and survive the nastiness of environment and adults. Assurance of survival, and the taste of humour and honey, sweeten the mammoth dose of dysfunction.

It is fascinating to observe J. K. Rowling's similarities with Dahl and the romping- away success of her Harry Potter books. For Potter, Hogwarts School replaces his immediate dysfunctional family with the Dursleys, although even there all is not calm, and he and his friends form their own nuclear family. Like Matilda, Harry is a hero, a survivor despite all odds, with support along the way.

Junk, by Melvin Burgess, darkly portrays adolescence which focuses on drug addiction, promiscuity and crime – not a pretty picture, but an honest portrayal of contemporary times although the setting is the 1980s – which fits the genre of contemporary realistic fiction. Like

Dahl's *Matilda*, *Junk* rises out of familial discord and moves on to the stage where teenagers almost drown in their struggle to assert themselves, to find self-image and identity. Compulsive reading for some adolescents, repulsive to others, it is more likely to heal than to destroy as it shows how, ultimately, despite a dysfunctional background, the young person must make choices.

David Almond's gripping fable, *Skellig*, begins with a bleak setting of family life in which a premature birth, surgery, fear of death and jealousy are rampant factors for a time, thus opening the way for emotionally neglected young Michael to discover, amid the debris and decay of a derelict garage, the strange being, Skellig, who supports and comforts him. His friendship with a girl, Mina, is positive and leads him into creativity which precedes deepening sensibility to the plight of his baby sister and his parents' distress. Thus he is then renewed to become a consoler, so the story becomes a celebration of a Phoenix arising from ashes; of inner strength, creativity and potential for healing that extends beyond the self.

At the end of the novel, as the time of family malfunction fades, as healing has begun, they are in a memorable scene:

> *We laid the baby on the table and sat around her. We didn't know what to say. Mum drank her tea. Dad let me have swigs of his beer. we just sat there looking at each other and touching each other and we laughed and laughed and we cried and cried.*
>
> Almond, 1998, 168.

10.2 Stepmothers and fathers

In contemporary society many children have a step-parent. Marion Howell writes: The stepmother still tends to be portrayed as evil and suspicious, and always with an ulterior motive for any charitable behaviour displayed. With the exception of *My Wicked Stepmother*, in which the stepmother is described and illustrated as a witch, most modern stepmothers now appear more 'normal.' Alongside this normalisation of the stepmother character, there has been an increase in the number of *stepfather* stories.

The stepmother character appears to have changed little over the centuries. She is still seen as wicked and cold-hearted, but it is my belief that there are acceptable explanations for most of her behaviour. For herself and her own children to survive the eradication of other family members was often her only means of survival. It has often been said that the stepmother is incapable of loving children. This may be so when it comes to loving another woman's children, but there seems very little doubt that a stepmother can be fiercely protective of her own offspring if their survival or position within their society is threatened. This seems to be very rational and acceptable behaviour.

Unfortunately, the stepmother character is going to change very little if present day authors insist on portraying her as evil and vindictive. There needs to be concerted effort by both authors and illustrators to portray the stepmother in a much more positive light. Perhaps as more and more children come to live in stepfamilies, they will begin to see that although the situation may not be ideal or even to their liking, that stepmothers are not all wicked characters.

11. Grieving Children

Myths tend to prevail about children and grief: that they do not grieve; they experience few losses; childhood is the happiest time of life. Yet the reality shows, according to Norma Osborn, reporting on the Grief Resource Foundation's findings, that they may grieve several times a day and may re-grieve throughout all the developmental stages, despite not understanding it is grief they feel. Certainly they can experience loss even on a daily basis, at *school*: in sports, or grades achieved, self-esteem and relationships; at *home*, in emotional control, understanding and in dysfunctional families. One in seven children loses a parent before the age of ten. War in the Baltic, Africa and Asia may have increased this ratio.

Stories about death and grief could hold possibilities to be told in a maudlin, sentimental way, but published writers for children reject this style. Rather they meet the vulnerable child with a strong storyline and characters to whom the reader can relate, but always with sensitivity concerning rites of passage.

11.1 Picture Books

present recognisable scenes of loss experienced by young children: *Losing a pet. Must Hurt A Lot: A Child's Book About Death* by Doris Sanford, tells the story of Joshua's puppy that died. Joshua misses his puppy so much that it hurts and makes him feel lonely. Gradually he discovers some 'secrets' that may also help another grieving child. Another picture book about the death of a family pet is the beautifully illustrated, sensitively told Alfie Story, *Alfie and the Birthday Surprise*. This is a book children really love even though it tackles a difficult subject. Another concerns the enduringly popular Mog who, in the twelfth and final story, feels the need to sleep forever. *Goodbe Mog* by Judith Kerr, is a story of hope and coping with the grief of parting.

11.2 Junior Fiction

Berlie Doherty is a skilful story teller and in *The Golden Bird* she is at her best as she writes about Andrew whose father has died. Jacqueline Wilson sensitively considers the death of Verity's mother, told in conjunction with the death of Mabel the cat in *The Cat Mummy*. Through her family coming to terms with one, they also accept the other. One other book of the bereavement genre for the Middle years should be noted: *The Crowstarver*, by Dick King-Smith, story of an abandoned baby adopted by a childless couple, presents a different focus that includes the adjustment of the child, Spider', as he grows up with physical and mental difficulties but with a remarkable rapport for animals.

11.3 Death of a Grandparent

This is an experience that comes to many children and there are picture books that talk about death, acknowledging it as legacy of living, yet helping young child readers in their grief. *The Grandad Tree* by Trish Cooke is a special story in which an Afro Caribbean brother and sister remember their grandfather's life; it is rather like an apple tree, backdrop to the setting, which changes over the years. Another is *Little Bear's Grandad* by Nigel Gray. The use of an endearing little bear helps to distance a child, a little, from death as an event in his/her own life, yet as David Parker argues, the use of animals allows authors to portray characters whose lives simultaneously embody childish and adult characteristics without seeming at all incongruous. So the young audience can delight in the friendship of Little Bear and his grandfather as they do special things together, like climbing the ladder to the tree house where they can survey the world and share special thoughts, until the last story and the final sleep.

12. Children in Hospital

There are books about hospitalisation for every stage of childhood, to help children understand what may seem at first like an alien environment For babies and pre-schoolers, Little Bill is a popular character who features in a series and also on television, so *A Trip to Hospital* by Kim Watson will present a familiar and loved little hero. Clifford the Big Red Dog is another series hero, in *Clifford Visits the Hospital*, a work more suited to the 4–8 year-old, Key Stage One child. Clifford imparts the reassurance of fictional animals that young children accept easily.

Jamie is the hero for Stage Two readers, about 9–12 years in *Jamie Drum's Massive Strike* in which he courageously and creatively fights life-threatening disease, and wins. Not all child patients will come through as Jamie does, but his story is inspirational. Of an informational nature, Diana Kimpton's *Hospital Highway Code* offers explanations of what goes on, give older children ideas for occupying themselves during their stay and even jokes to enjoy and banter in good fun with new friends.

13. Bullying

Picture books like *Hugo and the Bully Frogs* by Francesca Simon suit beginning readers, 4–6 years, the story of Timid Hugo who needs, and gets, an ally. Or, for Middle Years, *Camille and the Sunflowers* by Laurence Anholt which concerns a short period of oppression in Van Gogh's life, observed by Camille, the postmaster's son. Non-Fiction includes *Stop Picking on Me: A First Look at Bullying* by Pat Thomas, a well illustrated, sensitively told book that clarifies the issue for the child and suggests ways to cope, for child and also teachers and parents.

For junior fiction titles about bullying, *Buried Alive* by Jacqueline Wilson has both humour and sensitivity as Tim struggles to avoid bullies, as well as coping with his protective mother and his girl friend. For senior fiction re bullying, *Lost for Words* by Elizabeth Lutzeier, highlights what it is like for Bangladeshi Aysha, formerly regarded as clever and popular, to move to England where her peers bully her because she has difficulties with her new language. From Michelle Magorian and Alan Gibbons' facile pens, *A Spoonful of Jam* (Magorian) and *Chicken* (Gibbons) address the issue vividly. Magorian writes a story set in 1947 with her usual warmth about a girl protagonist, while Gibbons is strongly realistic, writing about Davy, newcomer to contemporary Liverpool where his life is made miserable by a gang of boys. In both books, family-support is important to the children.

14. Bibliotherapy

In its broadest historical context, the concept of 'bibliotherapy' forms part of the ancient dulcis et utile *debate, in which some scholars advocated a role for literature as 'useful' or 'instructive' in some moral sense, while others maintained that stories and books existed primarily or even purely to give pleasure.*

Crago, 1999, 166

Bibliotherapy is a twentieth century concept, much promoted in the Unites States, but also by some librarians and teachers in Britain. It is concerned with matching a child's condition – frequently coloured by deep emotions rather than essentially biological/genetic causes – with books that relate to the child's problem. The child may be in the disturbed situation for a moderate or long period, and where therapists are involved, these professionals intervene with selected, therapeutic stories, encourage discussion or role play, and recognise when the need diminishes.

When we consider bibliotherapy, we should keep in mind several considerations: *Firstly,* It is difficult to separate delight and instruction, for most literature offers both, feeding into both the logical left and affective right brain lobes described by Betty Edwards. Inevitably, responses to bibliotherapy differ from reader to reader, despite any one book's attempt to spotlight a particular issue. This is in accord with accepted Reader Response Theory.

Secondly, on the other hand, bibliotherapeutic theory seems insufficiently researched across a wide cross section of the community to provide pragmatic and precise epistemology. Anecdotal evidence in support of bibliotherapy indicates, however, that young people feel empowered by reading. The 1996 study, 'Young People Reading at the End of the Century', conducted by the National centre for Research in Children's Literature (NCRCL) tells that

. . . an impressive number of young people say that reading has already helped them solve problems in their lives – often very

difficult problems, ranging from bullying at school to parental divorce, sexual abuse, and what to do about the violent or addictive behaviour of someone close to them.

Reynolds, 1999, 13

Thirdly, children ultimately choose for themselves what they will either read or discard as 'boring'. Some children steer right away from dwelling on their immediate problems, and their choice should be respected, along with the child's uniqueness and individuality. They may self-select when the time is right for them to consciously or unconsciously, search for meaning, a need that may be at an incipient level, for, as Bettelheim says, 'In child or adult, the unconscious is a powerful determinant of behaviour.' However, as Crago points out, bibliotherapy may have ethical objections if imposed on older children who have not requested it, despite the possible values of comfort, enlightenment and guidance.

Fourthly, bibliotherapy has followers among therapists, teachers, librarians, parents and authors. It certainly has attracted publishers as a potential market, which accounts for general and specialist bibliotherapy lists which include a focus on such issues as: bullying, death and dying, medical and dental visits, family issues of many dimensions, moving house, starting school, going to war, violence, terrorism and war. Inasmuch as professionals in the library and classroom select books to offer to children, it is sensible for them to include books of a possible bibliotherapeutic nature, sometimes addressed by popular and award winning writers. These works can take their turn in a promotion programme or offered if a student requests work of a particular nature, thereby catering to all the community.

Finally, informational books major in instruction. Fiction, however, *demonstrates,* yet it is gently instructive at the same time for the reader who recognises the instruction because of his/her own need. For bibliotherapeutic purposes, fiction for most children is probably the more powerful medium. Its imagery and narration draws the reader in, to think and feel, to be there, like the protagonist of the story. It is in accord with an active rather than passive learning methodology.

In conclusion, this chapter indicates that further to the genres of Fiction, Non Fiction and the Informational or Biographic, there are also sub-genres. These range from the non-fiction, Informational genre, to biographic formats, to Series and Crossovers through books for reluctant male and other 'special' readers. Selection of publications challenges every librarian, teacher and parent who recognises a child's future may be in his/her hands. Stock should be available so the child can really explore.

Children's Sayings

"The Anthony Horrowitz series of books are my favourites because the boy hero has many adventures and it feels like REAL LIFE. (I've read *Stormbreaker, Point Blanc* and *Skeleton Key*)." Sian, 11 years.

"*True Shark Stories* " by Terry Dear is a really cool book because it tells you real shark stories and it has a fact file with Did you know?' Brian, 10 years.

"You can learn about the appendix and how it just sits there all your life in *Blood, Bones and Body Bits*., and about other countries food, like haggis, sheep eyes and frogs legs" *(sic)* Matthew, 10 years.

"I find *Sounds Dreadful* and many other books of its kind makes whatever they're talking about amazingly interesting. Also, if you hate science like me, then it ables you to see a subject you hate in a hole new light." *(sic)* Simone, 10 years.

"*More William* by Richmal Crompton was quite long. I liked the first chapter when it was Christmas and William got all his family a present each and he put them down in front of their bedroom doors. When he was doing it he shouted so they would get up, and then he went downstairs and saw his friend. He had lost some snails which were Christmas presents. I think William is kind but devious. Alys, 10.

"I used to read a lot but I don't now. I'm more interested in other stuff." Sarah, 16.

Tutorial Topics

1. Do you see any benefits in Bibliotherapy? Give reasons for your response. (Read Crago, pp. 170–171). Think of works that may provide healing. Give anecdotal evidence.
2. Read any book of the Bibliotherapy genre. In light of your text, consider and discuss how 'safe' should books recommended for

bibliotherapeutic purposes be? You may also consider the notion that a structured use of bibliotherapy abuses literature and sends out wrong reasons about reading. What do think? Substantiate your answer.

3. Should literature for children be 'good' for them? To guide you, read 'Essentials: What is Children's Literature? What is Childhood?' by Karin Lesnik-Oberstein, in *Understanding Children's Literature* edited by Peter Hunt, Routledge, 1999.

4. Explore books of the non-fiction genre. Are they published in an inviting format for young children/older children? Report on your findings.

Further Reading

Campbell, A. *Outstanding Sequence Stories: A Guide to Children's Books that Carry the Reader Forward*. Librarians of Institutes and Schools of Education, 1998. ISBN: 0901922323.

Daniels, J. 'Is a Series Reader a Serious Reader?', in Styles, M. et al (eds) *Voices Off: Texts, Contexts and Readers*. London: Cassell, 1996.

Hancock, S. (ed.) *A Guide to Children's Reference Books and Multimedia material*. Aldershot: Ashgate, 1998.

Nell, V. *Lost in a Book: The Psychology of Reading for Pleasure*. New Haven: Yale University Press, 1988.

Ott, P. *How to Detect and Manage Dyslexia. A Reference and Resource Manual*. Oxford: Heinemann Educational Publishers, 1997.

Stones, Rosemary (Ed.). *Guide to Children's Books About Bullying*. Reading: Co-published by *Books for Keeps* and The Reading and Language Information Centre Reading, 2000.

Watson, Victor. *Reading Series Fiction*. London: RoytledgeFalmer, 2000.

Children's Books Cited

Information

Blathwayt, Ben. *Ben's Big Book of Cars*. London: Hutchinson, 2002.

Brown, John. *Journey into the Desert*. Oxford: Oxford University Press, 2002.

Brownlie, A. *Why are People Vegetarian?* London: Wayland, 2002.

Corbishly, Mike *et al. The Young Oxford History of Britain and Ireland*. Oxford: Oxford University Press, 1996.

Delahunty, Andrew and Steve Cox. (eds). *Oxford First Thesaurus*. Oxford: Oxford University Press, 2002.

DK Children's Picture Encyclopaedia. London: Dorling Kindersley, 2002.

Gates, Phil. *Designer Genes.* Illustrated by Mark Thomas. London: Scholastic Press, 1998.

Goldsmith, Evelyn and Julie Park. (eds). *Oxford First Dictionary.* Oxford: Oxford University Press, 2002.

Green, Jen. *Racism.* London: Hodder Wayland, 2002.

Greenaway, Theresa. *The Wayland Book of Common British trees.* London: Hodder Wayland, 2002.

Howker, Janni. *Walk with a Wolf.* Illustrated by Sara Fox-Davies. London: Candlewick Press, 2002.

Hughes, Lisa. *Activators: Computers Unlimited.* London: Hodder Children's Books, 2000.

Kent, Peter. *Hidden Under the Ground.* London: Hodder Wayland, 1998.

Kirkwood, Jon. *Our Solar System.* London: Franklin Watts, 1998.

Llewellyn, Clare. *MaxFax: Great Apes.* London: Hodder Wayland, 2001.

Parker, Steve. *Lasers Now and Into the Future.* Morristown, NJ: Silver Burdett Press, 1999.

Ransford, Sandy. *The Otter.* London: Kingfisher 'Animal Lives.' 1999.

Robson, Pam and John York. *All About the Second World War.* London: Hodder Wayland, 1996.

Tagholm, Sally. *The Barn Owl.* Illustrated by Bert Kitchen. London: Kingfisher, 1999.

Tambini, Michael. *Eye Witness Guides: Future.* London: Dorling Kindersley, 1998.

Walker, Sally M. *Fossil Fish Found Alive.* Clinton, UT: Carolrhoda, 2002.

Wood, Richard. *Kitchens Through the Ages.* Illustrated by Tony de Saulles. London: Hodder Wayland, 1997.

Yass, Marion. *The Great Depression.* London: Hodder Wayland, 1988.

Biographies

Beckham, Victoria. *Learning to Fly.* London: Penguin, 2002.

Bitton-Jackson, Livia. *I Have Lived a Thousand Years.* New York: Simon and Schuster, 2000.

Buttino, Lou. *For the Love of Teddi: The Story Behind Camp Good Days and Happy Times.* Boston: Greenwood Press, 1990.

Frank, Anne. *The Diary of a Young Girl: The Definitive Edition.* Otto Frank, Mirjam Pressler, Eds. Susan Masotty, translator. London: Puffin 2002.

Gogerly, Liz. *Dian Fossey.* London: Hodder Wayland, 2002.

Goldsmith, Mike. *John Logie Baird.* London: Hodder Wayland, 2002.

—— *Guglielmo Marconi.* London: Hodder Wayland, 2003.

Marshall, Neil. *Letters to Henrietta.* Cambridge: Cambridge University Press, 1998.

Ross, Stewart. *Leonardo da Vinci.* London: Hodder Wayland, 2003.

—— *Michael Faraday.* London: Hodder Wayland, 2002.

Senker, Cath. *Rosalind Franklin.* London: Hodder Wayland, 2003.

Wheeler, Sara. *Dear Daniel: Letters from Antarctica*. London: Hodder Wayland, 1997.

Series
Belbin, David. *The Beat: Losers*. A Point Crime Book. London: Scholastic, 1997.
Blyton, Enid. *Go Ahead Secret Seven*. (Book 5 in the series) Illustrated by Bruno Kay. London: Brockhampton Press, 1953.
Cameron, Ann. *The Julian Stories*. London: Corgi Children's. (Various dates)
Daniels, Lucy. The *Animal Ark* series. London: Hodder Children's Books. (Various dates)
Grant, R. G. *The Great Depression*. London: Wayland, 2002.
Johnson, Paul. *Festivals*. London: A and C. Black, 2001.
Minarik, Else Holmelund. *Little Bear's Visit*. Illustrated by Maurice Sendak. New York: Harper and Row, 1961.
Nicoll, Helen and Jan Pienowski. *Meg and Mog*. London: Picture Puffins, 1975.

Horrible Histories
Deary, Terry and Neil Tonge. *The Terrible Tudors*. Illustrated by Martin Brown. London: Scholastic Children's Books, 1993.
—— and Peter Hepplewhite. *The Awesome Egyptians*. Illustrated by Martin Brown. London: Scholastic Children's Books, 1994.
Deary, Terry. *The Blitzed Brits*. Inside Illustrations by Kate Sheppard. London: Scholastic Children's Books, 1994.
—— *The Groovy Greeks*. Illustrated by Martin Brown. London: Scholastic Children's Books, 1996.
Deary, Terry *The Measly Middle Ages*. Illustrated by Martin Brown. London: Scholastic Children's Books, 1996.
—— *The Angry Aztecs*. Illustrated by Martin Brown. London: Scholastic Children's Books, 1997.
—— *The Cut-Throat Celts*. Illustrated by Martin Brown. London: Scholastic Children's Books, 1997.
—— *Rowdy Revolutions*. Illustrated by Philip Reeve. London: Scholastic Children's Books, 1999.
—— *The Woeful Second World War*. Illustrated by Martin Brown. London: Scholastic Children's Books, 1999.
—— *The Incredible Incas*. Illustrated by Philip Reeve. London: Scholastic Children's Books. 2000.
—— *The Balmy British Empire*. Illustrated by Martin Brown. London: Scholastic Children's Books, 2002.

Horrible Science
Arnold, Nick. *Bulging Brains*. Illustrated by Tony De Saulles. London: Scholastic Children's Books, 1999.

Dead Famous

Simpson Margaret. *Cleopatra and her Asp.* Illustrated by Philip Reeve. London: Scholastic Children's Books, 2000.

MacDonald, Alan. *Oliver Cromwell and his Warts.* Illustrated by Philip Reeve. London: Scholastic Children's Books, 2000.

Simpson, Margaret. *Mary Queen of Scots and her Hopeless Husbands.* Illustrated by Philip Reeve. London: Scholastic Children's Books, 2001.

The Knowledge

MacDonald, Alan. *Triffic Chocolate.* Illustrated by Clive Goddard. London: Scholastic Children's Books, 2000.

Arnold, Nick. *Awesome Archaeology.* Illustrated by Clive Goddard. London: Scholastic Children's Books, 2001.

Crossovers

de Saint-Exupery, Antoine. *The Little Prince.* London: William Heinemann Ltd, 1945.

Hearn, Lian. *Across the Nightingale Floor.* London: Pan Macmillan, 2002.

McKinley, Robin. *Beauty: A Retelling of the Story of Beauty and the Beast.* London: HarperCollins Library, 1985/ David Fickling Books, 2002.

O'Neill, Joan. *Daisy Chain War.* London: Hodder Children's Books, 2002.

—— *Bread and Sugar.* London: Hodder Children's Books, 2002.

—— *Daisy Chain Dream.* London: Hodder Children's Books, 2003.

Book Mates

Almond, David. *Kit's Wilderness.* London: Signature, 1999.

Arksey, Neil. *MacB.* London: Puffin, 1999.

Bryson, Bill. *Notes from a Small Island.* London: Perennial (Imprint of HarperCollins), 2001.

Brooks, Kevin. *Martyn Pig.* London: Scholastic, 2002.

Deary, Terry. *Dark Knight and Dingy Castles.* Illustrated by Philip Reeve. London: Scholastic, 1997.

—— *Savage Stoneage.* Illustrated by Martin Brown. Ontario: Schmidt Interactive Software, 1999.

Forsyth, Frederick. *No Come backs.* London: Arrow, 2001.

Horowitz, Anthony. *South by South east.* London: Walker, 1997.

—— *Stormbreaker.* Walker, 2002.

Jennings, Paul. *Unmentionable.* New York: Penguin USA, 1993.

Lawrence, Michael. *The Poltergoose: A Jiggy McCue Story.* New York: Penguin Putnam, 2002.

Mandela, Nelson. *Long Walk to Freedom.* London: Abacus, 2003.

Paulsen, Garry. *Hatchet.* London: Macmillan, 1996.

Pullman, Philip. *Northern Lights.* London: Scholastic, 1996.

Pratchett, Terry. *Johnny and the Dead.* London: Doubleday, 1993.

—— *Colour of Magic.* London: Corgi, 1985.

Swindells, Robert. *Stone Cold*. London: Puffin.
—— *Dosh*. London: Hamish Hamilton, 1999.
Townsend, Sue. *Adrian Mole: the Wilderness Years*. London: Penguin, 2003.
Useful w.w.w. sites
Terry Deary: <*www.terry-deary.com*>
Paul Jennings. <*www.pauljennings.com.au*>
Lawrence, Michael. <*www.wordybug.com.uk*>
Terry Pratchett: <*www.terrypratchettbooks.com*>
J. R. R. Tolkien. <*www.Tolkien.co.uk*>
<*www.hants.gov.uk*>

Dyslexics
Adeney, Anne. *Skulduggery: A Detective Story*. Tredwr: Dolphin, 1999.
Althea. *Dyslexia*. 'Talking it Through' Series. Happy Cat Books Ltd., 2003.
Childs, Rob. *Football Daft*. Illustrated by Aidan Potts. London: 'Soccer Mad' Series. Yearling, 1997.
Wiltshire, Paula. *Dyslexia*. London: Hodder Wayland. 'Health Issues' Series. 2002.
<*www.booktrusted.com/booklists/dyslexia*>

The Visually Impaired
Bloor, Edward. *Tangerine*. London: Harcourt Brace, 1997.
Burningham, John. *Mr Gumpy's Motor Car*. London: Jonathan Cape Children's Books, 1973; Red Fox, 2002.
Inkpen, Mick. *The Little Kipper Collection: Four Little Kipper Stories in One*. London: Hodder Children's Books, 2001.
<*www.livingpaintings.org*>
<*www.cnib.ca/library*>

The Disabled
Anderson, Rachel. *Best friends*. Illustrated by Shelagh McNicholas. London: Collins Jets, 1992.
Gantos, Jack. *Joey Pigza Swallowed the Key*. London: Corgi Yearling, 2000.
Hoopman, Kathy. *Blue Bottle Mystery*. London: Jessica Kingsley Publishers, 2000.
Laird, Elizabeth, ED. *Me and My Electric: A Collection of Short Stories*. London: Mammoth, 1998.

Bibliotherapy

The Dysfunctional Family
Almond, David. *Skellig*. London: Hodder Children's Books, 1998.
Burgess, Melvin. *Junk*. Introduction by Julia Eccleshare. London: Puffin Modern Classics, 2003.

Dahl, Roald. *Matilda.* Illustrated by Quentin Blake. London: Puffin, 2001.
Jones, Diana, Wynne. *The Ogre Downstairs.* London: Macmillan, 1974.
Wilson, Jacqueline. *The Suitcase Kid.* London: Corgi Yearling, 1992.

Stepmothers

Abercrombie, B. *Charlie Anderson.* London: Puffin Books, 1990.
Ahlberg, A. *Ten in a Bed.* London: Puffin Books, 1990.
Bawden, N. *The Outside Child.* London: Puffin Books, 1989.
Cross, G. *New World.* Oxford: Oxford University press, 1994.
Douthwaite, W. *The Christmas Pony.* London: Macmillan Children's Books, 1996.
Duncan, L. *Locked in Time.* London: Penguin Books, 1986.
Fine, A. *Step by Wicked Step.* London: Puffin Books, 1995.
Fisk, P. *Tyger Pool.* London: Random House, 1994.
Gardner, S. *A Book of Princesses.* London: Orion Children's Books, 1997.
Gavin, J. *The Wormholers.* London: Mammoth, 1996.
Geras, A. *Pictures of the Night.* London: Hamish Hamilton, 1992.
Grimm, J. L. C. and W. C. *Grimm's Fairy Tales.* Ware: Wordsworth Editions Ltd, 1993.
Hoffman, M. *Grace and Family.* London: Frances Lincoln, 1995.
Hooper, M. *Mad About the Boy.* London: Walker Books, 1996.
Impey, R. *Instant Sisters.* London: Orchard Books, 1989.
—— (Ed). *The Orchard Book of Fairy Tales*
Kerr Wilson, B. *Wishbones: A Tale from China. London:* Frances Lincoln, 1993.
Leach, N. *My Wicked Stepmother.* London: Julia MacRae Books, 1992.
Mahy, M. *Leaf Magic and Five Other Favourites.* London: Puffin Books, 1995.
Onyefulu, O. *Chinye; A West African Folktale.* London: Frances Lincoln, 1994.
Rainsbury, J. *The Seventh Seal.* Dyfed: Pont Books, 1993.
Rosen, M. *Snow White.* London: Firefly, 1989.
Welford, S. *Catch the Moon.* London: Macmillan Children's Books, 1989.
Wilson, J. *Double Act.* London: Doubleday, 1995.
—— *The Suitcase Kid.* London: Corgi Yearling Books, 1993.
<www.waterborolibrary.org/bklist>

Grieving Children

Cooke, Trish. *The Grandad Tree.* Illustrated by Sharon Wilson. London: Walker Books, 2000.
Doherty, Berlie. The Golden Bird. Illustrated by John Lawrence. London: Egmont, 2002.
Gray, Nigel. *Little Bear's Grandad.* London: Little Tiger Press, 2000.
Hughes, Shirley. *Alfie and the Birthday Surprise.* London: Red Fox, 1999.
Kerr, Judith. *Goodbye Mog.* London: Picture Lions, 2002.

King-Smith, Dick. *The Crowstarver*. Illustrated by Peter Bailey. London: Corgi, 1999.

Sanford, Doris. *It Must Hurt a Lot*. Portland, Ore: Multnomah Press, 1985.

Wilson, Jacqueline. *The Cat Mummy*. Illustrated by Nick Sharratt. London: Doubleday, 2001.

<http://wordpool.co.uk/ccb/feelings/pet.htm>
<http://www.booktrusted.com/booklists/deathjun fic.html>

Children in Hospital

Bridwell, Norman. *Clifford Visits the Hospital*. London: Scholastic, 2000.

Davies, Paul. *Jamie Drum's Massive Strike*. Shaftsbury: Element Books Ltd, 1998.

Kimpton, Diana. *The Hospital Highway Code*. Illustrated by Peter Kavanagh. London: Macmillan, 1994.

Watson, Kim. *A Trip to the Hospital (Little Bill)*. Illustrated by Mark Salisbury. New York: Simon Spotlight, 2001.

<www.umbc.edu/education/programs/early childhood>

Bullying

Arnholt, Laurence. *Camille and the Sunflowers*. London: Frances Lincoln, 1995.

Byrne, John. *The Bullybusters Joke Book*. London: Red Fox, 1996.

Gibbons, Alan. *Chicken*. London: Orion, 1998.

Lutzeler, Elizabeth. *Lost For Words*. Oxford: Oxford University Press, 1997.

Magorian, Michelle. *A Spoonful of Jam*. London: Mammoth, 1998.

Simon, Francesca. *Hugo and the Bully Frogs*. Illustrated by Caroline Jane Church. London: Gullane Children's Books, 2000.

Thomas, Pat. *Stop Picking On Me: A First Look At Bullying*. Illustrated by Lesley Harker. Hodder Wayland, 2000.

Wilson, Jacqueline. *Buried Alive*. Illustrated by Nick Sharratt and Sue Heap. London: Corgi, 1999.

<www.booktrusted.com/booklists/bullypic bks.html>
<www.booktrusted.com/booklists/bullyjun fic.html>

Bibliography

Almond, David. 'Writing for Boys?' In *Carousel*, Issue 12, Summer 1999, 29.

Bettelheim, B. *The Uses of Enchantment: The Meaning and Importance of Fairy Tales*. New York: Knopf, 1976, 7.

Crago, Hugh. "Can Stories Heal?' *Understanding Children's Literature,* Ed. Peter Hunt. London: Routledge,1999.

DfE. *Code of Practice on the Identification and Assessment of special Educational Needs*. London: Central Office of Information, 1994.

Eccleshare, Julia. 'Launching Young Readers: How to Navigate through the series,' *Books for Keeps* No. 138, January 2003, 6–7.

Edwards, Betty. *Drawing on the Right Side of the Brain.* London: Souvenir Press, 1992.

—— *A Guide to the Harry Potter Novels.* London: Continuum, 2002.

Gamble, Nicky. Review of the Daisy Chain War trilogy. In *Books for Keeps*, No. 140 May 2003, 29.

Graham Judith and Alison Kelly. *Reading Under Control: Teaching Reading in the Primary School.* Second edition. 2nd edition. Reprint. London: David Fulton Publishers Ltd. with University of Surrey, 2001.

Harris, T. L. and Hodges, R. W. (Eds.) *A Dictionary of Reading and Related Terms.* Newark, DE: International Reading Association, 1981.

Hollindale, Peter. Review of 'Beauty: A Retelling of the Story of Beauty and the Beast' in *Books for Keeps*, No. 140 May 2003, 30.

Howell, M. F. *'Damned if She Does and Damned If She Does Not': the step-mother in children's literature.* An unpublished Master's dissertation, Loughborough University, 1999.

Hunt, Peter. Ed. *Understanding Children's Literature.* London: Routledge, 1998

Hynd, G. W. and Hynd, C. R. 'Dyslexia: Neuroanatomical/neurolinguistic perspectives.' *Reading Research Quarterly*, 19, 482–498.

Lesnik-Oberstein, K. *Children's Literature: Criticism and the Fictional Child.* Oxford: Clarendon Press, 1994.

Mallett, Margaret. 'Life Cycles, Journeys and Historical Stories: Learning from Informational Narratives.' In *Books for Keeps,* No.117, July, 1999, 3–5.

Marley, Anne. 'Dads 'n' Lads: Reading Together.' In *Books for Keeps,* No.124 September, 2000.

Meek, M. *On Being Literate.* London: Bodley Head, 1991.

National Centre for Research in Children's Literature. *Young People Reading at the End of the Century.* London: NRCL 1996.

NCRCL. *Young People's Reading at the End of the Century.* London: Book Trust, 1996.

Nikolajeva, Maria. ' Exit Children's Literature.' *The Lion and the Unicorn,* 22 (2), 1998, 223.

Osborn, Norma. 'When Children are Grieving.' In *Ministry*, April 1998.

Parker, David. *'Animals are Nicer than People – they Can't Hurt You. A Child Development Perspective on the Portrayal of Animals in Children's Picture Books.* Unpublished Master's Dissertation, Loughborough University, 1999.

Percy, Ted. Book Reviews in *Books for Keeps*, No. 138, January 2003, 25.

Pressley, Michael. *Reading Instruction that Works.* The Guilford Press, 1998, 64–66.

Reid, G. *Dyslexia: a Practitioner's Handbook.* Chichester: Wiley, 1998.

Reynolds, Kimberley. 'Young People's Reading Habits at the End of the Century.' In *Research Bulletin*, Issue 1, Summer 1999, 13.

Samantha. 'Learning to Fly.' In *Books for Keeps*, No. 136, September 2002.

Schwartz, Wendy. 'Helping Underachieving Boys Read Well and Often.' *Eric Digest*, Number 176, 2002.

Shaywitz, S. E. 'Dyslexia.' *Scientific American*, 275 (5), 98–104.

Simpson, A. 'Fictions and Facts: An investigation of the Reading Practices of Girls and Boys. *English Education*, 28 (4) 1996, 268–79.

Smith, M. W. and Wilhelm, J. D. *'Reading Don't Fix No Chevys': Literacy in the Lives of Young Men*. Portsmouth, NH: Heinemann, 2002.

Treglown, J. *Roald Dahl: a Biography.* London: Faber and Faber, 1994.

Trim, Mary-Kate. *The Rights of the Child: A Teacher's Resource.* UNICEF, 1989.

Unstead, Sue. 'Book Reviews, Non Fiction', in *Books for Keeps,* No. 138, January 2003, 25–26.

Vellutino, F. R. *et al.* 'Cognitive profiles of difficult-to-remediate and readily remediated poor readers: Early intervention as a vehicle for distinguishing between cognitive and experiential deficits as a basic cause of specific reading disability.' *Journal of Educational Psychology,* 88, 601–638, 1996.

For Reading Champions, email: genevieve.clarke@literacytrust.org.uk

SECTION TWO

THE PROFESSIONAL: KNOWING AND GROWING

CHAPTER SIX

Selecting Activities: Focus on Library and School

1. The Library

> *A library where young people feel welcome can be their gateway to lifelong enjoyment of reading and learning.*

A library needs to give young people:

- *a space which they feel is theirs – where they can explore and search for what they want;*
- *Guidance tools to help in their search;*
- *Staff who can help them – and give them more ideas for their reading and learning.*

Libraries which work best for young people are those where library staffs have consulted with young people to get their ideas and feelings about what they want in a library, how they think it should look, and how it might work. (All this, of course, to be balanced with the budget available!)

So talk with young people – those already coming into the library and also those who don't. Visit school classes or youth clubs and ask what they think about the library, what they want from it, what would get them to use it for their reading and learning. This is an opportunity too to talk about what the library already offers – usually more than most people realize. This consultation should give you valuable information for thinking about

- **How the library can make a difference for young people:**
- Differences might include:
- *Young people using the library more;*
- *Young people using the library more confidently;*
- *Young people reading more widely.*

- **How you can change or improve the library. Activities:**
- Make the library more attractive, including using young people's ideas to do this;
- Make the library more accessible – in the widest sense;
- Changing the times when the library is open;
- Involving young people in choosing library books and materials;
- Running special library activities.

A particularly vital investment in the creation of a welcoming library is that made in the people who work in the library. Give special attention to staff recruitment and then to the training and support provided for library staff. Make sure that everyone who comes to work in the library enjoys being with all library users, children and adults – and make sure there are opportunities for all staff in developing their skills and knowledge in working with young people.

Remember when you are consulting young people to be aware of the sensitivities regarding talking to children. There is useful advice in 'A Safe Place for Children' – guidelines produced by CILIP

1.1 Making the Library Look Attractive and Welcoming

This does not have to involve an enormous amount of money. A smile is free, and time taken to make the library look as good as possible is well used. It shows people that you care and you want them to enjoy everything!

Here are some very practical suggestions for making a bright welcome to the library:

- Give some time to introducing young people to the library individually when they join. Prepare a simple 'Library Welcome Pack' to give them
- Arrange books face-on whenever you can. Put them in inviting piles on the tables. Don't have tightly packed shelves – people are more likely to explore and borrow if they can get at the books and

see their covers easily. Maybe take some books off the shelves and keep them handy, if possible, to top up the shelves once people start borrowing more books!

- Make the most of promotions from publishers and booksellers. You can often get attractive, classy posters, and also dumb pins which can give books that 'must have' aura.
- Have bright library displays including pictures and writing from users about their reading and activities. Local schools and under fives groups will often provide lovely displays of children's work. And keep the displays fresh and up-to-date.
- Consultation and partnership with schools, colleges or youth centres could also set off joint activity in brightening up the library – maybe a wall-painting work party or some design work on the shelves and kinderboxes?
- Think age and height. If you were 5 years old, could you see that display or reach that book?
- Look out for display ideas (your local party shop?!). One member of staff who attends a course can pass on ideas and skills to everyone else.
- Use PC screensavers to display welcoming messages: 'Welcome to your library!'
- A very useful exercise is to imagine you've never been in the library before and you're seeing it for the first time. What do you think?

1.2 Making the Library More Accessible

There are several points to consider here:

- The physical look and layout of the library
- Issues of disability
- Cultural considerations
- Library procedures: do they make barriers?

When you take look around the library as if you were seeing it for the first time, ask these questions:

- Are there any physical barriers? E.g. high and dominating counter; turnstile; 'Don't' notices on the walls
- Is it cluttered and overwhelming – too much to look at at once?
- Does the layout draw you in?
- Can you see straightaway where to ask for help?
- Is there a library plan – a guide to what's in the library?

- Does it feel as if the library belongs to everyone? E.g. displays by community groups, recommendations by readers, pictures of readers with their favorite reads
- Is it easy to see where the young people's section is? And is it easy
- to find any other section too?
- Do under fives, school age children, and teenagers each see that there's somewhere and something in the library especially for them?
- Does the library appeal to young people – is it current and relevant?
- Do under fives, school age children and teenagers each see that there's somewhere and something in the library especially for them?
- In considering access to the building and the library stock *you* will be consulting the library/school's equal opportunities policies, and also their implementation policy for the Disability Discrimination Act.
- Key points here include:
- Do you have the right stock and facilities for local needs? For example, large print, Braille, talking books, Kurzwell machine.
- Where have you put these facilities and stock? What would make them most accessible – integration or displayed separately?
- Work with local associations and schools and benefit from their specialist knowledge.
- See also the guidelines produced by disabled people's organizations. For example, the *National Library for the Blind: Best Practice Manual.*
- Use virtual services: ICT, Internet, video-conferencing. These will enhance access for all young people.
- Make sure you include the needs of disabled young people in the staff training programme.
- The books in your library must reflect the diversity of the young people who borrow them. A key reason why young people read is to find stories and information about people like themselves.
- To encourage a broad range of young people to use the library, stock needs to be rich and diverse, and in appropriate languages for the needs of the young people and their parents.
- *Other Considerations*
- Have a look at the lending procedures in your library. Fines and charges can put off many young people and their parents. Think

about the benefits that can come from relaxing reservation charges. It is not the children's fault that a library does not have the book they want; and the library is really wanting to encourage new readers and their wider reading – not to put them off!

- Many young people think the library is expensive, so get the message across that its free to join, and almost always free to use.

1.3 Inspiring Reading and Learning – and having fun

(i) Activities for Under Fives

In their early years children develop key skills they need for life, and stories, books and reading can help them in acquiring and building those skills.

Libraries work closely with parents and carers, and with all early years services and organizations, to inspire and support children's learning and development. This work is often part of national and local programmes such as Bookstart and Sure Start.

There are also numerous early years initiatives in libraries across the country which are being coordinated in a national network by CILIP (the Chartered Institute of Libraries and Information professionals)

Story and Rhyme Times

Sharing stories and rhymes with very young children is an especially enjoyable library activity which can make important and pleasurable differences for all involved. Evidence from programmes such as Bookstart is showing that children introduced to books and stories at an early age start school with an advantage that can last throughout their life.

Being read to

- Helps children learn to talk and develop language, and supports children in developing the skills to read themselves.
- Builds their listening skills and stimulates their imagination.
- Being read to, right from infancy, gives children the pleasure of sharing and communicating with others, and a sense of closeness

(ii) For parents and carers

Joining in a storytime

- Gives parents new rhymes and stories to share with their children
- Gives the pleasure of sharing in the activity with their children
- Gives the chance to meet with other parents and carers

(iii) For library staff

Running a storytime

- Develops storytelling skills and confidence
- Develops skills in planning and management
- Builds up knowledge about the books and stories

(iv) Rhymetimes

in libraries are becoming increasingly popular. Tiny babies can join in on an equal footing with toddlers and children who are ready for pre-school: at a few months they are smiling and bouncing on a lap to the sound and the rhythm of the rhymes; once they can sit up they share the library mat with other babies, clapping and jingling; and once they can walk, they dance!

See: *Take them to the library: Early years provision in libraries* Youth Libraries Group 0 946581 22 3

Contact: CILIP <www.cilip.org.uk> For information about the national network of Early Years work in libraries

1.4 Activities for School Age Children

(i) Storytimes

Joining in a storytime is special at any age. It gives all those benefits and skills listed above and is a wonderfully pleasurable thing to do.

As children get older stories and reading give them the chance to work through life's issues and changes at a safe distance. Traditional stories in particular both entertain and pass on messages about key life experiences and universal truths.

(ii) Storytrails

These are literature-based activities with a story at the centre. As children become involved in the activities they are able to relive the story, using their imagination as much as enjoying the skills of the storyteller.

This approach works especially well with stories about a quest or a journey – for example:

A Bhattacharia *The Enchanted Palace* J Ingham Associates 1854740121
A Barber *Catkin* Walker Books 0744577950
Colin McNaughton *Jolly Roger* Walker Books 074451732X

(iii) Activities which can link into these stories include
- Drawing picture maps of the journey (or a treasure map for 'Jolly Roger'
- Action games: 'Statues' when the characters in 'The Enchanted Palace' are turned to stone; 'Treasure Hunt' with 'Jolly Roger', hunting 'gold' coins around the library and getting to know it at the same time
- Singing: a lullaby, for Catkin to sing to the child Carrie

Try: Paul Geraghty *The Hunter* Red Fox 0099666316
Read the story to the children, then ask them to pretend they are being hunted. They have to lie on the ground and keep very still – the first one to move is out. Those who are out prowl around and try to spot any children who are moving.

Then they can hunt around the library for animals. Give them a list of animal names with the classification numbers of the books they are in – then hunt through the shelves. (The children could also look up the class. numbers themselves).

Tell a story about one of the animals the children find.

Draw together an African animals frieze based on the book. Pin up a background in yellow and black using the pictures in 'The Hunter' as inspiration. Then draw and cut out African animal silhouettes to stick onto the background.

Once you get the feel of which stories work well you can think of many more.

It is important to keep the story as a whole within this activity – the idea is for the children to feel even more a part of the story.

1.5 Reading Groups

Reading groups are a great way for children and library staff – and often parents and carers – to get together and talk about books.

An increasing number of libraries are setting these groups up for young people in libraries, aged from 4 years through to teenage. The groups often give children the chance to make new friends, from different schools, and to talk about their reading likes and dislikes in a way which is not always possible in the more structured, curriculum-focused work at school.

Schools are finding, however, that children joining in library reading groups are often becoming more confident and able readers.

In running reading groups libraries are working to make a difference for young people in all or some of the following ways:

- Providing new reading ideas for young people to widen and deepen their reading
- Developing young people's confidence about themselves as readers
- Developing young people's skills and confidence in formulating and expressing their opinions
- Developing peer to peer reading support
- Offering children the chance to interact positively with adults about reading (e.g. library staff and parents/carers)
- Increasing the time children spend reading and sharing books
- Increasing the sense of belonging to a community
- Providing an activity where children are having a really good time reading and talking about books

(These aims are those of the Orange Chatterbooks network of children's reading groups based in libraries)

Reading group sessions can include a range of activities, including:

- Talking about books read, maybe taking turns to talk in a circle, or discussing in small groups
- Writing or drawing something about books read, perhaps picking out 'The bit which stays in my mind most', or 'The character I liked best'.
- Book covers: do they really tell you what the book is like?
- Reading the beginning and/or last part of a book: now do you want to read the rest? Why?

- Comparing different formats of a story: book, film, video, story tape, TV version
- Joining up with an adult reading group to talk about favorite books, or about particular children's books
- Joining up with other young people's reading groups to share book feelings and opinions across the Internet

Family Reading Groups and Teenage Reading Groups work on the same principles as above.

1.6 Summer Reading Challenges

For many years libraries have run reading games and challenges, encouraging young people to

- Keep on reading during school holidays
- Come into the library to join in holiday activity programmes
- Talk with library staff about the books they have read

There is now a national UK summer reading challenge, encapsulating the above activities, coordinated by The Reading Agency and bought into by 85% of UK library authorities. Each year the challenge has a different theme, such as 'Reading Safari' and 'Reading Maze', and high quality publicity and activity materials are provided. The central activity of the challenge is simple but very effective: children are challenged to read (or have read to them) 6 books during the summer. They then come into the library and talk with library staff about their books and receive a sticker for their Challenge card for each book read. If they complete their card they win a medal and a certificate, presented to them at the end of the holidays. A bank of evidence is being collected, showing how this library activity too, is really making a difference for children and their reading.

Below are ideas for making the challenge work well.

- Create a focal point for summer reading: a 'reading challenge' point using promotional materials and children's own recommendations of 'must reads'
- Make a special summer 'book chat area' with comfy chairs or cushions

- Lots of inviting book displays, dumpbins, ideas about what to read next
- Have a point on the desk with the summer challenge publicity, that is just for young people, with staff there to talk with them about their reading

1.7 Ongoing Reading Schemes and Challenges

Public and school libraries often run reading challenges through term time on the same lines as the summer challenge described above.

These have the same benefits, not only in supporting and stimulating children's reading but also in developing the skills of the adults involved in talking with children about books.

Carnegie and Kate Greenaway Medals: Shadowing

The Carnegie Medal is awarded annually by children's librarians for an outstanding book for children and young people, and the Kate Greenaway is awarded for an outstanding children's book in terms of illustration.

Every year groups of children in schools and libraries all over the UK 'shadow' the judging by reading the shortlisted books themselves, discussing them in their groups and also over the Internet on the special Carnegie Greenaway Shadowing website. They then vote for the titles they think should win – and see how it compares with the adult judges selection!

This scheme has become increasingly popular and has significantly increased the profile and the debating around these medals ('The Booker of the playground'). In 2003 1200 groups of young people took part.

1.8 Author Visits to Libraries

An author visit is a special library event in several ways. It is anticipated and enjoyed – and actually meeting and talking with authors and illustrators often inspires children's reading, and also their own writing and illustration.

There is so much that a really good author, poet, storyteller or illustrator can bring to the reading and the library experience that it's well worth looking for ways to fund such a visit. This could be through a library and school sharing costs, or by contacting publishers who may be promoting new talent or putting together promotional tours.

A number of authors have their own, and often very good websites, where young people can talk with them via email. Or there may be possibilities with video-conferencing – perhaps sharing in an author session hundreds of miles away!

1.9 Using ICT

The marriage of ICT and reading can be really effective, with each enhancing access to the other. The internet offers innovative and dynamic ways of broadening reading opportunities, giving more reader choice and more possibilities for interaction with both authors and fellow readers.

Remember **virtual** meetings as well. A number of authors have their own, often very good websites, where young people can talk with them via email. Or there may be possibilities with video-conferencing – perhaps sharing in an author session hundreds of miles away.

Young people can talk with each other about reading via sites like Stories from the Web; they can write their own book reviews for sites like Cool Reads, and write their own stories on sites like Kids on the Net.

Library and school reading groups can set up virtual contact, emailing each other about their favorite – and not-so-favorite reads.

See*: Read Smarter Not Harder: reading promotions for children's libraries* Youth Libraries Group 0946581193

All Our Children: social inclusion and children's libraries Youth Libraries Group 0946581215

1.10 Making the Library a Helpful and Supportive Place for Children's Homework

In helping with children's homework, as in all library activity with young people, most important of all is the welcome, support and guidance provided by library staff. As described above, this is achieved by thoughtful staff recruitment and investment in staff training, focusing on the needs of young readers and learners.

To provide relevant materials and services to support children's homework the library needs to consult and work with:

- The local education service so that it has up-to-date knowledge of the curriculum and education priorities
- Local schools, so that the library can complement and support schools' work, and the school can encourage young people to use the library
- Young people themselves, so that the facilities and resources in the library are what they need

Activities and resources which the library could offer include:

Homework Collections

Most libraries now include collections of books to support young people's homework, housed in a dedicated area and often with titles held as 'reference only', or issued on short-term loans, so that they can be as available as possible for children coming in to study. The collection content will be based on curriculum needs and may also include GCSE/A Level subject study guides.

Study Areas

Where there is room in a library, study areas for young people are often provided, placed with the resources they are most likely to need, including Homework Collections and access to computers.

Homework Clubs

Many libraries now run Homework Clubs for young people. These can operate at several different levels:

- Special Homework Help time – e.g. after school/early evening – when a member of the library staff is available at the counter to help with children's homework enquiries
- Library Homework Club – e.g. one or more evenings a week – where children bring their homework to do in the library and dedicated helpers are available to work with them. These Clubs may also include activities to develop young people's information, learning and ICT skills.

- Study Support Centres, run in partnership with schools, education services, youth services

School Class Visits

School class visits to the library are a core area of library's work. This visits may well be a child's first opportunity to come to the library if they live at a distance, or if they have not come with their parents.

Libraries use these visits

- To welcome and introduce children to the library, its facilities, and the people who work there
- To encourage children to feel confident and at home in the library – and to enjoy it as their space
- To encourage and inspire them in their reading – through story-times, book talks, and other reading-based activities
- To help them develop their information and study skills – e.g. through activities based on the search tools available in the library: catalogue, subject index, library guiding.

All of this class visit content will provide a valuable foundation for building young people's confidence and competence in using the library for their homework.

1.11 Guidelines for a Storytime Session

Every children's librarian and teacher will want to share stories with children. Here are some helpful guidelines:

- Come to the storytime with more books than you need – all of them stories which you like and have practised reading out loud
- Clear the story corner of any distractions – toys etc
- Settle yourself and the group where the light is shining on you and not on children's eyes. Also try to sit where the children are not distracted by people passing by.
- Settle the children on the floor – they will be more comfortable and less fidgety! – and yourself at a level just a bit higher than them. You will then be able to se them easily, and they will be able to see the pictures in the book.
- Hold the book so they can see it clearly – check this out.

- Use as much eye contact as possible: make it seem as if you are actually telling the story.
- Acknowledge interruptions (e.g. 'we've got a new puppy . . .') but don't let them take over. You can pick those stories up at the end.
- Vary the tone and pace of your reading: keep it interesting.

Particularly with younger children

- Little ones have shorter concentration spans – the whole world around them is so exciting! Have lots of different kinds of stories in your bag: short, longer, funny, something to think about, noisy, lyrical . . . And don't worry if they don't always keep their attention on them – their concentration will grow!
- Include rhymes and simple action games in your storytime programme. Use soft toys and puppets if you like.
- And with very young children your storytime will be for parents too! Encourage mums and dads and carers to stay – maybe their children will want to sit on their lap and they can all enjoy the story and join in!

2. The School

> 'Of course you know your A B C?' said the Red Queen.
> 'To be sure I do,' said Alice.
> 'So do I,' the White Queen whispered . . . and I'll
> tell you a secret – I can read words of one letter!
> Isn't that grand!'
>
> *Carroll, 1994, 137*

The principle of immersion in language and literature continues beyond the home into school life. Here the wise and competent professional will relate literature across the curriculum. Not only will it be pleasurable for children – if used discreetly and without overt goals that have essential results to be scrutinized and measured – but it will also involve the development of children's multiple intelligences. Dianne Swenson Koehnecke, who teaches Curriculum and Instruction, demonstrates this principle when she says of her own pre-school experience:

> When I **listened** to . . . *folktales, I was using my linguistic intelligence. When my mother asked me to* **compare The Three Little Pigs** *with* **The Three Billy Goats Gruff**, *she was asking me to use*

*my mathematical intelligence. When I **drew** pictures about the stories, my spatial intelligence was working, and when I **reflected** about the tales before I fell asleep ... I used my intra personal intelligence.[1]*

Koehnecke, 1995, 243

Koehnecke continues to tell how the literature experience, which in her case focused on folktales, also contributed to *bodily-kinesthetic* intelligence while application to singing and rhyme developed *musical* intelligence.

Story reading, story writing and listening to stories that are told rather than read, all have a place in the classroom where children are immersed in language. The emphasis on Storytelling in this text applies to the classroom teacher just as much as it does to librarians, while in the home, children love to hear parents and grandparents tell about when were young and their adventures in the 'olden times'. Chamber points out that 'Storytelling is indispensable in enabling [people to become literary readers.'

Important aspects of literacy development in the primary school, such as Graham and Kelly point out, are:

- Everyone Reading in Class
- Reading Aloud to Children
- Shared Reading and Writing
- The Class Reader (a novel for the whole class, for the teacher to read aloud to children)
- Drama and playing in role
- Teaching specific, required skills. (In the case of reading, these are phonic and graphic knowledge) As is accepted today, there is good evidence that both whole language experiences and instruction in phonetics and decoding should be included in the curriculum.

Story telling also features because it offers another dimension of perceiving. Graham and Kelly state:

Of course, children need to have a full and varied exposure to print but we cannot ignore the 'bigger shapes' of literacy learning to which story-telling contributes.

Graham and Kelly, 2000, 77.

---

[1] Bold is mine – M. Trim.

A number of texts give advice on how to go about story telling. Many teachers enjoy telling stories to children and take to it naturally – and their well-told stories grip the attention of teens as well as younger children. Practice does help to make perfect, however, and the steps which manuals prescribe are well worth heeding.

Some points to remember are to: keep eye contact with the class, to visualize the action and the characters and hear their voices. Then you can tell the story as you see it – better than memorization, for it will flow easily with some of your own personality coming through which helps to make it believable. Use direct speech, act out some of the action and when it is applicable, use humour. The children will be saying 'Tell us another story, pl-eee-ase!'

Some 'Do Nots' concern: (i) pointing out a moral. Young children cannot think in abstract anyway, and older children will not want you to tell them what is obvious. (ii) And NEVER ask children questions in the middle of your story!

2.1 Favourite Literature-Related Activities

Here are some favourite classroom activities from Australia which not all teachers will know.

(i) *Story maps.* Young children enjoy illustrating a journey route, and many books, suited to children of all ages, lend themselves to this. For young children, try Michael Rosen's *We're Going on a Bear Hunt,* or John Burningham's *The Shopping Basket*, or *Rosie's Walk* by Pat Huitchins. Nursery Rhymes, such as 'Jack and Jill' or stories, for example 'Little Red Riding Hood', can be mapped, as also can Odyseus' journeys from legends of Ancient Greece. Older children can map out the secret parts of the house where *The Borrowers* lived, or the itinerary through the Chocolate Factory with Dahl's famous Charlie, or follow the route taken by David in Ann Holm's *I am David* or, by Sade and Feme in *The Other Side of Truth,* or the journeys in the Pullman series, *His Dark Materials.* The journey taken by Bunyan's Christian can be plotted out with appropriate illustration, as can events in the Shakespearian plays, *Romeo and Juliet,* and *A Midsummer Night's Dream.*

(ii) *Literary Passport* Make a booklet that resembles a passport. It should contain a sketch of the book character described and include the following headings for elaboration:

(iii) *Missing Person.* One student submitted the following work, set out as on a Missing Person poster, including illustration of the missing character.

> NAME: Wicked Witch of the West
> ADDRESS: Western Oz
> PHYSICAL DESCRIPTION: Ugly
> EYES: One telescopic
> HAIR: Long and black
> FEATURES: Owns a gold cap, enjoys enslaving Winkies and other unfortunate folk.
> Last seen in the company of a young female, Dorothy of Kansas. The witch is very afraid of water, so do not bother checking the ponds.
> If seen dead, bring peroof to the Wizard of Oz for REWARD.
> If seen alive, RUN!

(iv) *A Letter* (Written in role)

> The Eastern Forest
> The Land of Oz
> 30 February, 1911
>
> Dear Agony Aunt,
> I am a lion. I am supposed to be King of the Beasts, but I am too much of a coward. When I see a man, elephant or tiger, I am so scared I can't do anything but roar. Do you know any way for me to overcome these fearful feelings? Please answer as soon as possible.
>
> Sincerely scared,
> The Cowardly Lion
> (signed with foot prints)

(v) *Musicals/Dramas* help to bring literature to life. The story of Joseph in the musical version (with his dream coat) can involve many players. The story of Noah is brought marvelously to life through Benjamin Britten's *Noye's Fludde* in which about one hundred children can take part, many in masks and costumes to represent different animals and birds. One performance is described as follows:

> The Ark sailed through a terrible storm. Noah had to cling to the mast, and all the animals prayed as mighty waves lashed the vessel

and rain poured down. The man on the drums got tired arms from hitting the drums so hard, pretending it was thunder ... Noah woke Felicity who ... was playing the part of the dove. 'Fly out my dear, and see if there is land,' he said ... Because she shouldn't really fly, she had to dance like a bird flying ... She flew up the aisle, running lightly and came back with an olive branch in her hand ... the flood was receding!

Some books are available in play format for performance, as is *Charlie and the Chocolate Factory*. However, children of all ages enjoy scripting their own versions of stories, or acting them out spontaneously in unscripted drama. In drama as a way into learning, strongly pioneered by Dorothy Heathcote, it becomes more than mere play but a real, felt experience where children get inside of characters, are faced with decisions and consequences.

(vi) *Unscripted Drama*

Method. The teacher can make control and direction easy by taking on a *role* within the story. Inclusion of relevant props, some made beforehand by the children themselves, helps them to suspend their disbelief and become really involved. *Questions* guide the action if the children themselves are not forthcoming. Using *The Sea People* by Muller and Steiner, the following are examples of types of questions that open up the enactment as the teacher moves among the children of the Greater and Lesser Islands:

> *'Hello, my brother. Are you just back from fishing? Did you have a good catch?'*
> *"And who are you? I have lived so long on the Greater Island I thought I knew everyone., but I am growing old and I don't remember your face.'*
> *"May I visit you today? I could help you mend your nets. Or are you a nobleman?*
> *'Which do you think is the best market stall for fruit and vegetables? For tools?'*

The best questions begin with Who, How, Why, When, Where. Children need to know the story, or a particular incident, well before they improvise; beforehand they also need to have talked about the person they choose to become. There can always be onlookers to the plot who can be involved. Make stories live, even beyond the printed page!

Children's Sayings

'We all like it when Mr. John tells us stories. Some of them make us laugh! Some are sort-of serious, like Bible stories and from History. And he has pictures 'n puppets and things.' Pat's Primary -Assembly

Tutorial Activity

1. Librarians or teachers should work through Chapter Six together, selecting to read and discuss what is relevant to their situation.
2. Select two stories: one for preschoolers and one for an older age group. Prepare and share your story in a storytelling session. Keep your notes and post-story observations for future use.

Further Reading

Bauer, Caroline Feller. *Caroline Feller Bauer's New Handbook for Storytellers*. London: ALA, 1995.
—— *Leading Kids to Books through Puppets*. London: ALA, 1997.
Clipson-Boyles, S. 'The Role of Drama in the Literate Classroom', in Goodwin, P. (ed). *The Literate Classroom*. London: David Fulton Publishers, 1999.
Grugeon, E. and P. Gardner. *The Art of Storytelling for Teachers and Pupils*. London: David Fulton Publishers, 2000.
Kathleen T. Horning. *From Cover to Cover*: Evaluating and Reviewing Children's Books. London: HarperCollins Juvenile Books, 1997.

Suggested Titles for Storytime

Jez Alborough	*Duck in a truck*	Picture Lions	0006647170
	Can Duck's friends help him out of the mud?		
Quentin Blake	*Mr. Magnolia*	Red Fox	0099400421
	Mr. Magnolia has a dinosaur, parakeets … but only one boot!		
Ruth Brown	*A dark dark tale*	Red Fox	0099874008
	Follow the black cat through the dark wood & into the castle		
John Burningham	*Mr. Gumpy's outing*	Red Fox	0099408791
	Can the children & the animals all fit into Mr. Gumpy's boat?		

| Rod Campbell | *Dear Zoo* | Macmillan | 0333712781 |
| | I wrote to the zoo for a pet, could they get it right? | | |

| Rod Cambell | *Oh Dear!* | Macmillan | 0333733401 |
| | Buster goes round the farm in search of an egg for breakfast | | |

| Eric Carle | *The very hungry caterpillar* | Puffin Books | 0140569324 |
| | A newly hatched caterpillar eats its way through this book | | |

| *Lynley Dodd* | *Hairy Maclary* | Puffin Books | 0140505318 |
| | Hairy Maclary goes for a walk with some doggy friends | | |

| Julia Donaldson | *The Gruffalo* | Macmillan | 0333710932 |
| | What happens when mouse meets a Gruffalo in the forest? | | |

| Sarah Hayes | *This is the bear* | Walker Books | 0744509696 |
| | The adventures of a bear: a simple story in rhyme | | |

| Eric Hill | *Where's Spot?* | Puffin Books | 0140504206 |
| | Lift the flaps to join in Spot's adventure | | |

| Shirley Hughes | *Alfie gets in first* | Red Fox | 0099256053 |
| | Alfie is shut indoors with the key – how will Mum get in? | | |

| Pat Hutchins | *Rosie's walk* | Red Fox | 009941399X |
| | Rosie the hen went for a walk – with the fox behind her | | |

| Mick Inkpen | *The blue balloon* | Hodder | 0340757388 |
| | It's amazing what happens when you find a magic balloon | | |

| Judith Kerr | *The tiger who came to tea* | Picture Lions | 0006640613 |
| | A classic fantasy for young children's imaginations | | |

| Julie Lacome | *Walking through the jungle* | Walker Books | 074453643X |
| | Action and imagination in a jungle adventure | | |

| David McKee | *Elmer the patchwork elephant* | Red Fox | 0099697203 |
| | Elmer is different from other elephants, & equally lovable | | |

| Margaret Mahy | *A lion in the meadow* | Puffin Books | 0140506306 |
| | Is the lion in the meadow a real lion? | | |

| Jill Murphy | *Five minutes' peace* | Walker Books | 0744560012 |
| | Mrs. Large tries to get 5 minutes' peace from her family | | |

Jill Murphy   *Peace at last*   Macmillan   0333631986
                   How can Mr. Bear sleep when the night is so noisy?

Michael Rosen   *We're going on a bear hunt*   Walker Books0744523230
                   Lovely text & illustrations for this story with actions

Maurice Sendak   *Where the wild things are*   Red Fox   0099408392
                   A magic boat takes Max to the land of the wild things

Elfrida Vipont   *The elephant and the bad baby* Puffin Books 0140500480
                   A ride & treats for the baby – but he doesn't say please!

Martin Waddell   *Owl Babies*   Walker Books0744531675
                   Poor Percy misses his mum and is so glad to see her again

Shigeo Watanabe   *How do I put it on?*   Puffin Books 0140503609
                   A little bear isn't sure how he should put his clothes on

Titles for Older Children

Lots of lovely title to use – these below are just a taste.
And do include traditional folk tales and poetry

Quentin Blake   *The story of the dancing frog*   Red Fox   0099535513
                   A lovely fantasy about superstar George, the dancing frog

Tony Bradman   *Who's afraid of the big bad wolf?*   Mammoth
0749704136
                   Lift the flaps to find the wolf and the three little pigs

Jonathan Langley *Three billy-goats Gruff*   Collins   0001842145
                   Traditional story of the three goats and a troll at the bridge

Jonathan Long   *The dog that dug*   Red Fox   0099986108
                   A dog digs deep for his bone – and unearths amazing things

Susan Price   *Forbidden doors*   Faber   057116837X
                   Traditional stories of those who have dared to open
                   forbidden doors – includes 'Mr. Fox'

Jon Scieszka   *The true story of the three little pigs*
                                                      Puffin Books 0140540563
                   The whole big bad wolf thing was just a misunderstanding

Useful Sources for Further Information and Ideas

Publications

Elkin, J & Kinnell, M (2000) *A Place for children: public libraries as a major force in children's reading* Library Association Publishing 1856043207

Start with the child: report of CILIP Working Group on library provision for children and young people (2002) CILIP (Chartered Institute of Library and Information Professionals)

Framework for the Future: Libraries, Learning and Information in the Next Decade (2003) HMSO

Organizations

CILIP: Chartered Institute for Library and Information Professionals <www.cilip.org.uk>

School Libraries Group (SLG). A special interest group of CILIP which promotes school libraries and school library services as being essential to all areas of the curriculum, to enable the exploitation of a wide range of resources, develop pupils' information skills, encourage the reading habit and support equal opportunities and multi-cultural education. <www.cilip.org.uk/groups/slg/slg.html>

Youth Libraries Group (YLG) This is a special interest group of CILIP, which works to preserve and influence the provision of quality literature, library and information services for children and young people in public libraries and school library services. <www.cilip.org.uk/groups/ylg/index.html>

School Libraries Association: supports all those committed to the promotion and development of school libraries and information literacy. <www.sla.org.uk>

The Reading Agency: The Reading Agency is a library development agency and registered charity working to inspire and support libraries in creating the best possible access to books and reading for everyone. It is supported by The Arts Council of England, CILIP, and Southern and South East Arts. <www.readingagency.org.uk>

Their Reading Futures: This is a programme coordinated by The Reading Agency which is supports and enhances libraries' work in providing high quality reading services in libraries for all young people. Its website provides useful strategies and resources for this work, and also opportunities for library staff to network and share ideas for good practice. <www.theirreadingfutures.org.uk>

Bookstart: <www.bookstart.co.uk>

Booktrust: <www.booktrusted.com>

Federation of Children's Book Groups: <www.fcbg.org.uk>

Mencap: <www.mencap.org.uk>

National Library for the Blind: <www.nlb-online.org>

National Literacy Trust: <www.literacytrust.org.uk>

Sure Start: <www.surestart.gov.uk>

Websites about Children's Books and Reading

Achuka: Children's Books UK. Provides news, interviews, publication notices, author profiles, and more <www.achuka.co.uk>
Carnegie Greenaway Shadowing: <www.carnegiegreenaway.org.uk>
Cool Reads: <www.cool-reads.co.uk>
Kids on the Net: <www.kotn.ntu.ac.uk>
Stories from the Web: <www.storiesfromtheweb.org>

Bibliography

Burningham, John. *The Shopping Basket*. London: Red Fox, 2000.

Carroll, Lewis. *Through the Looking Glass*. Reissue. London: Puffin Books, 1994.

Chambers, Aidan. *The Reading Environment: How Adults Help Children Enjoy Books*. South Woodchester: Thimble Press, 1991, 46.

Farrelly, Alan and Ron Morrison. *Two By Two*. Adelaide: Rigby ~Ltd, 1962.

Graham, Judith and Alison Kelly. *Reading Under Control: Teaching Reading in the Primary School*. Second edition, reprint. London: David Fulton, in association with University of Surrey Roehampton, 2001.

Hutchins, Pat. *Rosie's Walk*. Reprint. London: Picture Puffins, 1982.

Johnson, Terry D. and Daphne R. Louis. *Literacy Through Literature*. Sydney: Methuen, 1985.

Koehnecke Dianne Swenson. 'Folklore and the Multiple Intelligences.' In *Children's Literature in Education*, Volume 26, Number 4, December 1995, 243.

Muller, Jorg and Jorg Steiner. *The Sea People*. London: Victor Gollancz, 1982.

Pressley, Michael. *Reading Instruction that Works*. New York: The Guilford Press, 1998.

Rosen, Michael and Helen Oxenbury. *We're Going on a Bear Hunt*. London: Walker Books, 1989.

Wagner, Betty Jane. *Dorothy Heathcote: Drama as a Learning Medium*. Reprint. London: Hutchinson, 1984.

CHAPTER SEVEN

Selecting Electronic Books

'and what is the use of a book,' thought Alice, 'with pixels but no pagination?'

(Finn, 1999, XI)

The significance of literacy and children being able to develop reading skills is universally accepted (see, for instance, the National Literacy Strategy (Department for Education and Employment, 1998); the Government funded National Year of Reading 1998–99 (Attenborough, 1999) and the National Reading Campaign (2000)). However, concerns have been expressed about the effect on children of the increasing emphasis on and importance of modern technologies such as film, television and video. The preponderance of such new technologies has led to the emergence of a generation accustomed to experiencing other media in addition to print as part of everyday life. Often termed the "television generation," or the "computer generation", these young people are said to be exposed to a large number of images via the visual media. There is no doubt that television viewing is a significant part of children's lives, as demonstrated by *Fact File 2002*, 2001 figures for the UK which state that, in 2000 55% of children (persons aged under 16) had a television and 19% had a video recorder in their bedroom. In addition, children are now able to use computers for an abundance of purposes, and have become so computer literate, according to Meek, 1991 and Bromley, 1996, that they are often more conversant with computers than their parents.

The predominance of, and children's great interest in, the visual media such as video, audio, comics and magazines, film, television and

Illustration 7: 'Pixels but no pagination.' Front cover from ALICE'S ADVEN-TURES IN WONDERLAND AND THROUGH THE LOOKING GLASS by Lewis Carroll (Puffin 1997). Cover illustration by James Marsh. Cover image used by licence from Penguin Press.

computers necessarily leads to them experiencing a large number of images. This is said to be causing children to develop a more sophisticated level of "visual literacy" than they might formerly have done. This phrase means "the ability to find meaning in imagery" (Yenawine, 1997), and it has been argued that constructing meaning from the enormous variety of images present in contemporary culture calls upon a variety of different skills. For example, "a straightforward news photo requires fewer, simpler operations than a psychologically manipulative ad (and) an illustration engages the viewer differently from abstract painting . . ." (Yenawine, 1997, 845). The combination of these skills is called visual literacy, or alternatively "media literacy" (Desmond, 1997). One result of the increasing significance of visual literacy is that more importance is being placed on extending the definition of literacy to include the reading of electronic formats (Meek, 1991; Adams, 1986). Furthermore, the substantial influence which the digital world may be having on printed literature for young people has been noted by Dresang (1997) – a natural and inevitable transformation of form and content in the arena of texts for children in an increasingly electronic society.

Arguments have been put stating that the increase in concentration on images and the more sophisticated levels of visual literacy affect both children's attention span and their desire to read. This is aptly illustrated by one particular finding of a study investigating the relationship between young people and new media. Children participating in the study described books as being "old-fashioned, boring, frustrating, and on their way out . . . Books, we were told . . . are too long, take too much effort . . . They have too many words and don't get to the point, the action is too slow, and there are no pictures." (Livingstone and Bovill, 1999). For children to whom visual literacy has become very significant, a relatively new medium – the electronic book – might appear rather attractive.

1. Defining the Electronic Book

As its name suggests, an electronic book is ". . . a text analogous to a book, that is in digital form to be displayed on a computer screen . . ." (Feather and Sturges, 1997). This useful definition introduces the idea that the content is electronic, and that it is contained in a similar way to the contents of a conventional or printed book. The origin of the term "electronic book" can be traced back as far as the late 1960s (van

Dam, 1966) and also to a reference in 1979 (Goldberg, 1979). Indeed, it has been suggested that the concept of the electronic book goes back to at least 1945, when Vannevar Bush (1945) postulated an imaginary system called the Memex, which could store large amounts of text and allowed users to index and organize information (Reynolds and DeRose, 1992). However, the concept of an electronic book has only comparatively recently been realised physically as a result of the evolution of technologies such as the Internet and the introduction of hypertext and data storage media such as CD-ROM (Compact Disc Read Only Memory).

The electronic book is therefore a significant new medium, which can offer added value to the perhaps more familiar printed book through its potential for including other media in addition to text on its pages. The electronic book can offer such extra features as animation, sound, hypertext connectivity, customizability and rapid information retrieval through quick searching facilities. These elements represent interactivity, which distinguishes the electronic book from its more static printed counterpart (Kafai and Soloway, 1994; Parham, 1995). Electronic books may be available on a variety of media, for example, on the Internet, on dedicated, portable reading devices and on CD-ROM. They have the capability to include a variety of types of content (e.g. fiction, non fiction), and to vary in both their presentation (e.g. book metaphor, input and output devices) and their functionalities (e.g. audio, animation). These are the significant features of an electronic book, which operate independently by overlaying each other.

The same electronic book can be presented either on CD-ROM or via the Internet, and the various electronic books which are currently presented on CD-ROM offer differing functionalities, and so on. This is an important point: because of the speed at which new technology changes, the medium on which electronic books are available is also subject to rapid change. The dominant medium has previously been CD-ROM (see Figure 1), however, e-book readers have now become more prevalent. An e-book (or sometimes e-Book) is the electronic text which is displayed on a reader – a device for reading electronic books which has emerged from the improving technology of laptop computers or subnotebooks (McKenna, 1998). Readers could be considered to be a descendant of the less successful Sony Data Discman (Vinzant, 1998), and approach the ideal of the portable electronic book. There are three types of reader: handheld (computers such as Personal Digital Assistants (PDAs) which can be used to read

The first little pig found some straw.
"This will make a good house," he said.
He bundled and tied and made a house of straw.

Figure 7.1: The Three Little Pigs – CD-ROM, © Europress Software 1997

e-books), dedicated (designed solely for reading e-books) and desktop readers (software installed on a standard PC or laptop) (Ormes, 2001).

2. The Book Metaphor

The electronic book is so called because it takes the printed book as its model and adds electronic features. The main reason for taking the printed book as the model is because of its universal interface, that is, the majority of people know how to use a printed book, and there are well-established mental models and manipulation skills (Carroll et al, 1988) associated with printed books which makes them easy to use. As a result, electronic books make use of the book metaphor, that is, they preserve the logical structure of printed books, e.g. chapters and indexes, and their physical and logical aspects, e.g. pages, book thickness analogies (Barker, 1997; Catenazzi and Sommaruga, 1994; Landoni et al, 1993). The intention is to make the electronic book easier to use, an important factor to consider if young people are to be

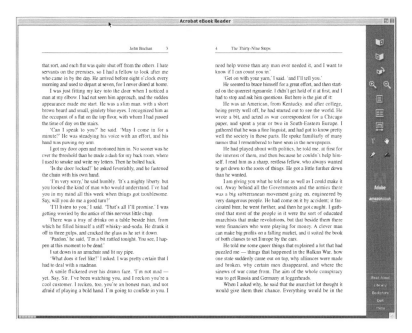

Figure 7.2: Extract from The Thirty-Nine Steps by John Buchan, as viewed on a desktop reader – Adobe Acrobat eBook Reader

the end users. The benefits of the book metaphor have been demonstrated recently by the favorable results which have been obtained from an evaluation of an electronic book which employs it by Landoni and Gibb (2000). Having kept some of the characteristics of the printed book, the electronic book adds the features and functionalities noted earlier. The use of the book metaphor can be seen in Figure 2, which features a page from a CD-ROM version of *Alice's Adventures in Wonderland*. The contents take the form of numbered chapters, and each screen is set out like the page of a book, having a white background with black text, and a turned-down corner to suggest the qualities of a printed page. The menus are shaped liked printed books and the graphics surrounding each screen or page depict an open book. A bookmark with a tasselled end, depicted in computer graphics, may be inserted to keep a note of a particular page.

Researchers have suggested that, in order to produce the most effective electronic book, attempts should be made to identify all the advantages and disadvantages of the printed book. By retaining the

Figure 7.3: Alice's Adventures in Wonderland – CD-ROM, © Europress Software 1997

advantages, eradicating the disadvantages, and incorporating the benefits of the electronic medium an efficient electronic book can be developed (Catenazzi et al, 1993; Benest, 1991). This concept is taken further with the proposition that the electronic book can only become widely accepted if it can offer the same properties as the conventional book, for example, rendering the computer screen as readable as paper (Landoni et al, 1993), and making electronic books as portable as conventional books (Goodman, 1993). Such concerns involve the problems of hardware and software development (Landoni et al, 1993), of which a large part are now being addressed by the appropriate advances in technology (Collier, 1993). With regard to the problems associated with reading from screens, however, it could be argued that the children of the present time are less likely to experience problems, since they are so accustomed to looking at screens of all shapes and sizes while interacting with new technology and new media. Indeed, the suggestion has been made that, for the child who has grown up with handheld computer games machines, using PDA technology might appear to be more "natural and desirable than using the printed book" (Gosling, 1998).

3. Advantages of Electronic Books for Children

An electronic book which employs the book metaphor will therefore be quite similar to a printed one in that it will have pages incorporating text and pictures, but it will offer an extra dimension in having the potential to include additional media on its pages. Therefore, the electronic book represents the combination of the advantages of the printed book with the capabilities of the computer, adding more to the text and pictures in terms of animation, sounds, and a narrator. It has been quite widely argued, therefore, that electronic books might have the power to bridge the 'gap' between print and other media, thereby encouraging reading in those children who are reluctant readers (Adams, 1986; Balajthy, 1988; Jacobson, 1992; Meyer, 1994; Chu, 1995; Meakin, 1997). An illustration of this possibility can be seen in the increasing emphasis which is now being placed on the electronic environment in the teaching of reading (Chu, 1995).

There is much material on the subject of the attractions offered by electronic books to young readers (Graham, 1994; Kafai and Soloway, 1994; Sefton-Green, 1994, Bennett, 1994; Jacobson, 1992). These attractions make the process of reading more like playing a game. However, some writers doubt that the makers of electronic books have fully exploited the computer medium as yet (Kafai and Soloway, 1994; Shade, 1994). It seems that the attractions of the electronic book do delight children (Talley et al., 1997; Chu, 1995), however, in many cases this may be on a first encounter when the concept is new, so that the initial fascination with the special effects inevitably wears off (Chu, 1995).

Some work has also considered whether electronic books could help children to learn to read (Talley et al., 1997; Medwell, 1996; Meyer, 1994), while Miller et al (1994) have noted some improvements in children's reading through the use of storybooks presented on CD-ROM. The educational value of electronic books can be seen, for example, in text being read aloud to help children with reading, and help can be given with difficult words both in terms of pronunciation and meaning, the latter via online dictionaries. Animation can also show concepts in more than one dimension, for example, a diagram of a human heart could be animated to show how the blood flows in and out. However, there have been some doubts about the impact of the visual media in schooling (Sefton-Green, 1994, Shade, 1994; Kafai and Soloway, 1994). Moreover, even if electronic books do help in the teaching and learning of reading, it may not necessarily mean that children will find them an encouragement to read more.

There are two issues within the question of whether electronic books can encourage children to read: whether they encourage children to read more in the form of other electronic texts, and whether they encourage children to read more printed books.

4. Can Electronic Books Encourage Children to Read Other Electronic Texts?

Concerning whether children like reading electronic books, the Children's Literature Research Centre (1996) surveyed 8,800 UK children aged between 4 and 16 on whether they preferred to read electronic books on a computer, to read printed books, or whether they liked to read both equally. The study found that 31% of the boys preferred to read electronic books (with 31% preferring printed books and 38% showing no preference). Of the girls, 7% preferred to read electronic books and 62% preferred printed books, while 31% showed no preference for either format. It was therefore concluded that "Boys exhibit a stronger tendency than girls to use electronic texts" (p230). This may be explained, at least in part, by the fact that boys traditionally prefer to read non-fiction, while girls traditionally prefer to read fiction, and the choice and quality of electronic reference books were thought by the authors of the report to be superior to those of electronic story books at that time. The survey also found that the younger children were reading more electronic fiction than the adolescents. This can be explained by the fact that there was more choice for younger readers than for older readers with regard to story books in the electronic medium.

As to the reasons for preferring one or other medium, more children (31%) rationalized their preference for printed books in anti-computer terms than did children who explained their preference for electronic books as a dislike of printed books (0.78%). This suggests that the children who preferred reading electronic books had no resistance to printed books, but they did have a preference for computers. Conversely, those who preferred to read printed books did exhibit a certain level of resistance to computers. It was also found that the children were emphatic about the virtues of the portability and privacy of the printed book. These results could mean that those children who preferred reading printed books because of their resistance to computers would be unlikely to wish to read other electronic texts. However, having experienced a text they like in the electronic format, they might be encouraged to read the same or similar texts in printed format.

Kafai and Soloway (1994) give an example of a child who reads her printed books over and over again, but reads each of her electronic books only once. Indeed, Graham (1994) feels it unlikely that, as an adult, she would revisit electronic texts, because all the illustrations in the book which she viewed had been enhanced with effects, leading to a lack of the need for creativity on the part of the reader. She suggests there is evidence that children feel the same way, that is, ". . . the work the reader has to do has all been done for them." (p 16). Graham notes that the re-reading of texts is important as a way of helping children to become readers, and does allow that children might want to revisit an electronic text in order either to share the added effects with others, or to experience the effects again themselves. However, being so interested in the pictures, animation and computer effects may mean that the text itself will be largely ignored, so that the book is not really being read.

5. Can Electronic Books Encourage Children to Read More Printed Texts?

With regard to the second issue of whether electronic books can encourage children to read more printed texts, it should first be reiterated that the electronic version of a book can offer a text which is fairly close to the original one, with the added extras available to the medium. However, by its very nature, the electronic version of a text will not be the same as the printed version – the extra dimensions will cause the difference and will act as the enticement to children. Electronic versions of texts are often abridged – such treatment will obviously render the electronic book different from its printed origin. It has been suggested, however, that the parts omitted from an abridged text might be seen as "extras", available to children as they move on to the original version (Waterland, 1989). In the case of electronic versions, they could certainly be seen as an incentive for those children who go on to read the original texts. These issues and others are discussed in detail in Maynard et al (1999).

It is interesting to note that the electronic environment is being used as a means of encouraging children to read more and to share their views on the books they read in the *Stories from the Web* project (1999). There is no other evidence that reading electronic books can encourage the reading of printed texts, so in order to consider this issue further, a comparison could be made with the effects of children's exposure to other non-print versions of literary texts. It is widely accepted that television and film versions of books encourage the reading (or re-reading) of the original text, in the case of both adults and children. For example, the survey by the Children's Literature Research Centre (1996) argues that, ". . . since the early days of radio and television it has clearly been established that . . . hearing/viewing a version of a book stimulates young people to read it for themselves." (p. 95)

The Children's Literature Research Centre report points out that reading a book after or at the same time as listening to or viewing another version of it can make young readers more sure about enjoying and more able to deal with the language, period, and narrative experimentation involved. Indeed, the survey found that experiencing a film version of a book encouraged children to choose to read it. Another survey of children's reading choices (Hall and Coles, 1999) found that "the visual media have a strong influence" (p. 133) on those choices. The survey, carried out in 1994/95, discovered that of the list of books that children had read in the four weeks previous to the survey date, approximately one in seven books had some sort of media tie-in. Watkins and Sutherland (1995) point out how television has been able to encourage reading, and to revitalize such "classics" as *Thomas the Tank Engine*, *The Borrowers* and the Narnia series by C.S. Lewis. They also highlight the fact that television characters have featured in tied-in books, for example, Postman Pat. Indeed, there are many instances of the placing of television and film characters in books, for example, *Teletubbies* (BBC Children's Books, 1997), *Tweenies* (BBC, 1999), *Toy Story 2* (Disney, 2000) and *A Bug's Life* (Disney, 1999). Although this may be seen as a marketing ploy to ensure that the most is made of temporarily popular products, these do have the power to encourage children to read books. In addition, Bradman (1995) discusses current reissues of children's classics, and finds countless versions of *Little Women*, which have been "very likely influenced by the recent film" (Dir. Armstrong, 1995). Furthermore, it is quite plausible that the link between the visual media of television and film and the printed medium might apply the other way round, that is, reading a book might encourage a reader to view a film or television version of the text (Waterland, 1989).

6. Audio Books

Turning to another non-print medium – audio books – the Children's Literature Research Centre (1996) survey found that children who described themselves as 'reluctant' readers were more likely to say they liked listening to tapes as much as, or more than, reading to themselves than those children who described themselves as 'enthusiastic' readers. Perhaps more importantly, the survey also found that, ". . . at all Key Stages significant numbers of respondents said they were stimulated (by listening to a book) not only to read the same book but also to read other books by the same author and other books which they think will be similar" (p 95). It therefore seems that audio books have as much power to encourage children to read printed texts as do television and film.

There is no doubt of the appeal of television and film/video to children. There are also indications that electronic books have many attractions for children, however, these may be temporary in nature. Although claims have been made for the ability of electronic books to utilise these attractions to encourage reluctant readers as well as to encourage children to read more generally, there is no evidence of their having such an influence. If electronic books are sufficiently similar to these media by being equally entertaining and attractive, children should enjoy them as much and, having experienced one electronic book, be encouraged to read more. More time is spent by children watching television than using computers (Livingstone and Bovill, 1999), however, this is very likely to be as a result of access problems, since there are fewer computers in homes than there are televisions. It could be a result of the relative cheapness of televisions, and the fact that they have been available for longer than computers, and have therefore had more time to achieve market penetration.

7. Disadvantages of Electronic Books for Children

A rise in the use of electronic books leads to the question of how they compare with printed books. The added attractions have led to concerns about how children's comprehension of electronic books compares with their comprehension of printed books (Talley et al, 1997; Trushell et al, 2001). The view has been expressed that children will be so interested in the pictures, animation and computer effects that the text itself will be largely ignored (Graham, 1994). On the other hand, Wartella et al (2000) discuss whether "active involvement with computer–based content" increases children's comprehension and retention, and whether it influences "their perceptions of the task so that they are more highly motivated to sustain their attention and engagement". A third argument has been that the special effects have an initial attraction which quite quickly wears off, leading to children ultimately treating computer books as printed books (Chu, 1995).

Some recent research has considered the issue of children's comprehension of electronic books. Greenlee-Moore and Smith (1996) investigated the effects on the reading comprehension of nine and ten year old children of printed narrative texts of different length and complexity, compared to the same narrative texts presented on interactive CD-ROM software on the computer. The fact that only children of above average ability were involved limits the study, as does the fact that it was designed to compare different narrative text types. The authors admit the need for further research into the effects of interactive CD-ROM software when reading narratives.

A UK study by Trushell et al (2001) took as its basis research indicating that reading an electronic book can have beneficial outcomes for pupil's reading. The aim of the study was to investigate small groups reading an electronic book (or as they describe it, an "interactive storybook") without teacher intervention, and to observe whether pupils' recall was affected by a number of factors. There were seven groups, each made up of three children aged 9–10 years, these being of mixed ability and mixed gender. The data which were collected comprised observation schedules noting screen-by-screen progress, recordings of the groups' verbal recall of the story and individual pupils' responses to multiple choice questions concerning the story. The electronic book involved in the study was entitled *Kiyeko and the Lost Night* (LudiMedia/Ubi Soft, 1995). This book is presented on CD-ROM. It offers a linear progression through the text, and features cued animations and effects, which are either incidental and irrelevant to the storyline, or which may provide supplemental information to it. The effects, or interactive details in the illustrations are often described as "hot spots", and respond in various ways when clicked on by a mouse (see Maynard and McKnight, 2001).

Trushell et al (2001) found that participants' recall of the storyline was "poor", and that, although the interface seemed to facilitate linear progression within the text, few of the participant groups read the book from start to finish. They suggest that such reading behaviour might have had an adverse effect on the children's recall of book. With regard to the multiple choice questions, the researchers noted a high incidence of incorrect answers to questions where it was necessary to infer the answer from the book. They concluded that participants' recollections of the book were affected by their descriptions and memories of the hot spots, and that a more intensive choice of hot spots appeared to correspond with pupils exhibiting poorer comprehension.

Maynard and McKnight (2001) carried out a study of user interaction with electronic books, which investigated the effect of the electronic medium on both comprehension and reading speed. The authors compared children reading an electronic book version of Jules Verne's *Journey to the Centre of the Earth* with children reading the same text in two different printed versions. Thirty participants from the UK and aged 9–11 years were involved in this study, and were matched in three groups of ten according to both gender and reading ability. Their comprehension of the book was tested using multiple choice questions about the story. A positive correlation was found between participants' scores for the multiple choice questions and their reading score. It was expected that those with a higher reading score were likely to have better general comprehension skills than those with a lower reading score. The positive correlation confirms this expectation. No evidence was found to suggest that the added effects and visual dimension offered by the electronic book reduced participants' comprehension of the text. Indeed, there was an indication that electronic books of this kind might actually aid the reader's comprehension of a text – this was perceived via a trend for those reading the electronic book to score higher on the multiple choice questions than those reading the other two versions of the text.

The added effects which could be considered to be a distraction might therefore actually be beneficial to readers in their comprehension of electronic books. One possible reason for this is that an animated illustration in conjunction with the text could make particular parts of the story more memorable. There are various ways in which this might be achieved: firstly, if the story is made more interesting by animation, it will engage the reader's attention more and therefore be better remembered. Secondly, the animation might supplement comprehension and render the story less ambiguous, which will also make it more memorable. Lastly, the animation may make concrete temporal and sequential incidents in the story which might supplement comprehension and render the story clearer, thus making it more memorable (Lansdale, 1999). An animated illustration could also mean that it would not be necessary to read the text thoroughly in order to know the answer to a question about it.

8. Particular Disadvantages of Electronic Books

Perhaps the most significant potential disadvantage of electronic books for children is unequal access to the necessary technology in the home, at school and in public libraries. A detailed discussion of this subject will not be included here. However, recent research carried out by the author has shown that, with regard to access in schools, pupils in secondary schools are more likely to have access to both computer equipment and CD-ROM drives than pupils in primary schools. This clearly disadvantages younger children, in whom it is important to engender an early interest in books and computers. As for access in the home, the latest figures at the time of writing show that a relatively large proportion (between one third and one half) of households contain a computer. In addition to this, homes with children are the type of household most likely to own a computer (Office for National Statistics, 2000). Given the additional fact that there will be comparatively less competition for a computer at home, it can be argued children's access to a PC at home is therefore more assured than it is at school. General access to computers in libraries is good in terms of both hardware and software. Taking into account new developments in the field of electronic books, however, it will soon perhaps be more relevant to investigate the levels of access to e-book readers and the Internet. Evidence suggests that access to both of these types of electronic book is either increasing or set to increase within the public library sector (People's Network Online, 1999; Ormes, 2001).

Another disadvantage of electronic books for children lies in the potential for gender differences. There is a generally held view that girls experience limited access to electronic media and are therefore disadvantaged by a lack of the skills required to make use of them (e.g. Spender, 1996; Livingstone and Bovill, 1999). It has been argued that young girls and boys have an equal liking for computers, but that ". . . after about 10–11 girls turn away and their attitude becomes . . . less confident" (Livingstone and Bovill, 1999). Encouragingly, the study by Maynard and McKnight (2001) found that the female participants did not encounter any particular difficulties with reading the electronic text, and that their comprehension of the story was not affected by reading it in the electronic format. Since the female participants in this study were aged between nine years and one month and ten years and nine months, according to Livingstone and Bovill's finding, they were at the age just before their enthusiasm for computers will begin to decline. It is therefore likely that the female participants in the study had a roughly equal level of enthusiasm for computers as did the male participants.

9. The Effect of New Technology On Children's Reading

It is often suggested that children's interest in reading is in decline, and the increasing dominance of the more visual media, particularly among young people, is cited as the main cause. An investigation of this theory was carried out in early 1995, when the Children's Literature Research Centre (1996 – see above) questioned participants about their out of school and after school activities, and it was clear from the responses that those who spent most time reading were also those who were busiest across the range of activities, including watching television and videos and using a computer. However, the findings suggested that the reciprocal to this was not true, that is, those who did not watch a great deal of television were not necessarily active readers.

Hall and Coles (1999) noted that watching the television displaces time spent doing something else, and attempted to test the theory that reading was the activity being superseded. To this end, participants were asked how much television they had watched on the evening prior to the survey, and it was found that children generally reported spending significantly more time watching television than reading. Furthermore, "heavy" readers were more likely than others to have watched no television the previous evening, and an inverse relationship between the amount of television viewing and the amount of book reading was generally the case in this survey. However, the authors found that this relationship is not as simple as it may appear, and some children "manage to accommodate a considerable amount of television viewing and a considerable amount of reading in their leisure time activities." (p. 125) This last finding agrees with that of the Children's Literature Research Centre (1996).

As part of his survey of children's leisure reading habits, Benton (1995a) discusses the theory that television in particular is displacing reading, and finds it likely that there is an increasing link between reading and viewing. He notes that the result of the growth in the amount of television and video machines situated in children's bedrooms has been that children now have a far greater level of control over their viewing than formerly. He is also concerned about the view that boys are reading less than girls as a result of the former's increasing interest in computer games, and indeed found a greater interest in computer games among the boys than among the girls.

Hall and Coles (1999) also studied current concerns about the relationship between reading and the use of computers. To this end, participants were asked about their computer use on the evening prior to the survey, and 44.5% reported some such use. No significant relationship was found between the participants' reported use of a computer and whether or not they had been reading that same evening. The findings did not suggest that using a computer has any notably adverse effects on children's reading.

A study of the reading habits and attitudes of both adults and children (Book Marketing Ltd, 2000) involved a postal survey among a nationally representative sample of approximately 1,000 British households (2,500 adults and children). Amongst many other issues, the survey investigated the reasons why respondents either did not read books, or did so only occasionally. The survey found that 17% of the children (aged up to 16 years) who answered the question gave the reason that they used electronic media instead. Notably, this was twice as many as the number of adults who mentioned using electronic media instead of reading books.

Benton (1995b) concludes that reading is not necessarily in decline, but that the type of literature which is being read is changing along with the times. If this is true, it is likely that electronic books will be one of the new types of literature which will increase in popularity. Furthermore, Hall and Coles (1999) conclude that the television and the computer should not be seen in opposition to the book, but that each should be seen as one element in the range of media available to children of the present time. Their findings, and those of other research, support the position that, ". . . children, on the whole, do not consider their use of different media in a hierarchical relationship with one another either in relation to the use of their spare time, or the satisfactions they gain." (p. 132–133) Hall and Coles believe that children who have grown up with television can integrate the extensive use of it into their lives without having to exclude other activities.

Conclusion

In conclusion, it can be argued that the electronic book is a significant new medium, which exhibits some of the characteristics of the printed book whilst adding various electronic features and functionalities. Electronic books are attractive to young readers, having the potential to overcome perceived differences between print and other media. Evidence suggests that electronic books may have some effect on children's reading patterns. However, far from being a threat to their reading, the electronic book can contribute another dimension towards opening up the worlds of imagination and fact for children.

Selection criteria for electronic books

The same criteria as those for printed books of a similar type should be borne in mind, for example, selecting for the appropriate age group, suitable subject matter, the number and proportion of pictures, and so on. In electronic books which include pictures, the quality of the illustrations is, not surprisingly, as important as in printed picture books. This is particularly true for electronic adaptations of printed books. An interesting example can be found in an electronic version of *Alice's Adventures in Wonderland* (see Fig. 7.3) published by Europress Software (Carroll, 1997). The publishers aimed to reproduce Tenniel's original illustrations, adding colour and animation, and altering only Alice herself. As the only "real" person in Wonderland, Alice was rendered in 3D to stand out against all the other characters. However, this did not have the anticipated effect, with one reviewer describing her as being "more reminiscent of a Star Trek alien" (Meakin, 1997).

Since computer technology will be involved in the presentation of the electronic book, it will be important to consider the *usability*, or how *user-friendly*, the electronic book is. In practice, this will require a thorough consideration of a wide range of issues relating to the user-interface, such as: does the electronic book possess a clear and obvious means of navigation (e.g. consistent use of back and forward buttons, orientation cues, easy scrolling)? Is the text easy to read (e.g. good contrast and size, simple fonts)? Can the interface be adapted to cater for individual differences (e.g. increasing text/icon size, increasing audio volume)? Are colours used in an appropriate fashion (e.g. avoiding poor colour combinations, such as red and green)? Are on-screen buttons readily identifiable as such, and of a suitable size for the intended age range? Is the interface flexible, enabling interaction for children with a wide range of reading abilities (e.g. utilizing good, readily understandable icons, as well as text, use of audio)? In addition, and as discussed previously, use of the book metaphor is significant in making electronic books easier to use – an important factor to consider if young people are to be the end users.

If the electronic book has been abridged, as is often the case, it is important to consider very carefully the extent of the abridgement, and whether a full text would be preferred. It has been suggested that the parts omitted from an abridged text might be seen as "extras", available to children as they move on to the original version (Waterland, 1989). In the case of electronic versions, they could be seen as "rewards" for those children who go on to read the original texts.

The electronic book should be compatible with the medium on which you wish to read it – this includes software and hardware. For example, books intended for Microsoft Reader may not be readable with Acrobat Reader (and vice versa); some CD-ROM books are compatible with PCs, but not with Macintosh computers; some e-books may be compatible with Acrobat Reader, but not with Pocket PCs, PDAs, or other handheld devices, and so on.

It should be clear that the extras (e.g. animation, sound, hypertext connectivity, customizability and rapid information retrieval) offered by an electronic book correspond with the needs of the reader(s). Of particular note for younger readers are aids to reading such as audio narration, and online dictionaries and thesauri to help with the pronunciation and meaning of difficult words.

10. Publishers

The field of the publication of electronic books is a fast moving and diverse one. For example, an indication that CD-ROM had not lived up to initial expectations came with the news that several publishers – Dorling Kindersley, News Multimedia, McGraw-Hill and Quarto – were scaling down their multimedia operations (Newman, 1997; Reguly, 1996). It is also sometimes difficult to make a distinction between educational software or games software and electronic books, particularly when considering those published on CD-ROM. Electronic books may include games within them, for example, *Green Eggs and Ham* (Softkey – see below), and it is possible that educational software may exhibit some book-like attributes.

At the time of writing, the following are notable publishers of electronic texts for children:

Softkey

Part of Mindscape Ltd, Softkey publishes stories which often include a focus on education. Examples of Softkey titles include: *Just Grandma and Me* by Mercer Mayer, *Arthur's Reading Race* by Marc Brown (featured on *Arthur's Reading Games*) *Dr Seuss's ABC* and *Green Eggs and Ham*, both by Dr Seuss, and *The Three Little Pigs* (traditional). Contact details: Softkey, Elm Park Court, Tilgate Forest Business Centre, Brighton Road, Crawley, West Sussex, RH11 9BP, UK. <http://www.mindscape.co.uk, enquiries@mindscape.com>.

Dorling Kindersley

The Dorling Kindersley (DK) range of CD-ROMs is now published by GSP (Global Software Publishing). The company publishes some interactive storybooks, for example, *Alice in Wonderland*, *Oz: the Magical Adventure*, and *The 3 Little Pigs*. Well-known for its printed non-fiction for children, DK's Electronic non-fiction includes *My First Dictionary*, *Children's Encyclopedia*, and other educational titles. Contact details: GSP Ltd, Meadow Lane, St Ives, Cambridgeshire, PE27 4LG, UK. <http://uk.dk.com/>.

iPicturebooks

Part of the larger publisher Time Warner and based in America, iPicturebooks offers products which are readily available in the UK. The company specializes in picture books via digital download which may be read with either Acrobat Reader or Microsoft Reader. iPicturebooks is dedicated to providing high-quality e-books based on printed children's books from many publishers, and to creating new books and making books available in electronic form that have been out of print for years in print form. Examples of titles by authors and author/illustrators familiar to British readers are as follows: *My Flower* by Brian Wildsmith, *Nicky* written by Tony Ross and illustrated by Zoe Ross, *I Don't Want to Go to the Hospital*, by Tony Ross, *Frog is Frog* by Max Velthuijs, and *King Rollo and the New Stockings* by David McKee. Contact details: iPicturebooks, 24 West 25th Street, New York, New York 10010, USA. info@ipicturebooks.com, <http://www.ipicturebooks.com>.

Pocket Books, Pocket Pulse and Simon Pulse

Simon & Schuster has an e-book division which publishes books under the imprints entitled Pocket Books, Pocket Pulse and Simon Pulse. The books are available via digital download and represent mainly juvenile fiction, particularly relating to television series, and some titles include: the *Buffy the Vampire Slayer* series by various authors, *Head Games* by Christopher Golden, *Violet Eyes* by Nicole Luiken, *The Gypsy Enchantment* (from the *Charmed* television series) by Carla Jablonski and Constance M. Burge, and *Hollywood Noir* (from the *Angel* television series) by Jeff Mariotte. Contact details: Simon & Schuster UK Ltd, Africa House, 64–78 Kingsway, London WC2B 6AH, UK. <http://www.simonsays.co.uk>, enquiries@simonandschuster.co.uk.

PerfectBound

HarperCollins publishes e-books under the global imprint called PerfectBound, which publishes a wide range of fiction and non-fiction including middle grade and young adult fiction. The books are available via digital download, and titles include *The Magicians of Caprona* by Diana Wynne Jones, *The Adventures of Spider-Man* by Michael Teitelbaum, and the *Circle of Three* series by Isobel Bird. Contact details: HarperCollins Publishers, 77–85 Fulham Palace Road, Hammersmith, London, W6 8JB, UK. <http://uk.perfectbound.com>.

Amazon Press

Amazon Press is noteworthy as a publisher of digitally downloadable juvenile classics such as *The Light Princess* written by George MacDonald and illustrated by Maurice Sendak, *Through the Looking Glass* by Lewis Carroll, *The Jungle Book* by Rudyard Kipling, *The Princess and the Goblin* by George MacDonald, and *White Fang* by Jack London. Contact details: <www.amazon.co.uk>.

References

Attenborough, Liz. *National Year of Reading 1998 – 1999*, available from <http://www.yearofreading.org.uk/campaign/lizarticle.html>, 1999.

Balajthy, Ernest. "Encouraging Recreational Reading." *Reading Teacher* 42.2 (1988): 158.

Barker, Philip. "Electronic Libraries of the Future." In *Encyclopedia of Library and Information Science* Vol 59 (supplement 22), ed. Allen Kent. New York: Marcel Dekker Inc., 1997. 119–153.

BBC. *Tweenies: I'm not scared*. Text by Diane Redmond and illustrations by Leo Hartas. London: BBC Worldwide Ltd, 1999.

BBC Children's Books. *Teletubbies: The Flying Toast*. Adapted from the original script by Andrew Davenport. London: BBC Children's Publishing, 1997.

Benest, Ian D. "An Alternative Approach to Hypertext." *Educational and Training Technology International* 28.4 (1991): 341–346.

Bennett, H. "To Instruct and Delight: Children's and Young Adults' Literature on CD-ROM." *CD-ROM Professional* 7.4 (1994): 84–94.

Benton, Peter. " 'Recipe Fictions . . . Literary Fast Food?' Reading Interests in Year 8." *Oxford Review of Education* 21.1 (1995a): 99–111.

Benton, Peter. "Conflicting Cultures: reflections on the reading and viewing of secondary-school pupils." *Oxford Review of Education* 21.4 (1995b): 457–470.

Book Marketing Ltd. *Reading the Situation: Book Reading, Buying and Borrowing Habits in Britain*. Library and Information Commission Research Report 34. London: Book Marketing Ltd, 2000.

Bradman, Tony. "Black Beauty Still a Frontrunner." *Daily Telegraph* 18 July 1995: A8.

Bromley, Helen. " 'Did You Know there's no Such Thing as Never Land?' Working with Video Narratives in the Early Years." In *Potent Fictions*: *Children's Literacy and the Challenge of Popular Culture*, ed. M. Hilton. London: Routledge, 1996. 71–91.

Bush, Vannevar "As We May Think." *The Atlantic Monthly* 176 (1945): 101–108.

Carroll, John et al. "Interface Metaphors and User Interface Design." In *Handbook of Human-Computer Interaction*, ed. M. Helander. New York: Elsevier Science Publishers, 1988. 67–85.

Carroll, Lewis. *Alice's Adventures in Wonderland*, 1865. Macclesfield: Europress Software, 1997. PC 486, Windows 95 or 3.1, 8Mb RAM, CD-ROM.

Catenazzi, Nadia et al. "Design issues in the production of *hyper-books* and *visual-books*." *ALT-J (Association for Learning Technology Journal)* 1.2 (1993): 40–54.

Catenazzi, Nadia and Lorenzo Sommaruga. "Hyper-book: A Formal Model for Electronic Books." *Journal of Documentation* 50.4 (1994): 316–332.

Children's Literature Research Centre. *Young People's Reading at the End of the Century*. London: Roehampton Institute, 1996.

Chu, Meei-Ling Liaw. "Reader Response to Interactive Computer Books: Examining Literary Responses in a Non-Traditional Reading Setting." *Reading Research and Instruction* 34. 4 (1995): 352–366.

Collier, Harry. *Strategies in the Electronic Information Industry – A guide for the 1990s.* Infonortics In-Depth Briefings, 1993.

Department for Education and Employment. *The National Literacy Strategy.* Sudbury, Suffolk: DfEE Publications, 1998.

Desmond, Roger. "TV Viewing, Reading and Media Literacy." In *Handbook of Research on Teaching Literacy through the Communicative and Visual Arts*, eds. J. Flood, S. Brice Heath and Diane Lapp. London: Macmillan, 1997. 23–30.

Disney. *A Bug's Life.* London: Ladybird Books, 1999.

Disney. *Toy Story 2: Book of the Film.* London: Ladybird Books, 2000.

Dresang, Eliza. "Influence of the Digital Environment on Literature for Youth: Radical Change in the Handheld Book." *Library Trends* 45.4 (1997): 639–663.

Europress Software. *The Three Little Pigs.* Macclesfield: Europress Software, 1997. PC 486, Windows 95 or 3.1, 8Mb RAM, CD-ROM.

Fact File 2002. Carlisle: Carel Press, 2001.

Feather, John and Paul Sturges (Eds.) *International Encyclopedia of Information and Library Science.* London: Routledge, 1997.

Finn, Holly. "A Library in the Palm of Your Hand." *Financial Times Weekend*, 2nd/3rd October, (1999): XI.

Goldberg, Adele. "Educational Uses of a Dynabook." *Computers and Education* 3.4 (1979): 247–266.

Goodman, E. "Computers, Libraries and the Future of the Book." *AB Bookmans Weekly* 91 4th January (1993): 5–10.

Gosling, Ju. "The E-Book and the Future of Reading", available from <http://www.netmatters.co.uk/ju90/frm.htm>, 1998.

Graham, Judith. "Trouble for Arthur's Teacher." *English and Media Magazine* 31 (1994): 15–17.

Greenlee-Moore, Marilyn and Lawrence Smith. "Interactive Computer Software: The Effects on Young Children's Reading Achievement." *Reading Psychology* 17 (1996): 43–64.

Hall, Christine and Martin Coles. *Children's Reading Choices.* London: Routledge, 1999.

Jacobson, Frances. "Computerized Children's Literature: Beyond Electronic Page Turning." *Journal of Youth Services in Libraries* 5.4 (1992): 411–416.

Kafai, Yasmin and Elliot Soloway. "Computational Gifts for the Barney Generation." *Communications of the ACM* 37.9 (1994): 19–22.

Kiyeko and the Lost Night. Wimbledon: UbiSoft Entertainment, 1995. PC 486, Windows 95 or 3.1, 4 MB RAM, double speed CD-ROM drive.

Landoni, Monica et al. "Hyper-books and Visual-books in an Electronic Library." *The Electronic Library* 11.3 (1993): 175–186

Landoni, Monica and Forbes Gibb. "The Role of Visual Rhetoric in the Design and Production of Electronic Books: the Visual Book." *The Electronic Library* 18.3 (2000): 190–201.

Little Women. Dir. Gillian Armstrong. Screenplay by Robin Swicord. Columbia Pictures, 1995.

Livingstone, Sonia and Moira Bovill. *Young People New Media*. London: London School of Economics and Political Science, 1999.

Mayer, Mercer. *Just Grandma and Me*. New York: Golden Books, 1975.

Mayer, Mercer. *Just Grandma and Me*. Crawley, West Sussex, UK: Softkey, 1997. PC 486SX+, Windows 3.1, 95 or 98, 8Mb RAM, CD-ROM. Macintosh and Power PC System 7.0.1+, 8 Mb RAM, CD-ROM.

Maynard, Sally et al. "Children's Classics in the Electronic Medium." *The Lion and the Unicorn* 23.2 (1999): 184–201.

Maynard, S and C McKnight. "Children's Comprehension of Electronic Books: An Empirical Study." *New Review of Children's Literature and Librarianship* 7 (2001): 29–53.

McKenna, Brian. "The Coming of the Electronic Book." *Online & CD-ROM Review* 22.5 (1998): 346–348.

Meakin, Derek. "Breathing electronic life into children's classics: the 1997 Woodfield Lecture." *The New Review of Children's Literature and Librarianship* 3 (1997): 1–9.

Medwell, Jane. "Talking Books and Reading." *Reading* 30.1 (1996): 41–46.

Meek, Margaret. *On Being Literate*. London: Bodley Head, 1991.

Meyer, Nadean. "Hypertext and Its Role in Reading." *Youth Services in Libraries* 7.2 (1994): 133–139.

Miller, Larry et al. "An Exploratory Study into the Use Of CD-ROM Storybooks." *Computers and Education* 22.1–2 (1994): 187–204.

National Reading Campaign, <http://www.year ofreading.org.uk/campaign/index.html>, 2000.

Newman, Cathy. "Revolution falters as CD-ROMs fail to excite the young." *The Independent* 19 December 1997: 3.

Office for National Statistics. *Social Trends 30*, eds. Jil Matheson and Carol Summerfield. London: The Stationery Office, 2000.

Ormes, Sarah. "*An E-book Primer*: An issue paper from the Networked Services Policy Taskgroup" available from <http://www.earl.org.uk/policy/issuepapers/ebook.html>, 2001.

Parham, Charles. "CD-ROM Storybooks Revisited." *Technology and Learning* 15.6 (1995): 14–18.

People's Network Online, <http://www.peoplesnetwork.gov.uk>, 2000.

Reguly, Eric. "Quarto Plays by the Book." *The Times* 3 September 1996: 26.

Reynolds, L and S. DeRose. "Electronic Books." *Byte* 17.6 (1992): 263–268.

Sefton-Green, Julian. "From Real Books to Play Books to Un-Books." *The English and Media Magazine* 30 Summer (1994): 32–37.

Shade, Daniel. "Here We Go Again: Compact Disc Technology for Young Children." *Day Care and Early Education* 22.1 (1994): 44–46.

Spender, Dale. *Nattering on the Net: Women, Power and Cyberspace*. Toronto: Garamond Press, 1996.

Stories from the Web. (URL: http://hosted.ukoln.ac.uk/stories/), 1999.

Talley, Susan et al. "Children, Storybooks and Computers." *Reading Horizons* 38.2 (1997): 116–128.

Trushell, John et al. "Year 5 pupils reading an "Interactive Storybook" on CD-ROM: losing the plot?" *British Journal of Educational Technology* 32.4 (2001): 389–401.

van Dam, Andries. Unpublished PhD thesis: *A Study of Digital Processing of Pictorial Data*. University of Pennsylvania, USA, 1966.

Vinzant, Carol. "Electronic Books Are Coming At Last!" *Fortune* 138.1 (1998): 119–121.

Wartella, Ellen et al. "Growing up with Interactive Media. What we know and what we don't about the impact of new media on children. An executive summary of a report to the Markle Foundation' (May 2000). *Children and Interactive Media A Compendium of Current Research and Directions for the Future*." Available from <http://www.markle.org/news/digital_kids.pdf>, 2000 [accessed 25/06/02].

Waterland, Liz. "Reading Classics with Young Children." *Signal* 60 September (1989): 187–194.

Watkins, Tony and Zena Sutherland. "Contemporary Children's Literature (1970 – present). In *Children's Literature: An Illustrated History*, ed Peter Hunt. Oxford: Oxford University Press, 1995.

Yenawine, Philip. "Thoughts on Visual Literacy." In *Handbook of Research on Teaching Literacy through the Communicative and Visual Arts*, eds. J. Flood, S. Brice Heath and Diane Lapp. London: Macmillan, 1997. 845–846.

CHAPTER EIGHT

Selecting for All Communities

Unless children are to develop an inward-looking insular perspective, educating them for the future implies educating them to live and play a positive role in society where cultural diversity and equal opportunity are recognised and respected and a global perspective assumed.

Elkin and Lonsdale, 1996, 3.

1. Every Child in Every Community is Special

The selection of books by librarians and teachers must always keep in mind the premise that *every child is special,* and that discrimination in any form is both harmful to the child and opposed to the principles of the United Nations Declaration of the Rights of the Child (1959, 1989). It is also contrary to current library practice, in which, as Tricia Kings points out in Chapter 6, cultural considerations should be kept in mind when making the library accessible to everyone. Findings of research by Roach and Morrison (1997) pointed the way to change, which is now being put into practice, when they indicated that library objectives and standards in the late twentieth century rarely addressed racial equality or ethnic diversity. The excellent work done by the International Board of Books for Young People (IBBY) in promoting books from many cultures is a great step toward children from diverse lands and cultures meeting each other through stories that portray different life styles, problems and solutions; also the commonality of the human spirit, emotions, loyalty and need to belong – to be rooted in faith for important aspects of life.

The contemporary child in the UK reflects the diversity of a shrinking world, with a portrait that is recognisable in other countries across the globe. Not only has the UK a long tradition of welcoming the oppressed and homeless refugee, but the population was also largely influenced in the past by immigration from English-speaking Commonwealth countries. Beyond the year 2000, however, a world disturbed by war and economic distress has prompted the arrival of many non-English speaking children from Eastern Europe, the Middle East and parts of Africa. Therefore the contemporary picture is of a child who may originate from cultures which are very different from traditional white Anglo. Moreover, the child may belong to any one of a variety of religions, e.g.: Anglican, Buddhist, Catholic, Hindu, Jewish, Muslim, Nonconformist Protestant, Sikh, or to a microculture within any group. Additionally they may be children of post-modern, humanist homes where New-Age customs prevail.

Inasmuch as some religious and cultural adult communities hold distinct concerns about their children's reading, despite the fact that they do not reflect the majority in the population, the professional should try to understood their views and provide for them where it is possible. The child will, in time, make his/her own choices, but parental standards should be recognised in a multicultural, multi-faith society.

In Chapter One, various theories of child development are set out, all of which can give a framework to understanding the child. Highly relevant to the topic of Communities there is one theory, not considered as yet, which has implications for the child and children's literature. This concerns the development of the characteristic commonly called faith.

2. Faith Development

James W. Fowler, a developmental psychologist and Director of the Centre for Faith Development at Emory University, USA is considered the Father of Faith Development Theory. Certainly his pioneer study, *Stages of Faith* (1981) is regarded as a ground-breaking classic. In it, Fowler builds on the influences of Piaget's cognitive development and Kohlberg's theory of moral development, and, like them, claims stages that are 'hierarchical, sequential and invariant.', but unlike them he does not propose that his developmental stages of faith are universal, thus leaving the way open for further research. He is also influenced by Erikson's psychosocial stages which begins with an emphasis on trust versus mistrust in infancy; that the onslaught of new experiences triggers disequalibrium (conflict) and movement to the next stage. Despite some criticism, extensive research shows that Fowler's theory is the most well known and accepted.

2.1 Fowler's Stages of Faith

Faith, according to Fowler's perspective, is:

- an innate potential with which every child is born;
- 'a way of knowing, of construing, or of interpreting experience.' It concerns actual images, values, beliefs, symbols and rituals;
- always *relational* within a background of shared meaning and purpose. It thus embraces many aspects of living such as family and shared communities of commitment or interest;
- of central importance in informing behaviour and shaping personality;
- distinct from *belief,* or 'faith' as it is used in theological language;
- is a characteristic of all human beings, regardless of whether they apply it to religion or not.

2.2 Faith Development and Children's Literature

There are three stages in Fowler's theory which apply to children, that can be seen to hold implications for the selection of children's literature. The first thing to understand is that these three stages are linked with, and driven by, the child's evolving cognitive abilities – as in the first three stages of Piaget's theory, i.e. sensorimotor, preoperational, and concrete operational.

STAGE 0. (Infancy). This is the period when the foundations of a balanced character, trust and love, are being established – and trust is foundational for all forms of faith. Picture books which show children in happy relationships with their parents or caregivers, shared together at story times in physical and emotional closeness, contribute staunch building blocks to this foundation. Not yet master of communication through spoken language, yet understanding much from early on, the infant nevertheless develops the incorporative self.

STAGE ONE **Intuitive-Projective Faith**

The child continues dependence on the care, security and love that flow from parents or surrogates. These figures are his/her reference in the construction of a meaningful world.

This is the time when imagination flourishes, when stories stimulate and rituals and symbols fascinate, so books should be selected which contain images of good and evil, life and death, threat and protection; also images of the achieving child and community. Greenaway Award winners can be counted on to suit this stage of development.

Fowler concurs with Bruno Bettelheim that fairy tales and myths assist young children in the process of externalising fear, and fear of monsters, the dark, death, separation and other aspects common in the preoperational child, can be met through the reassuring world of children's literature.

STAGE TWO **Mythic-Literal Faith**

Fowler suggests 6 +1/2 years to eleven for this stage of 'the imperial self', but as with Piaget's sequence, it is *stages not ages* that are to be emphasised and there will be individual differences, although seven years is recognised by many as a turning point in a child's development:

- The more narrow, nursery world has extended to become more ordered and dependable and now includes significant others whom the child accepts as 'like us': teachers, ethnic, social and religious leaders, customs, also traditions, the media, books and the ideas of peers. S/he can take on the role of the group but does not see self through the eyes of the group.
- They respond to anthropomorphic symbols for deity, are also interested in myths and heroic images.

STAGE THREE **Synthetic-Conventional Faith**

The average ages for this stage are 12 to adulthood, coinciding with adolescence, but as stressed previously, individuals vary. With growing teenage cognition there are number of changes, all contributing to a watershed in faith development:

- Mutual perspective taking is now possible;
- Integration begins of distinct self-images into a coherent identity of the self, yet they are still seeking;
- their synthesis of values and beliefs is largely intuitive, rather than examined and reflected upon; they are simultaneously idealistic and highly judgemental.

- peer pressure and conformity are characteristic as the 'interpersonal self' emerges.

Fowler admits that many individuals, communities and congregations never develop beyond this stage.

Award winners for older readers, such as by Philip Pullman, frequently take aboard the considerations that characterise Fowler's Stage Three. Many other books for teenagers and young adults also demonstrate the changes, challenges, disillusionments and decisions demanded of the growing-up years, all of which affect faith development.

3. The Christian Community

The UK, like much of Europe and the Western World, has a tradition of Christian belief, but 'belief' is not to be confused with 'faith', as Ed Stephenson and others point out, for *belief* concerns assent in creedal statements of a religious tradition. Before belief, however, there must be faith or trust.

3.1 Christmas

Books about Christmas, an important Christian festival, are published by both secular and denominational publishing houses. Some general favourites are:

- *The Night before Christmas,* by Clement Clarke Moore. ISBN 0–689–83683-X
- *Twelve Days of Christmas*, compiled by Rachel Griffin. ISBN 1–84148–938–7
- *The Lighthouse Keeper's Christmas,* by Rhonda and David Armitage. ISBN 0–439–98144–1
- *It's Christmas: Stories About Christmas* (Quids for Kids). ISBN 1858815959

Stories based on the biblical account of the stable birth also feature, as in:

- *The Nativity* by Jane Ray, which has its own stand-up nativity scene. ISBN 1 86039 852 9

- Crafts for Christmas, carols and stories for four to seven-year-olds are in *First Festivals: Christmas.* ISBN 07459 3907 4
- *My First Book About Christmas (My First Bible Collection)* – a rag book, for infants. ISBN 1856083500.
- *Christmas Story* by Heather Amery, a bright board book. ISBN 0 7460
- *The First Christmas* by Georgie Adams. A traditional narrative. ISBN 1 85881 188 0
- *The Christmas Star* by Marcus Pfister, imaginatively told. ISBN 1 5585
- *Sleepy Jesus* by Pennie Kidd, another imaginative version. ISBN 0 7459 3764 0

A factual book for older readers by Philip Ardagh, *The Truth About Christmas: Its traditions Unravelled,* answers a variety of questions ranging from Who decided to celebrate Jesus' birthday on 25 December? through questions about Saint Nicholas (Santa Claus), to the origins of Christmas trees in England and Why have a fairy, not an angel at the top of the Tree?

3.2 Bible Characters

Stories about **Bible characters** are published by Usborne, Lions, Macmillan and others. Humorously written *Daniel and the Dark Arts* by Earnest Spellbinder, published by Scripture Union for eight to twelve-year-olds, attempts a Rowling style, retelling the story of how Daniel of the Old Testament maintains his integrity while a student of magic. Ralph Gower, an RE teacher, wonders if some imaginative retellings tend to equate Bible stories with fairy tale favourites so that they lose their true significance, so becoming reduced to folk lore and later discarded as is Santa Claus.

The Christian tradition has long influenced English literature, and thereby, world literature, including literature for children. This was especially so from medieval times until the mid-twentieth century, as the history of children's literature reveals. One very beautifully and sensitively illustrated work by Pauline Baynes presents the Nicene Creed which is the most widely accepted statement of Christian faith. Entitled with the four opening words of the creed, here is a book called *I Believe in God*, for any child of the Christian tradition, for RE educational purpose, or for any adult who wants to own a book with some breathtaking images that endeavour to extol creation, death and resurrection.

3.3 Narnia

The *Narnia* series by C. S. Lewis, published in the 1950s, is an outstanding example of Christian influence. The seven books can be read on two levels, either as straightforward fantasies, or as allegorical tales. It is at the level of allegory that Christian readers recognise Aslan, the great lion, as representative of the Lion of the Tribe of Judah, an image of Christ. They recognise the parallels between the redemptive deaths of Aslan and Jesus Christ and the ultimate home he provides at the end of their journeys.

Lewis maintained that he wrote the sort of books he would have liked to read himself when young, so they draw on fantastic characters that children from Bunyan's day to Harry Potter enjoy: talking beasts, dragons, dwarves, magicians, satyrs, fauns, giants . . . and child heroes in the contention of good against evil, especially the four Pevensies who resemble the four boys of *The Pilgrim's Progress* Part II in that they are four distinct character types who change and develop through the story, some transformed from foolishness to goodness and purposefulness, though not all will complete the journey into Aslan's country. Lewis reports that he wrote *The Lion, the Witch and the Wardrobe* to answer the question: 'What might Christ be like if there really were a world like Narnia?' In a letter to a child, Carroll, he says:

> *I found the name in the notes to Lane's Arabian Nights: it is the Turkish for lion. I pronounce it Ass-lan myself. And of course I meant the Lion of Judah.*
>
> *Lewis, 1986, 29.*

3.4 Harry Potter

The Harry Potter series has aroused widespread passionate public and professional debate, as an overwhelming number of publications and web-sites indicate. Some Christian leaders and communities applaud Harry as a force for good against evil, praise Rowling's imaginative story telling and the series' mythic structure, recognising that even the Bible is a narrative that is largely based on mythic structure, though not mythical. John Houghton, a Christian writer likens Harry to Dorothy in *The Wizard of Oz*, for both enter a parallel world. Harry's is a dark journey to face the shadow of his past, meeting Dumbledore, his very wise mentor, allying himself with Ron, Hermione and Hagrid. Snape and McGonagill are the 'gatekeepers', while Malfoy is the trickster and Voldemort, the shadow – a world where shapeshifters abound.

3.5 Critics, chiefly from Christian fundamentalists, are concerned that:

(i) the emphasis on wizardry and the occult, used by both good and evil wizards in the Potter saga, repeatedly portray, in a positive way, activities which the Old and New Testament denounce; they see spiritual forces of darkness seeking to overshadow Christian values and practice;

(ii) children absorb for hours on end, in the form of fiction, activities that some parents would not permit them to practise or observe in reality;

(iii) librarians in diverse settings report increasing numbers of children who request occult materials;

(iv) paganation of children's culture is the end-product, a reflection of the prevailing world view: of the post-Cold War, post-Christian, post-modern society <harrypotterguide.co.uk>.

Main stream reviewers recognise the tremendous imaginative force behind Rowling's work, her skill in drawing together clues that are implanted in text and her rightful place in a tradition of writing that demonstrates the battle between good and evil. Ingeniously she has applied it in another dimension. It is a memorable work in the fantasy field, and of course it must reflect, to some extent, the societal background against which the author writes, as does any piece of creative writing from mediaeval times and subsequent centuries. Those in opposition may not be viewing the full picture, not seeing it as a masterpiece of a literary form, but getting bound up in matters which concern some adult minds. Children worldwide have given their opinions, and to them, Harry Potter is a *winner.*

3.6 Fantasy Worlds

Worlds of fantasy appeal to the child of the 'imperial self' in Fowler's Stage Two -Mythic-Liberal Faith – at about seven to twelve years. This is the stage when a child begins to distinguish and make clear choices about basic moral situations; when they separate fact from fantasy, although they are not yet able to stand back and to objectively reflect, for literal interpretations are typical; when myths provide coherence at a subconscious level, to their own experience. Thus one can understand the appeal of fantasy at this developmental stage, and also the danger inherent in the way 'attitudes are absorbed and adopted; beliefs are appropriated with literal interpretations, as are moral rules and attitudes' according to Fowler. It is the older child who is moving toward Stage Three in Fowler, and into Piaget's Stage Three of cognition, who has increasing skill in discernment, synthesis and evaluation.

It should be clear that Professionals and parents should not take rampant sides in the Harry Potter debate, but have tolerant understanding of where each is coming from. This is helpful for parents when they make group decisions for their children in a school community. For example, one group of parents at a public school in the Midlands, UK, discussed using a Harry Potter theme for an end-of term party. They knew the children's fascination for wands and some suggested that children compete for a prize for the best wand. A minority demurred out of concern for the occult, others for reasons of safety: 'Imagine a hundred of them racing around with their wands, poking them at each other . . .' After rational consideration of all the points of view, they chose another theme.

Robert Frost is said to have stated:

> *Education is the ability to listen to almost anything without losing your temper or self-confidence.*

4. Muslims

Muslims share the same interest in character development and in passing on knowledge of the same middle eastern characters as by Christians, it is the sources that differ: *Qur'an*, or Old Testament of the *Bible*. *Stories of the Prophets from the Qur'an* is a series of six board books for young children, using Islamic names but telling a similar story. So IBRAHIIM equates Abraham, ISA is the name for Jesus, MUSA, the equivalent of Moses and NUH equates Noah.

The Muslim Educational Trust provides informational materials that are designed for children of the Muslim community but which can be useful to RE teachers, to children of other backgrounds and to adults who want to make friends across society. Their titles concern Islam beliefs and teachings, the importance of daily prayers which they regard as an important pillar of Islam, Sex Education, from a Muslim Perspective, and the magazine for teenagers, *Reflect.*

Zarafa is another UK based distributor of Islamic resources for home and school. It offers a range of colourful picture books for the early years, which pictorially look much like those from any publishing house; which endeavour to be imaginative rather than purely didactic. The difference lies in the textual emphases, for these are written for Muslim children who look to Allah in thankfulness and as their authority. This sets them in accord with Fowler's Stage One when the faith of primal others comes to the four to seven year-old child through the language, symbol and ritual of religious tradition. Other books that affirm the Islamic way of life are: *What do we Say* . . . a guide to manners; *Assalamu Alaykum* by M. S. Kayani, in which little children, Abdullah and Aminah, demonstrate Muslim greetings. Another, *Faisal and Friends* has a colourful, attractive cover showing Faisal the Frog and his friends, Saleem the grasshopper and Leila the butterfly. Like the other books mentioned, it is designed to teach, using Islamic character names with which a Muslin child can identify. Most of the Zarafa publications are instructional, but there are also some categorised as 'Stories to Inspire.' These are novels for Key Stage 2 in which the heroes are Muslim children.

Lutterworth do not confine themselves to publications concerning Christianity for they publish *Loving Letters: As Islamic alphabet* by Riad Nourallah, another of their beautifully presented books for the young, an ABC with illustrations of scenes and themes from Islam, along with poems.

5. The Jewish Community

Jewry shares with Christians and Muslims the same basic values of faith in an omnipotent, omniscient, omnipresent deity – God. They also value their children highly and seek to educate them for the good of their own and the wider community. They hold their own significant festivals:

(i) Passover, celebrated in *Four Special Questions*;
(ii) Purim, illustrating the festival of Purim in *It's Party Time;*
(iii)Rosh Hashanah, described in *Apples and Honey*;

(iv) Chanukah, explained in *Eight Candles to light,* which features a Jewish type, glowing candle with an orthodox family seated about it. These are a series of four brightly illustrated pre-school books called *Festival Time,* by Johnny Zucker. *Rebecca's Passover,* also a picture book tells the story of Rebecca and her brother Josh who help Granny Sarah to prepare for the Jewish festival which commemorates the escape from Egypt of Jewish slaves.

The worldwide Jewish community holds another important festival, a weekly one which they celebrate on the seventh-day of the week, Saturday, or Shabatt, the Sabbath day. This is in accordance with their belief in the command and promises related to the *Torah,* believed to have been entrusted to the Hebrew race. A board book called *Shabatt Shalom* is a board book for children, showing in a positive way a family as it prepares for, and celebrates the Sabbath.

The persecution of the Jewish people by Nazi Germany will never be forgotten by their own community for it has touched all their lives. Many stories have come out of the holocaust experience which can be read along with RE classes as well as language arts. One recent biographic book for children in the eight years and above range is *Elsie's War: A Story of Courage in Nazi Germany.* Actual photographs convey the courage of the story.

6. The Hindu Community

How Hindu young people, aged 14 years and over, feel about themselves in relationship to their community in Britain, is revealed through a research project of the Oxford Centre for Vaishnava and Hindu Studies, 2001.[1] A sample of 400 participants completed a survey, followed up by group discussions. Awareness of the findings provides a backdrop to non-Hindu understanding, and relating to, the Hindu community. When little is known about another culture or religious group, suspicion is rife and few hands of friendship or cooperation are offered.

The majority, 93%, said they were happy to be Hindu. Of these, 84% considered themselves religious, while 83% agreed that it was

[1] Search for 'Hindu Community' on www.

important for them to practise their religious/spiritual beliefs. When asked to indicate if they considered it important to pass on the Hindu tradition to future generations, 90% gave a positive response. At the same time 89% considered it important to work with people of other faiths, indicating a positive stance toward maintaining good relations with people of other faiths and living harmoniously in an homogenised society. Finally, 88% considered Hinduism relevant in the modern world.

The Hindu community is concerned to promote spirituality among their children and youth. Numerous organisations indicate this in their goals. The Auromira Centre UK Youth, for example, which conducts workshops for children, has as its aim 'to promote spiritual progress in its entirety for everyone, irrespective of caste, creed or colour.' Another organisation, The *Bochasanwasi Shree Akshar Purushottam Swaminarayan Sanstha* (BAPS), a socio-spiritual group, 'reaches out far and wide to clear the confusions and questions that crowd the moral, social and material world of today. Other groups express interest in 'young minds', and 'every individual.' Part of their approach to the young includes teaching different aspects of Hindu culture, representative of a number of Hindu deities and areas of the Indian and African continent. Some of the subjects offered are music, drama, story, dance and vegetarian cooking, languages of India, along with philosophy, yoga and meditation. The largest weekend school in the UK operates on Saturday mornings from the Stanburn School, Stanmore, Middlesex.

With recognition of the large body of Hindus who have made the UK their home and who are genuinely trying to assimilate while not forgetting their roots, it is not surprising to find their interest in literature for children. Back in India, *The Hindu*, India's national newspaper, announces Kerala State's annual awards for children's literature in national languages. Interestingly, the award for the best translated children's work in 2002 was for a Malayalam translation of Rudyard Kipling's *Jungle Book*. A www. search for 'Hindu children's literature' indicates a number of websites, including The National Book Trust of India, Book India and Asia for Kids. The National Book Trust of India has books in 18 Indian languages, but most of the books listed are in English. They cover the usual genres: traditional myths and legends, picture books, fiction, non fiction. Prema Srinivasan's work, *Children's Fiction in English in India: trends and Motifs* give an informative survey of the history of children's literature in India and includes a survey of children's leisure reading. She also points out that the publishers of Penguin India have realised the potential market found in the large numbers of Asian children in the UK.

Available in the UK are books about the Indian festivals of Divali and Holi. *The Divali Story* by Anita Ganesi honours the goddess, Lakshmi and includes special recipes for children to make for the occasion. Another book, told as a story rather than as information, is *Here Comes Holi: the Festival of Colours* by Meenal Pandya. Centred around a boy and his friends, It is suited to any child in a multicultural society and gives the Hindu way to welcome springtime.

For the contemporary child of an Indian family, the story of *Anita and Me* by Meera Syal looks back at what growing up was like for nine year-old Meena in the 1960s when being caught between two cultures was more challenging. It was especially so because Meena's family were the only Punjabi family in a Midlands mining village and she is the only daughter. Meena survives with some help from her friend and her dog.

7. The Travellers

A minority community, but a vibrant one nevertheless, Travellers have now reacted to discrimination by producing their own stories for children. Thomas Acton describes the situation and writes about *Traveller Education Publications* in *Books for Keeps* (2002), citing three books in particular that librarians and teachers should know about. They are:

*Gypsies and Travellers in their Own Words. I*SBN: 0 9508029 9 9
The Travelling People. ISBN: 0 9538008
Where's Mouse? (No ISBN)

Who exactly the Travellers are is explained in *The Travelling People* as New Travellers, Showmen, Romani asylum-seekers plus the territorially defined Gypsy and Traveller groups. It is knowledge not commonly known in society.

Acton commends the Resource Fair that is conducted biannually by the National Association of Teachers with Travellers, where, he suggests, they offer not only quality but also innovation. Although not yet many in number, they are a welcome addition to books for children that affirm background, heritage and uniqueness.

Young adult readers, particularly male, may enjoy *King of the Gypsies: Undefeated Bareknuckle Champion of Great Britain and*

Ireland by Bartley Gorman and Peter Walsh. Also about bareknuckle fighting is the true story of another bareknuckle champion of the Gypsy community: *Tarmac Warrior: The Violent World of Extreme Fighting* by Billy Cobb. Superior to any television supposedly real-life, violent drama and more astounding than any fiction, both of these biographies are part of Romany history.

For those professionals who want to understand Romany ethnicity and the background of children who may appear in their classroom or library from time to time, and want to know how the state deals with Gypsies and Travellers, read *Gypsy Politics and Traveller Identity.* From this work and others, such as *Romanichal Gypsies* by Thomas and David Gallant, it becomes clear that they, like all communities are concerned to maintain their children's faith. Certainly, these publications confirm the Traveller's place in society, divergent though it may be.

8. Across the Cultures

In addition to those religious and cultural groups identified in this chapter, there are others – for example the world-wide community of Buddhists, the many races of the African continent, the Far East, and those of Black Britain who have no affiliation with Christianity or any 'ism.' Another book that crosses cultures, using a universally common theme is *Celebrations: Christmas, Divali, Hanukah/Birthday Celebrations,* a book suggested for Foundation to Key Stage 1 children, which shows how each child has his/her own festival that makes them feel special. In contrast is *Whose God is it anyway?*

For mature Key Stage 4 students *Whose God is it, Anyway?* introduces Buddhism, Confucianism, Zoroastrianism, Taoism, Tribal religions and the religions of Native Americans. It is written by a Jewish rabbi and a Roman Catholic priest with a preface by the Dalai Lama. It offers a perspective for students who will probably be at Fowler's Stage Three; perhaps fifteen to seventeen year-olds at the stage of Synthetic-Conventional Faith; young people at the cusp of adulthood. From a Piagetian perspective, they are proceeding in the development and practice of reasoning and the application of abstract thought. In Fowler's terms, they still see authority as external to the self, though they accept personal responsibility for determining choice and to weigh up sources of guidance.

Conclusion

Community programmes make every effort to meet the entire community. The Boots Books for Babies programme, 2001–2006, for example, which runs a programme similar to those of Book Start, Sure Start etc., has the following aim:

Total inclusivity for its reading packs for babies in Nottinghamshire. This means that every infant receives through liaison with Health Visitors, a canvas bag which contains two books, a placemat, rhyme cards and cassette tape of songs, and an application to join the library. These are provided for:

- Travellers' nursery school
- Muslim Women's Centre
- Women's Homeless Centre
- Special Needs workers
- Looked after children
- Travellers' education team
- Teenage parent group

To children everywhere applies a principle which communities recognise and interpret from their own perspectives of faith, one expressed by renowned psychoanalyst, Bruno Bettelheim. He said, when confronted with deducing what experiences help a child to find meaning (i.e. faith) in his/her life:

> . . . *nothing is more important than the impact of* **parents and others who take care of the child***; second in importance is . . .* **cultural heritage***, when transmitted to the child in the right manner. When children are young, it is* **literature**[2] *that carries such information best.*

> *Bettelheim, 1978, 4.*

Children's Sayings

"I have read four Harry Potter books. I like it when he is an 11 year-old in the first book and Harry and his friends outsmart all the charms

[2] Bold is mine

protecting the philosopher's stone. Then he is 12 and in his second year at Hogwarts in the next book . . . the stories are funny, mysterious and very adventurous." Sarah, eight-years-old.

I've read all the Harry Potter books, and I've got the video. *Of course* I know that the Harry Potter books are not true! But I've been reading fairy stories and fantasy all my life and I talk about it with my parents. (They read them too). I want to be an English teacher. Thingy, 12 years

Referring to 'Jabberwocky' by Lewis Carroll: "Somehow it fills my head with ideas – only I don't know exactly what they are." Alice, from *Through the Looking Glass*.

Tutorial Topics

1. Discuss Judy Blume's observation from *The New York Times*, October 22, 1999:

   > *In Minnesota, Michigan, New York, California and South Carolina, parents who feel the books promote interest in the occult have called for their removal from classrooms and school libraries ... I'm not exactly unfamiliar with this line of thinking, having had various books of mine banned from schools over the last 20 years. In my books, it's reality that's seen as corrupting. With Harry Potter, the perceived danger is fantasy.*

   See the full text on <http://www.neac.org/harrypotter.html>
2. Based on reading one book of criticism, consider the pros and cons of the Harry Potter debate.
3. Consider Fowler's Theory. Identify its similarities to other developmental theories, and relate to children's literature of your choice.

Further Reading

Campbell, Joseph. *The Hero with a Thousand Faces.* 2nd edition. 3rd printing. Princeton: Princeton University Press, 1973.

Heilman, Elizabeth, ed. *Harry Potter's World: Multidisciplinary Critical Perspectives.* London: Routledge, 2002.

Hunt, Peter and Millicent Lenz. *Alternative Worlds in Fantasy Fiction.* London: Continuum, 2001.

Lonsdale, S. 'Faith Development Across the Life Span. Fowler's Integrative Work.' In *Journal of Psychology and Theology,* 25 (1), 49–63.

Children's Books which Build trust in their Communities

GENERAL

All Things Bright and Beautiful. Illustrated by Pauline Baynes. Cambridge: Lutterworth, 2000.

Armitage, Ronda and David. *The Lighthouse Keeper's Christmas.* London: Scholastic, 2002.

Baby World. Series of four books: *Good Morning; Playtime; Bathtime; Goodnight.* London: Dorling Kindersley, 2002.

Brown, Margaret Wise. *Goodnight Moon.* Illustrated by Clement Hurd. London: Macmillan, 2001.

Celebrations: Christmas, Divali, Hanukah, Birthdays.

Cope, Wendy. *Is that the New Moon?* London: Collins, 2002.

Gellman, Marc, and Thomas Hartman. *Whose God is it, Anyway?* London: The Bodley Head, 1998.

Griffin, Rachel. *Twelve Days of Christmas.* Bristol: Barefoot Books, 2002.

Mahy, Margaret. *Alchemy.* London: Flamingo: Harper Collins, 2002.

Moore, Clement Clarke. *The Night Before Christmas: The Original Story.* Illustrated by James Rice. Gretna, Louis: Pelican Publishing Company, 1989.

Oborne, Martine. *One Gorgeous Baby.* London: Macmillan, 2001.

Thistlewaite, Diane. *Baby World.* A series of four books. Photography by Zara Ronchi and Steve Gorton. Dorling Kindersley, 2002.

Wilson, Jacqueline. *The Worry Website.* London: Corgi, 2003.

—— *Lola Rose.* Illustrated by Nick Sharratt. London: Doubleday, 2003.

CHRISTIAN

Ardagh, Philip. *The Truth About Christmas: Its traditions Unravelled.* London: Macmillan Children's Books, 2001.

Encounter Christianity. London: Church House Publishing. n.d.

Gaudrat, Marie-Agnes. *What is God like?* Illustrated by Ulises Wensell. Cambridge: The Lutterworth Press, 1998.

Lee, Kathy. *Fabulous Phoebe; Phoebe's Book of Body Image, Boys and Bible Bits; Phoebe's Fortune.* Series of three books. Milton Keynes: Scripture Union, 2003.

Mackenzie, Cairn. *Our Loving God.* Illustrated by Fred Apps. Fearn: Christian Focus, 1997.

—— *My God is So Big.* Illustrated by Andy Orb. Fearn: Christian Focus, 2001.

Maclean, Ruth. *Joseph's Journal.* Fern: Christian Focus, 1997.

Parry, Alan and Linda. *The Evergreen Wood: an Adaptation of The Pilgrim's Progress for Children.* Reprint. Alresford: Hunt and Thorpe, 1994.

Reason, Joyce. *To be a Pilgrim: The Story of John Bunyan.* Faith and Fame series. Cambridge: Lutterworth Press, 1961.

Spellbinder, Earnest. *Daniel and the Dark Arts.* Milton Keynes: Scripture Union, 2002.

Watts Murray. *Bible for Children.* (Retelling). Illustrated by Helen Cann. London: Lion, 2002.

MUSLIM

Eccleshall, Anne. *Faisal and Friends.* Illustrated by Rachel Verity. Watford: Zarafa 2002.

Kayani, M. S. *Assalamu Alaykum.* Watford: Zarafa, 2002.

Juma, Siddiqa. *Stories of the Prophets from the Qur'an.* A series of six board books: Ibrahim, Adam, Isa, Musa, Muhammad, Nuh. Watford: Zarafa Publishing, 2002.

Khan, Saniyasnain. *Tell Me About Hajj.* Watford: Zarafa, 2002.

Nourallah, Riad. *Loving Letters: An Islamic Alphabet.* Cambridge: Lutterworth Press, 1996.

JEWISH

Geras, Adele. *Rebecca's Passover.* London: Frances Lincoln, 2003.

Gold-Vukson, Marji. *The Sounds of My Jewish Year.* Minneapolis: Kar-Ben Publishing, 2003.

—— *The Shapes of My Jewish Year.* Minneapolis: Kar-Ben Publishing, 2003.

Smith, Frank Dabba. *Elsie's War: A Story of Courage in Nazi Germany.* London: Frances Lincoln, 2003.

Yaffa. *Shabatt Shalom.* Minneapolis: Kar-Ben Copies Inc., 1995.

Zucker, Jonny. *Festival Time!* (Series). Illustrated by Jan Barger Cohen. London, 2003.

HINDU

Garnesi, Anita. *The Divali Story.* Illustrated by Carole Gray. London: Evans Brothers, 2002.

Pandya, Meenal. *Here Comes Holi: the Festival of Colours.* Wellesley, MA; Meera Publications, 2003.

Syal, Meera. *Anita and Me.* London: Flamingo, 1997.

TRAVELLERS

Acton, Thomas and David Gallant. *Romanichal Gypsies.* London: Hodder Wayland, 2001.

Cribb, Billy. *Tarmac Warrior: The Violent World of Extreme Fighting Today.* Edinburgh: Mainstream Publishing, 2001.

Gorman, Bartley and Peter Walsh. *King of the Gypsies: Undefeated Bareknuckle Champion of Great Britain and Ireland*. Milo Books, 2001.

Hawksworth, Val, Jean Flynn and Sylvia Murphy. *Where's Mouse?* Cardiff Traveller Education Service, 2000.

Saunders, Peter et al. *Gypsies and Travellers in their Own Words*. Leeds Traveller Service, 2000.

Wormington, Anthea, Stan Newman and Chris Lilly. *The Travelling People*. Newham, Hackney and Tower Hamlets Traveller Education Services, 2001.

OTHERS

Celebrations: Christmas, Divali, Hannukah, Birthday Celebrations. San Diego: Raintree/Harcourt, 2003.

Gellman, Marc and Thomas Hartman. *Whose God is it Anyway?* London: Bodley Head, 1998.

Onyefulu, Ifeoma. *Welcome, Dede!: An African Naming Ceremony*. London: Frances Lincoln, 2003.

Bibliography

Abanes, Harry. *Harry Potter and the Bible*: The Menace Behind the Magic. Camp Hill: Horizon Books, 2001.

Acton, Thomas, ed. *Gypsy Politics and Traveller Identity*. University of Herefordshire Press, 1997.

Bettelheim, Bruno. *The Uses of Enchantment: The Meaning and Importance of Fairy Tales*. London: Peregrine Books, 1978.

Carroll, Lewis. *Through the Looking Glass*. London: Puffin, 1994, 15–18.

Eccleshare, Julia. *A Guide to the Harry Potter Novels*. London: Continuum, 2002.

Elkin, Judith and Ray Lonsdale. *Focus on the Child: Libraries, Literacy and Learning*. London: Library Association Publishing, 1996.

Fowler, J. W. *Stages of Faith: The Psychology of Human Development and the Quest for Meaning*. New York: Harper and Row, 1981.

Fowler, James W. 'Stages in Faith: The Structural -Developmental Approach.' In *Values and Moral Development*. Thomas C. Hennessy, Ed. New York: Paulist Press, 1976.

Gilligan, Carol. *In a Different Voice*. Cambridge MA: Harvard University Press, 1982.

Gower, Ralph. 'Biblical Books for Children.' In *Books for Keeps*, No. 115, March 1999.

Houghton, John. *A Closer Look at Harry Potter: Bending and Shaping the Minds of Our Children*. Eastbourne: Kingsway Publications, 2001.

Lewis, C. S. *Letters to Children*. London: Fount paperbacks, 1986, 29.

Mattarasso, Francois. *Learning Development: Valuing the Social Impact of Libraries*. The British Library Board, 1998.

Piper, Edward. 'Faith Development: A Critique of Fowler's Model and a Proposed Alternative.' In *The Journal of Liberal Religion*. Vol. 3 Number 1, Winter 2002, 1–16.

Roach, Patrick and Marlene Morrison. *Public Libraries, Ethnic Diversity and Citizenship*. University of Warwick, 1997.

Stephenson, Ed. 'Introduction to the Stages of Faith'. *Wesley Conventicle*, June 23, 2002. See: fumch@fumch.org

Smith, Wilfred Cantwell. *Faith and Belief: The Difference Between Them*. Princeton: Princeton University Press, 1979.

Srinivasan, Prema. *Children's Fiction in English in India*. T. Nagar: T.R Publications, 1998.

Trim Mary-Kate. *The Rights of the Child: A Teacher's Resource*. UNICEF Australia/Save the Children Fund, 1989. ISBN 0 949346 04 7; also 0 9594641 1 5

<http://www.lifesite.net/features/harrypotter/obrienpotter.html>
<www.hinduyouthuk.org/researchproject.htm>

Index